How it all began

with love, Chen

FULL CIRCLE

A MEMOIR

GWEN LEIGH

taliesin press

Published in 2004 by Taliesin Press

Taliesin Press
11 Kensington Place
Brighton BN1 4EJ

info@taliesin-press.co.uk

ISBN 0-9547790-0-2

Designed by Barry Leigh
Original Illustrations and drawings by Gwen Leigh
Title page photograph by Henry Klyne

Typset in Palatino Linotype by Caravan of Dreams
Printed by Antony Rowe of Chippenham

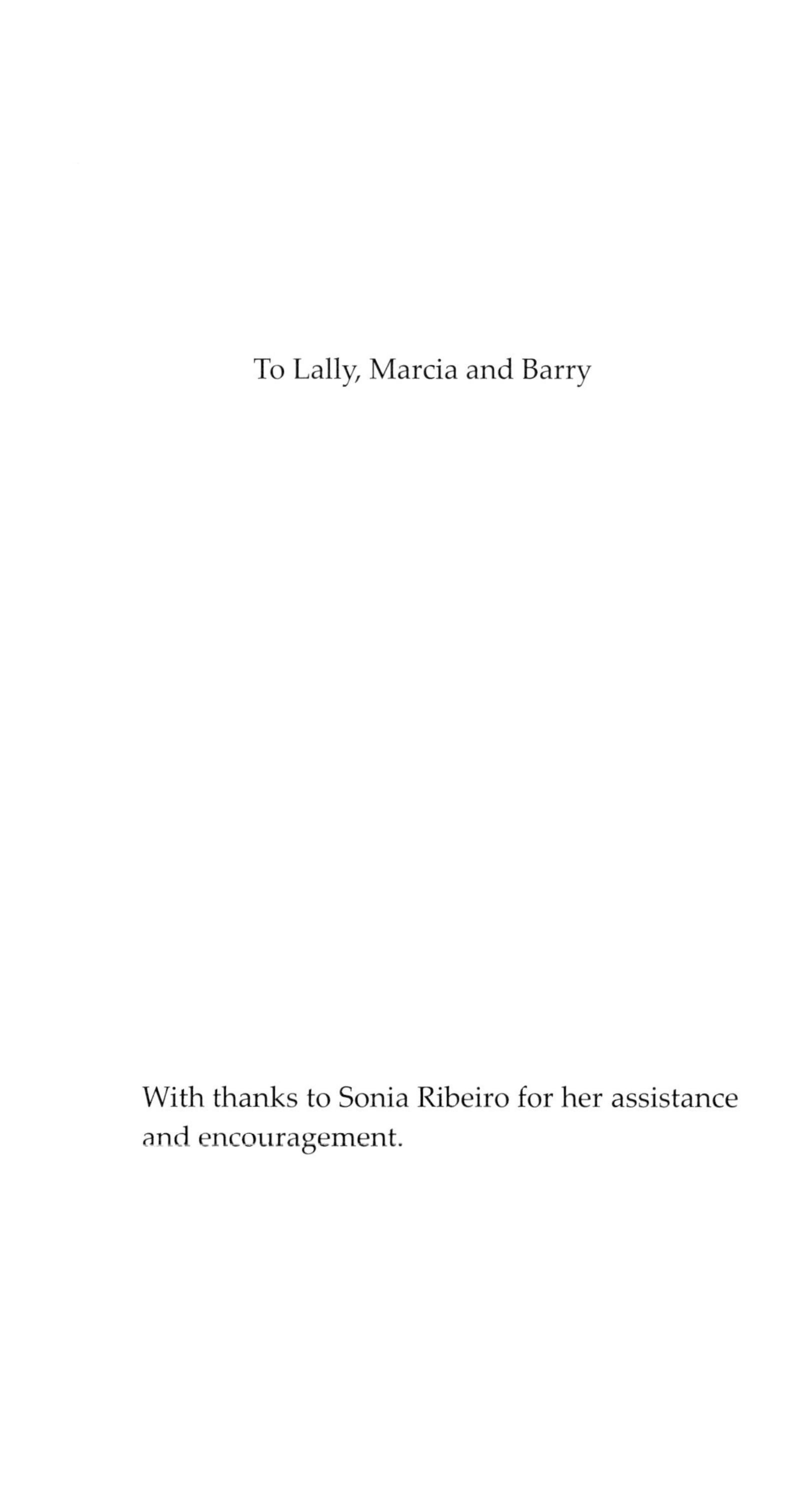

To Lally, Marcia and Barry

With thanks to Sonia Ribeiro for her assistance and encouragement.

Preface

We felt that we could not allow the occasion of the publication of our mother's book to pass without some comment from her children. We are very proud of her achievement. Whilst most might have expected her to take things more easy in her later years, she has been typing away on her lap-top, or editing previously written material, for many months.

Our mother has always been someone who has been motivated to achieve goals she has set herself, starting off as a successful dress designer and later as a painter and sculptor, interior and graphic designer, and finally as a 'something special' shopkeeper, which she only gave up when she became ill. And then she started this book.

She was of a generation where mothers were not expected to work and, whilst she freely gave up her successful profession to start a family, in retrospect she would probably have been more fulfilled had she felt able to continue with her work.

The book is our mother's personal recollections and others may find their recollection of events differing from those written. We include ourselves as remembering certain events differently but are happy to accept our mother's account as we celebrate with her the double achievement of the publication of this memoir and her elevated status as an author and octogenarian.

Barry Leigh
Marcia Mishcon
July 2004

Full Circle

INTRODUCTION TO THE STORY

"Shingles?" I was surprised. I didn't know much about shingles, but in my mind it conjured up the image of a cove, the sandy beach sheltered by rugged cliffs, the sea gently surfing on the pebbled shore. That couldn't be bad.

"Is that all?" I asked.

Dr Dodds looked up. "Try to rest as much as possible," she commanded. "It could affect your nervous system."

I nodded as I got up. I had come to the surgery with a cold and cough. It was just by chance that I pointed out the wreath-shaped spots on my chest.

"There's no treatment," she continued. "You've been under a lot of stress recently. That probably brought it on. Can you take a holiday?"

"Maybe," I replied.

I made my way home and went to bed. By the evening I felt worse; I was devoid of energy. I recalled Dr Dodds' words: "There's no treatment. Rest as much as possible."

I took a compulsory rest, but alas, with little relief. One week stretched into one month and continued into the second month. I felt ready for the dustbin. Gazing at the ceiling, which was now my main pastime, I reflected, "This isn't like me! I'm positive thinking." Yes, that was true. "Remember?" I asked myself.

"Yes, I remember." Misty pictures filtered through my mind and memories returned to comfort me. I had locked away the past and thrown away the key, but this illness broke the lock as hidden memories came flooding out.

PART ONE

~ The Roots: Papa ~

Papa was a rebel, fired by the beliefs of an ideological world of high principles and a quest for knowledge, following in the footsteps of his forebears. My roots begin with Papa and his attitude to life, which began in Russia during the period of the pogroms.

During the late nineteenth century, it was not unusual for Cossacks to attack villagers just for the sport of causing havoc to Jewish families. It was on one such occasion that Papa's father and brother were killed, leaving his mother widowed, with five children to bring up alone.

Papa's four uncles were teachers and philosophers, the sages of the community, wise men who studied the Torah and prayed in the synagogue. People would go to them with their problems and they would find the answers in the Talmud. The law of the land was that the eldest son of every family, when he reached a certain age, was conscripted to serve the Czar in the Russian army. In their wisdom, they registered the death of the firstborn and that is how it came to pass that my father took on the name and identity of his younger brother, who had been killed, and had the trauma of living a lie.

His uncles, all learned men, arranged for Papa to study the Torah. The family ties were based on knowledge and Papa entered the rabbinical world to study and become a rabbi. He was sent to a Yeshiva and in time became a scribe. He had a fine hand, but while he enjoyed preparing the skins and writing, he was not happy being a long way from his family in the village near Rega, in Lithuania. It saddened him that they were not at the shtetl to share his bar mitzvah. He didn't settle into religious life and when he was mature enough, he rejected his religious learning, maintaining that if there was a God, he could not witness the atrocities without doing something about it. Turning his back on God, he renounced his belief and became an agnostic.

News reached him that his four uncles were emigrating to America with their families. His mother and her five children were being left behind. Without a breadwinner, they couldn't undertake the extra burden. If and when they could, they would send for her. As soon as he could, he followed in his uncles' footsteps and was welcomed in Toronto by his Uncle Morris and cousins Hilda, Rose and Betty. Shortly after, Uncle Morris was offered a teaching position in Portland, Oregon, and the family moved, leaving Papa alone in Toronto.

The Goldblatt family were recognized for their knowledge and achievements through generations, producing exceptionally clever or talented individuals. I wish Papa had spoken more freely about his family background, but any reference to it in the early years was a closed book. However, in later years I learnt much more about them and discovered that the ancestry of our family was quite extraordinary, including an early forebear who designed the first dollar bill. My early recollections recall achievements made by the offspring of Papa's uncles. Uncle Philip's son, Harry, became a doctor who attained world recognition in the early 1920s when he was a relatively young man – for his discovery of a cure for rickets; he went on to become a world authority on kidney research. His sister, Alta, was the driving force in establishing the B'nai B'rith in Canada. She was a tireless worker. The committee honoured her on her eightieth birthday by planning a trip for her to Israel; as an afterthought, they arranged for someone to meet her and show her around, to which she replied: "Don't worry. I have a friend meeting me." The friend was Golda Meir. She spent two weeks with the President of Israel, her close friend and colleague from their early schooldays.

I was about six when Uncle Nathan's daughter, Rose, won a scholarship to study music in London. Her stay was extended twice and we were amusingly told of her playing piano for the King and Queen at Buckingham Palace. She became Professor of Music at McGill University. My brother Albert and I had lessons with the same teacher, to no avail, even though we acquired, and still have, the piano she learnt on. Hilda, daughter of Uncle Bernard, was a marine artist in Chicago; I spent a week working with her in her studio and was amazed at her stamina. It was she who told me about the forebear who designed the dollar bill, giving me information I cannot recall. She was the matriarch of the family, proud of her heritage and making every effort to keep our far-flung family in touch with each other.

Papa was proud of his heritage. I'm probably wrong, and speaking off the top of my head, but I think he always resented the fact that his name was not Goldblatt. His mother was a Goldblatt, and he felt he was one too, but without the name he was so proud of, I think he felt cheated. Nevertheless, he was a clever pioneer and an achiever. He was a truly good man. He had gone to Canada penniless and alone, and then one by one, sent for his mother, two brothers and two sisters and brought each member of his family to Canada.

Papa's life was a constant battle in coming to terms with the duality of his nature. He was what was then termed a member of the intelligentsia, spending all his spare time reading or mulling over, in discussion, the fate of the world, mainly with patriots who were, like himself, interested in making the world a better place. He was basically an academic with a keen, enquiring mind, interested in new projects and progress, totally opposed to violence. In his Utopia, everyone would speak the same language, and he learnt, and tried to encourage us to learn, Esperanto, the proposed Universal Language in the thirties. He rarely spoke of his Russian background, or I should really say Lithuanian, but he did occasionally talk about his early years. He was proud of being a scribe and would delight in telling how he first had to prepare the skins in order to make the scrolls and then demonstrate how he then would write them. He took pride too, in his beautiful, flowing handwriting. It slipped out only once that he was bar mitzvahed in another town, away from his family, but could never be drawn to speak of it again, as if the memory was too painful.

Starting a new life in a strange country, without knowing the language, is a challenge. Couple that with a training which you no longer wish to pursue and you indeed have a problem. Papa had no trade, but he was ready to learn. Through necessity, he was tied to a life in the commercial world to which he wasn't really suited.

The "new world", as he called it, excited and inspired Papa. He found himself in the centre of the clothing industry and secured a position with the T. Eaton Company, the largest and most progressive manufacturing firm in the city, and like so many other immigrants, discovered that he was among friends who were in the same plight. Clever and quick to learn, he worked his way through the different stages of manufacturing, experiencing the skills required in each stage. By the time he reached the cutting department, he realized that everything depended on the pattern. Pattern-making was in its infancy, and with his disciplined mind and imaginative flair, he determined to become a pattern-maker. In fact, he progressed even further and became a designer. He was not a businessman, far from it, but he was clever technically and in time became very successful. I'm proud to say that he was one of the pioneers of pattern-making in the clothing industry, treating pattern-making as a science. When Papa made a pattern, there was no hit or miss factor; everything went together like clockwork. He dispensed with muslin drapery on a figure or dummy and devised a method of calculation on the pattern itself, to attain the design and measurements required, and to include details such as pleats, collars or fullness for a gathered skirt. He introduced a system of grading sizes which are standard today. Through sheer dedication, he earned himself a reputation as one of the major pioneers of dress designing for the mass production market. My brother Henry and I have the benefit of his knowledge and followed in his footsteps.

Papa was a modest man, a private person who didn't allow his emotions to show; he was meticulous to the most minute detail, with every 'i' dotted and every 't' crossed. He abhorred gossip, was not a great conversationalist and only spoke when there was something worth saying; he didn't believe in wasting words. He was a devoted father and a demanding parent, expecting the utmost from my two brothers and me. He was economical with praise, usually implying that something could have been done better. We each had our own reaction to Papa's demands. My brother, Henry, was defiant and aroused Papa's wrath, by questioning him with, "Why should I do something I don't agree with, just because you say so?"

Albert had more tact, replying, "Sure, but I don't think it's right." He could wind Papa around his little finger with, "Pop, it's modern humour," which made Papa laugh.

But I was in awe of Papa; I never answered back.

Papa's idea of fun was to have a spelling quiz. Sport and leisure were considered a waste of time and novels were frowned upon. Classics and the *Book Of Knowledge* were proper reading. Reference to the *Encyclopaedia Britannica* was encouraged. Papa treated books with reverence, insisting that we maintained the same respect. It's understandable that one of the first things I purchased when I set up my own home was the *Encyclopaedia Britannica*, followed by the *Book of Knowledge* as soon as my children appeared.

Papa was an honourable man and one to be proud of. I doubt if anyone could say a bad word about him, unless it was to say he was Victorian in his attitude to discipline and a stickler for doing one's duty.

And so, as the legacy reaches out, handed down from Papa to me, I feel myself following in Papa's footsteps. I look like Papa and inherit his enthusiasm for a challenge. I span a different era but the tenacity remains the same.

~ Grandma and Mama ~

It was around the turn of the century when my widowed grandmother decided that she and her youngest daughter, Mary, would emigrate to Canada to join her two married daughters, Chaika and Annie. This was Grandma's second experience of picking up roots in search of a better life.

Grandma and Grandpa were among the multitude who escaped from the tyranny of the pogroms in Russia in the latter half of the nineteenth century, when they fled from Rega, with their four young children, to London. Grandpa was a cabinetmaker, and they settled in Whitechapel, where he was able to find work in small workshops. Mama, their daughter Mary, was born in London and home was in the Brady Street Buildings, a vast Victorian tenement in Whitechapel, built by one of the generous philanthropists who donated dwelling housing for poor immigrants who crowded into the east end of London.

I know very little about those early years except that life was hard after Grandpa died. I pick up the trail when Mama was seventeen, in the late Victorian era, when the suffragettes were active and women were campaigning for equality and votes for women. She took an active part and interest in the emancipation of women, enjoying the camaraderie she found in London. Working hours found her in a cigarette factory, rolling the tobacco and sliding it in to the paper tubes with a tortoiseshell instrument. Later years would find her making cigarettes for my father, using vile-smelling Turkish tobacco. A popular place for meeting young people was at Gardiner's Corner, quite near to the market, where food stalls abounded in Petticoat Lane.

Conditions in London were bleak, with few prospects; Mama's two sisters, Annie and Chaska, had emigrated to Toronto, in Canada, with their families. America beckoned with promises of more prospects for a good future. Permission to marry was refused to her sister Yetta, and Ben, because they were first cousins. They ran off and eloped and to everyone's surprise, went to Chattanooga, where his uncle gave him a share in a shop. Her brother Max took his bride to Baltimore, where her family had settled.

Grandma was a domineering woman, used to getting her own way. She brought up five children and considered that it was now their duty to look after her. When Grandma suggested going to Canada, though Mama loved London, she agreed that it would be better for Grandma to be nearer her children and grandchildren.

It displeased Grandma to find, on their arrival in Toronto, that arrangements had been made for them to stay in lodgings. Times were difficult and money was scarce for Annie and her husband, Nathan, who lived in dire circumstances with their disabled daughter, Jean. Chaika lived in Montreal, and they too, were struggling to make ends meet.

It was the custom in those days, and considered their duty, for the youngest daughter to care for her elderly parents in their old age. It was easy to identify an old maid aunt, confidante and friend to nieces and nephews not much younger than herself. That was the situation Mama found herself in: a teenager, untrained and unskilled, in a strange new country, with a mother to support.

Times were hard in those days for immigrants. They arrived by the boatload, mostly unskilled and penniless, looking for work. Still, her attitude to life was to do her best under the circumstances and when she found herself in the middle of the clothing industry, she looked around at the opportunities. She discovered that reasonably high wages could be earned on the sewing machines. It didn't take her long to develop the skills that made her an experienced machinist. She enjoyed the comradeship of working in the factory and her cheerful disposition endeared her to everyone. She found accommodation for her mother and herself, and when she began earning money, her sisters withdrew the responsibility for supporting their mother, which cast the burden firmly onto her young shoulders. Life was full of promise; she was young, on the threshold of adulthood and in a new country. She made friends easily and she was earning enough to support her mother and herself. The responsibility for her mother restricted her somewhat, but she believed in progressive and free thinking, joining in the movement of votes for women, akin to the suffragettes. Life was good and she was happy.

By this time, Papa had worked his way up the ladder and was now a qualified pattern-maker. He held a high position and was esteemed by the management. His fastidious appearance had the elegance of the man about town, never seen without the stiff white collar and tie, waistcoat, sporting the gold watch and chain and grey spats. Well-defined features, with curling brown hair scrupulously brushed back, revealed the aquiline nose topped by inquisitive brown eyes. He was the epitome of the Victorian gentleman.

Papa had disciplined his life from boyhood, not allowing himself to stray from reaching his goal, but deep down lurked the soul of a romantic. Mama had triggered his emotions and though he didn't believe such things happened, he found himself making excuses to go to the machine room. Each time he found the visit more compelling. In his eyes, she was the most beautiful and desirable girl he had ever seen. Papa was captivated by Mama's effervescent zest for life. He absorbed the details of her wide-set eyes, twinkling as she chatted to the girls around her. Her brown wavy hair cascaded halfway down her back, except for the top which was twisted in a knot to keep it safe from the whirring needle. Occasionally, he caught a glimpse of her standing and admired her gracefulness; he was determined to meet her.

Papa was ten years her senior and he wanted a wife. She was surprised to be introduced to the highly respected pattern-maker, and at first she thought it was to do with her work, but he apologised for the deception and asked if he could take her out, arranging to call for her later at her home. That was when he met Grandma. The meeting with her mother put him at ease. He knew at once that in her, he would have an ally. He courted Mama with determination, taking her to theatres, concerts and picnics and he found himself wanting to give her the moon.

When he proposed marriage, she pointed out that they were not at all compatible. She told him that he needed a wife to run his home efficiently and to cook and sew for him. She herself was young and frivolous and not nearly good enough.

He insisted that he did not want a housekeeper; he wanted a wife and he was in love with her. He would try his best to make her happy. He wouldn't try to stifle her personality. That was what he loved and admired about her. He would respect and treat her as an equal; his wife would be his partner. He maintained that though she didn't love him, he felt his love and devotion might be enough for both of them. It was the era when a husband expected to receive a large dowry and she had nothing but the liability of a dependant mother. He promised to provide a good home for her and her mother. The combined pressure of her domineering mother, and Papa's persistence, broke down Mama's resistance and they were married on Papa's birthday, May 7, 1911. Papa was twenty-nine and Mama was nineteen.

They had a good marriage, founded on respect, admiration, love and devotion. They were opposites, but it proved to be a good balance. Mama catered to Papa's fastidious routine, but was not backward in expressing her opinion. She brought sunshine into

Papa's austere existence. They never argued, nor disagreed with a decision made by one or the other, in front of my brothers or me, but they did have heated discussions, sometimes deep into the night, and respected each other's opinion. I suspect that in many cases Papa agreed with Mama, but he loved a two-sided discourse, and so did she.

I can say without a moment's hesitation that Papa loved and adored Mama until the day she died and long after.

Henry, their firstborn, in 1912, was followed two years later by Pearl. When Pearl was three years old, tragedy struck, and she died of appendicitis. Mama was bereft and inconsolable. She could not bear to remain in the same place and they moved from Toronto to Montreal. Both of her sisters were now in Montreal and their presence was a comfort to her in her grief. It proved to be a good move as the clothing industry was growing rapidly and Montreal was the centre. Papa soon established himself and then, after a few years, Albert arrived. Two years later, I appeared, on July 15th, 1924.

~ *The Early Years* ~

My challenge began the day I was born; the longed-for daughter who would fill the void left by the sister who had died seven years earlier. Mama referred to me as a "blue baby", the meaning of which I never fully understood, but surmised that it was because I was poorly. I was just a few months old when a mastoid was diagnosed. The doctor was reluctant to operate on a child so small. The year was 1924, when doctors' instruments were little more than butchers' knives. He maintained that there was no alternative. Without the operation, I would surely die. I survived, but not without problems: paralysis down the right side of my face and deaf in one ear. Only time would tell if the damaged nerves and muscles would respond to treatment. Mama nurtured me with love and devotion and her faith in the face of adversity was unfailing.

Not a stone was left unturned in Mama's search to find out and learn how to do the best for me. Papa's cousin, Doctor Harry Goldblatt, was making a name for himself in the medical world. His work in London was receiving universal recognition as an authority for sick children. He came to Montreal to see me, and young as I was, I remember. The room had a sheet hanging from wall to wall, forming a screen, with me behind in a high sided cot.

After the examination, I stood in the cot listening to their hushed voices and then he came in to say goodbye. The emotion in the room was probably what made the impression so vivid.

I was to spend many years in the safety of that room and though I was a mere child, certainly under five, much of it remains in my memory: glass doors that opened wide onto the balcony, and the upright piano, with its round-topped stool, that wound up and down. My brother Albert loved winding it to the top until it fell off, much to Mama's annoyance. The large, glass-domed brass clock was company as it chimed each hour, while the four balls of the pendulum twisted from side to side. On each side of the clock were a pair of brass vases, the bases of which were cannon shells of World War One. I couldn't bear to touch them as the metal left my hands with the odour of death. I recall slipping on the polished floor, and the carpet, with squiggles of orange, black and white. I loved the large brown chesterfield and two enormous chairs. My favourite game was building a house on the settee with the large cushion seats, where I would sit in the dark, curled up in a corner until someone came looking for me.

My early years were lonely years. I don't remember playing with children. I did a lot of drawing, cutting things out, and playing on the large balcony overlooking Main Street, watching the clanging street-cars making sparks on the overhead wires as they went by, just about level with the wrought-iron balustrade. Beyond the road was a park, called Fletcher's Field, where people walked and children played. To the right, across Esplanade, the wide main street, and rising upwards, was Mount Royal. The mountain rose proudly and clearly visible at the summit, was the large cross, a beacon for navigation on the river. But the mountain had much more meaning for me. Henry, my elder brother, used to ski there and I would watch for him on the large ski jump. That meant more to me than the Olympics.

I was enveloped and protected with love and devotion by all the family. Papa treated me like a piece of delicate porcelain.

Henry, my older brother, was my mentor, and Albert was my playmate. Each in turn, in their own way, would talk or do things to spur my imagination. Occasionally, I would respond and I became aware of their pleasure at any reaction from me. Mama was my rock; always there with a big smile, comforting me and telling stories. Her boundless repertoire ranged from fairytales like *Cinderella* and *The Emperor's New Clothes*, to stories of England when she was a little girl. Sometimes she would sing, her beautiful voice filling my head and heart with song. Light operettas were popular at the time and our was home stocked with sheet music: *Rose Marie, The Desert Song, Ramona . . .* Records, too, were played on our His Master's Voice gramophone, including Caruso's recording from *Pagliacci.* Mama would hold me in her arms at the end of the day and sing a lullaby. My favourite was the Russian lullaby:

"*Just a simple little tune when baby starts to cry . . . rock-a-by my baby . . . some day there may be . . . a land that's free for you and me . . .*"

Mama was always inventing games concentrated on exercising the muscles of my face, making funny faces, or seeing who could make the biggest yawn. All the family joined in and I was never really made to feel I was odd.

One day, she produced a hook. We all asked what she intended to do with it, but she gave one of her mysterious smiles and said, "You'll see. Come here Albert, you try it first." She caught one side of his mouth with the hook and then we could see that something else was attached to it. Tucking that extra piece around his ear, she held a little loop by the side and gently pulled it and drew back the side of his mouth to make him smile. We all laughed and clapped our hands. Then it was my turn, and by then we knew what it was all about. Of all the gadgets devised for me – and there were many – this was the most successful, and I used it for years.

As I grew older, my brother Henry began to help. He concentrated on making me wink.

"What are you doing?" I asked.

"I'm winking," he replied. "Look at my eyes."

I watched as he closed one eye and quickly opened it.

"It's a silent message to tell a girl that I like her. I wink, to let her know," he explained. I laughed as he continued, "If you like me, give me a wink."

Every day that had to be my greeting, first one eye, which was easy, and then the other.

"That right eye of yours is so convincing. Do it again," he would say.

My brother Henry was my hero. He was twelve years my senior and I looked up to him and adored him. He was a great influence on my life and looking back, a remarkable fellow. Good-looking, with straight black hair brushed back from a square forehead, long curling lashes on warm brown eyes complemented his athletic physique. He was an avid reader with a mind that absorbed everything. Papa occasionally made the remark that he was a fund of useless information, but everything that Henry did and said was magic for me.

It was from that flat that I remember my first day at kindergarten. We had to make a picture. I made a sailing boat on a wavy sea. The teacher wouldn't let me take my picture home, which upset me very much, as all the other children took theirs home. She told me that she was going to hang it on the wall, as an example, but I thought it was a punishment.

The security of the familiar room was replaced by a paved area between two entrances, when we moved from the flat in Mount Royal to the middle floor of a three-storey, red-brick building on Rue La Joie, in Outremont. Albert went to Guy Drummond School, which was close by, but I was too young. Mama arranged for me to go one day a week to the Convent, which was just a short walk away. Mama called it "elocution", but it was really speech therapy. It was there that I learnt how to pronounce sounds and to speak properly.

I was fascinated by the nuns; their scrubbed cheeks and their chins bound with stiff white material held by the stiff band across their forehead, just peeping out of the black hood attached to their long robe. They would glide along, arms joined together by hands hidden in voluminous sleeves. The rustling of their long black robes shattered the stillness of the silent white corridors, as I was guided to the small room where I waited until the Mother Superior called her greeting: "Come in, child."

Mother Superior was very regal. Her beautiful black robe had a stiff white bib at the front on which a large cross dangled on a long chain. Her kind face and gentle manner put me at ease as we sat face-to-face. At first, I had to repeat what she said, which progressed to learning how to make specific sounds. The clarity of her words made me aware of my inability to enunciate each sound, but I progressed under her guidance. She gently encouraged me to use the dormant facial muscles unaffected by the paralysis.

"Now put your tongue between your teeth," she would say as she demonstrated. As I imitated, she would nod in approval and follow on with the phonetic sound, "Thu.. u . . . u . . . u . . .

"Good," she'd say encouragingly, followed by words: "Th . . . ank you . . . th . . . ree. th . . . ere . . ."

Mama was always waiting. "What did you learn today?" she would ask.

When I answered, "This . . . and . . . that," a big smile flashed across her face and she gave me a big hug. I was responding! I looked forward to the lessons.

"Teeth together." Mother Superior demonstrated and I followed her example.

"Good, now with your lips together, like you're telling someone to keep quiet. Sh . . . uh . . . uh . . ."

I followed every move.

"Good, very good. Now say sh . . . oo . . . oo . . . oo."

When I mastered that, she asked, "What do you wear on your feet?"

I smiled as I replied, "Shoo . . . es."

Mother Superior kept me interested with every lesson. "This will be easier, so smile as you do it. Teeth together and make a hissing sound . . . ss . . . ss . . . ss . . ."

Before long, I was able to say the tongue twister: "She sells seashells by the seashore." And went on to "Peter Piper picked a peck of pickled peppers." Thanks to Mother Superior, I could speak properly when I eventually went to school.

Elocution lessons continued long after the speech therapy. Exercising by using the facial muscles was proving beneficial in overcoming the paralysis. Mama was always so enthusiastic about how much fun it was, that I didn't realize the real implication. I learnt story after story, and had to say the pieces daily. Sometimes the family would be an audience and at other times Mama would inflict my recitations as entertainment for her friends. They, too, were enthusiastic. Mama had very good friends.

Saying I did not like the La Joie flat is an understatement. The murky, dimly lit staircase was witness to a thwarted, obscene attack on me by a grubby delivery boy, fortunately interrupted by Mama. It left me with an intense loathing of the place, a negative period in which I was just biding time. The day we moved was most gratifying.

~ A Glimpse Of Home In The 30s ~

Stuart, a tree-lined road in the suburb of Outremont, was the site of our new home. 784 indicated our own front door, the upper floor flat of the two-storey duplex. The Levine family lived downstairs at 782, where Mrs Levine, a boisterous busybody, and her daughter Annabelle, kept an inquisitive watch on everyone coming and going, which gave Mama a sense of security.

A buzzer from upstairs opened the front door – a novel feature in 1929 – and one ascended the long staircase, turning left with the last three stairs, to the glazed door which allowed the light to filter into the square entrance hall. The warmth of the Persian carpet and the telephone on the hall table was welcoming as you entered. To the left was the spacious den, where I spent most of my time, and straight ahead was the lounge, referred to as the "front room". The brown chesterfield and armchairs from Mount Royal looked much better here. The glass-domed clock, standing elegantly in the centre of the mantelpiece, still chimed the hour which resounded throughout the flat. The brass vases with cannon-shell bases, which I disliked, stood each side of the clock and brought focus to the fireplace. I was intrigued by the artificial fire and amber glass coals that sparkled and looked like flames.

"What makes it burn?" I asked my brother Henry.

He explained: "The heat of the lamp makes the deflector revolve, which changes the pattern of diffused light through the glass, and creates the illusion."

Clever, I thought, as I watched the changing patterns it made.

The grand piano, on which Papa's cousin Rose won her scholarship, stood by the window. Albert and I both had lessons from Mr Gardner, her teacher, but the magic didn't rub off on either of us. It did, however, help to fill our lives with music, which played a large part in our family background. Mama had a beautiful voice, as did Henry, who sang in a Barber Shop quartet.

The 1930s was a wonderful period for musical operettas and shows. They were at their height, especially on Broadway, where there were composers like George Gershwin, Irving Berlin, Jerome Kern and Sigmund Romberg; our home had stacks of sheet music, with records echoing songs from shows and films. They boosted the musical evenings in our own front room, with Mama usually the prime performer and everyone else joining in. Papa would sit there transfixed; he didn't participate, but he enjoyed listening.

Mama spent time every day with me; elocution lessons continued and I had to stand and do recitations, speaking out loud and clear, with expression. One piece, 'When the liner reached the New World' became a party piece which I had to recite to one and all: Mama's friends, her bridge friends, aunts, uncles . . . anyone who would listen. She'd produce a scarf for me to tie on my head and I'd hunch myself over, in the guise of an old woman:

> *I come a longa way to dis beeg countree, America, to be wid my boy. He ees so fina boy ees Joe. Ee worka 'ard for many years and sava money to bring 'is poor ol' mudder across de sea to liva wid 'im.*

Some onlookers were moved by the drama when she was refused entry because of her eyes, but with hindsight, I think it must have been the strain of sitting through my monologue.

The den was my domain. Mama kept the room supplied with materials for drawing. I played with paper dolls, making paper clothes for them, and listened to music. The wooden cabinet of the His Master's Voice gramophone had a handle at the side to wind it up. I could choose from the extensive selection of records and would play records over and over until I knew all the words. Other times, I'd cut out figures and watch them dance round and round on the record. I didn't mind playing alone. Mama invited Annabelle from downstairs to play with me, but she didn't come. I didn't like her, anyway.

We were a close family, with Mama and Papa joined in making a good cultural background. Mealtimes usually included discussions on current topics and reports on day-to-day activities. We all played chess or watched games being played to gain an insight into the art of strategy. The *Reader's Digest* was Papa's bible. We didn't necessarily have to read it, but one of the features were unusual words, their spelling and meaning. Papa would give a prize if we knew the answers. We were encouraged to use reference books, be they dictionaries or encyclopaedia. I admit I was an also-ran competitor to my two brainy brothers.

Mama was a marvellous cook and the house always had a welcoming aroma of something succulent on the hob. Once a week, usually a Thursday, the smell of freshly baked bread filled the air. Mama was baking buns. One would find Mama in the kitchen kneading dough, which was then left to rise in large covered bowls while she busied herself making mandelbrot, crisp, sponge-textured biscuits. When the dough was ready, Mama cut off a little piece at a time, rolled it into a small rope and twisted it into a knot. Each small round tin held eight buns. She made enough to feed a hungry family and their friends for a week.

The floors throughout the flat were polished wood and I know it was a chore keeping them clean and polished, but Mama nurtured them with love. They were her pride and joy.

And that brings me to my first memory of Maritza, our French-Canadian maid and Mama's "Girl Friday". Maritza was full of life, anxious to please, and new to the city, a sibling from a large family in a remote Quebec village. She shared Mama's enthusiasm, singing merrily as she removed black marks by rubbing the wooden floor with wire wool and spirit. One day, as I was watching, the friction set her alight.

"Maritza's on fire!" I shouted, which brought everyone running, to find the bucket aflame. Maritza thought it was very funny and laughed about her singed hair, but Mama was adamant: "You're not to use spirit on the floors again, even if it does leave black marks. I want you to be more careful."

I can't think of 784 without thinking of Maritza. She made the flat a haven for me, always around, patient and understanding. She befriended me with a warmth that broke down barriers to my private world that revolved within my family circle, into which no one could enter. Maritza was the exception. I well remember the night she heard my cry of terror which stemmed from a fear of being attacked in the dark, and came to see if I was all right.

"Don't go," I begged.

Maritza had a sixth sense of my fear. "Would you like me to sleep in here with you?" she asked.

I nodded and from then on she shared my room, for which I was very grateful.

"It's nothing, I like your pretty room," she would say.

Time was very important to Papa. His life was ruled by the clock. Each time the chiming clock would strike in our lounge, Papa would take the watch from his pocket and check it. Routine was paramount and he was adamant that everything had to happen to the minute. If dinner was not ready on time, we all kept out of his way. To that end, Mama, my brothers and myself, adhered to his demands without question. Dinner was always ready as he walked in the door. The message would be passed around, "Papa is home" and we would each down tools no matter what we were doing and take our place at the table.

Papa was Victorian in his attitude to bringing up children, demanding and expecting complete obedience. Time not spent in useful pursuits was worthless. Henry's high spirits and athletic pastimes annoyed Papa, who considered skiing, swimming and tennis were time-wasting. Many were the times Henry felt Papa's strap, but it never broke his spirit. My cousins, contemporaries of Henry, received the same treatment and recalled in later years how they regarded Papa with terror. He put the fear of God in them, but his bark was worse than his bite, and really unfounded. Papa was the father-figure Mel needed after his father died. Papa took Mel under his wing, giving him advice and teaching him a trade, as he did with Henry.

Papa laid down rules, but Mama was at the helm. Mama's zest for life was irrepressible, with large rooms and an open plan creating a happy home filled with love and respect. Cousins of similar ages to my brother Henry treated our home as their own. Mama was their agony aunt, broad-minded and a good confidante and they came to her for guidance. Her understanding and unquestionable advice was readily forthcoming. Queenie was gorgeous and invited trouble, relying on Mama to rescue her. Attempts to restrain her usually fell on deaf ears, but her high spirits amused Mama and she gave her help unflinchingly. Mama was a tireless charity worker, with time for anyone in need. Mama was special; and loved by all who knew her.

I watched with curiosity when Henry took up oil painting, waiting patiently for his return to see what he had done. Most of his paintings included colours of the setting sun as a background to stark branches of trees reaching up to the sky. Imagine my surprise when he gave me my own set of oil paints. I opened the black metal box and gazed at the small tubes in a row, displaying the colours of the rainbow: small bottles of oil and turpentine, clip-on containers, four brushes, and a palette which slipped into the lid and kept all the items in place. I couldn't express my joy as we set out for my first day's painting and made our way to a large field. We trudged a little way through woodland and settled in a glade awash with wild flowers, and set up our easels. I copied as he squeezed paint in rotation of colour onto his palette.

Henry laughed at my effort to hold my small, square palette: "Look," he said as he demonstrated how to put my thumb through the strategically placed hole, "let it rest on your arm."

I watched as he began outlining a small cluster of flowers and proceeded to copy him.

"Don't copy my painting! You have to paint what you see." He grinned at my puzzled face and continued, "It's called observation and it's very important. The flowers must look different from where you're sitting."

I looked at his painting and I could see that the flowers did not look the same. "I see what you mean," I replied. It was a lesson I never forgot.

Henry had my finished painting framed and I gave it to Mama for a present.

My brother Albert was two years older than I. He was everything I wanted to be, but wasn't: good-looking, with brown curly hair, loved by everybody, full of high spirits and fun, free and easy, never lost for words. He could chat to anybody, whether he knew them or not. Everybody was his friend, and to top all that, he was clever. When I was old enough, Mama insisted that he had to take me with when he played with friends.

"Sure, Mama," he said, giving me a reassuring smile and taking me by the hand. We headed for the park very close to our home, where he normally played with the local children.

"Hi kids!" he said in greeting. "This is my kid sister and she's going to play with us. OK?"

I was now part of the gang. Albert continued to look after me and I felt secure in his shadow. He was my mouthpiece as well as my guardian and little by little I gained my confidence.

Religion played a strange role in our home, with controversial parents who “agreed to disagree”. We were brought up to be free-thinking, not subjected to “because I say so”. We had a choice. Papa was not averse to observing the Jewish traditions, in fact I can say he was proud of them, but he would maintain that he didn't believe in God. Mama wasn't sure. She wasn't convinced, so she followed her own convictions and filled our lives with tradition to the best of her ability.

Passover was an experience in our home. Mama would clear the kitchen and change the dishes to a special set kept just for Pesach: white plates with narrow yellow squares in a black border. The larder was filled with boxes of matzos, cinnamon balls, plava and masses of eggs. We'd have special tea and jam and a special traditional dinner, reflecting dishes of the Seder service: egg soup with spring onions and salt water; chopped apples and nuts with honey; chicken with green vegetables and chrane, made with freshly grated horseradish. Papa always grated the horseradish for Mama. We'd end with sponge cake and stewed fruit. Pesach breakfast was fried matzos smothered in cinnamon-flavoured sugar, and tea, a special treat, as we rarely had tea. Papa did not join in observing Pesach, although he would sometimes speak about the slavery in Egypt and of the Exodus. Papa insisted on having his usual cereal and eating bread, despite Mama's efforts to make it a special week, but Mama didn't mind.

Chanukah had a different slant for Papa. The death of the Maccabees upset him. He hated violence and unnecessary death. He felt they wasted their lives for a God who allowed it to happen, which he couldn't condone. We didn't light candles, but Mama always gave us Chanukah gelt, gold-wrapped chocolate coins, for the eight days.

We missed going to shul. Our cousins looked forward to dressing up and meeting there, but Papa said shul was for prayers to God and it was wrong to go there just to meet friends. He felt that it was hypocritical; Papa had very high principles. Though Mama didn't share his views, she wouldn't embarrass him by showing their differences in public. She was true to herself, respectful of Papa's feelings and made sure that we were not repressed by Papa's demands, as we learnt to cope with the situation.

~ *A Cameo Of Early 30s In Montreal* ~

No one ventured into the kitchen on Sunday mornings when Papa was sharpening his razors. He'd put a drop of oil on the sharp stone and gently grind each razor's edge. Every so often he would pull a hair from his head to check that the blade had made a clean sharp cut, then finish off by propelling each razor back and forth on a leather strop.

Papa would then wash and polish his car till it gleamed. The recollection of Papa's car cleaning fills me with shame and I feel sure that my brother Albert echoes the emotion. We were larking about, probably playing hide-and-seek, when one of us inadvertently shut one of the doors, locking in Papa's fingers. Fearful of his temper, we hid behind the car. Papa called out for help, but we remained trembling with fear. Papa knew we were there and calmly begged, "Please open the door. I promise I won't punish you. Please release my fingers."

The thought that we made him suffer that way nauseates me to this day, but strangely enough, it made a change in Papa. He hadn't been aware of the terror he had created by his strict punishment and after that he rarely, if ever, used his strap again.

If we weren't entertaining or visiting relatives on a weekend, we would be taken out for a meal, always to the same large restaurant, Moishe's, situated on Main Street, in the heart of Montreal's immigrant population. This was a haven and reminder of home to those who still missed their old country. Waiters with white starched aprons would hold their steaming trays high above their heads and set the delicacies down on starched white tablecloths. Smoked meat, goulash, borscht, chicken fricassee, meat balls, tzimmes and cheese blintzes with sour cream, to name just a few. The atmosphere was always like one big family, friendly and noisy. Papa treated every meal as a ritual, never hurried, savouring every mouthful and counting every bite.

Visiting family was always interesting, and one I revered was an occasional visit to Papa's Uncle Nechemyah. They lived on Park Avenue, near to Mount Royal, and going to their home was like walking into another world. A dark room, the Russian furniture covered with embroidered cloths and dark, highly polished chairs. It was similar to entering a sanctuary: calm, distinguished and comfortable.

Uncle Nechemyah was a small man, an older edition of Papa, with a small pointed beard and twinkling eyes. He would stand up, his arms outstretched and greet each one in turn: "Victor, so good to see you, and Mary, more beautiful than ever," he enthused. "Albert, you get more like your Papa every time I see you!", looking back and forth at Papa. Gazing at me, he smiled and nodded, "A shaina maidle, a pretty girl."

Papa always seemed to glow when he was with his uncle. Their love for each other was a joy to see. His wife was very quiet and I suspect she spoke very little English. Their two daughters, Fanny and Jenny, served tea, plain or with lemon, with lump sugar, from a samovar on the sideboard. Papa and Uncle Nechemyah sipped their tea through the sugar, smiling broadly and exchanging conversation at the same time. There was always news of other uncles and cousins who were spread right across America, one in Portland and others in Cleveland and New York. There was always news too, of their daughter Rose, and her progress in London, where she had won a scholarship to study music, which in time led to a professorship at McGill University. Sometimes we just watched as Papa and Uncle Nechemyah played chess.

Visiting Aunt Chaika couldn't be a greater contrast. We called her Fat Auntie Annie, as a way of identification when referring to her, as her sister's name was Annie. It was a mystery to everyone as to why she chose to be called the same name. Fat Auntie Annie was Mama's middle sister. They lived in downtown Montreal, close to the market. Barrows of food with barrels of herrings and pickled cucumbers, bread, cheeses and live chickens, lined the street. People laughing created a colourful and friendly atmosphere.

Aunt Annie's house was chaos; whenever we arrived, she would be spread out on the settee, with a box of chocolates by her side. She was always happy, as were her children, bright and cheerful, abounding in high spirits. It was a complex family structure. She had been widowed with four children, Queenie, Marie, Freda and Hy, but was now married to Uncle Sam, a tall, thin man with ginger hair. As a couple they looked like Jack Sprat, who could eat no fat, and his wife, who probably ate fat as well as chocolates. Marie, the eldest daughter, was married to Uncle Sam's son, Bill. They lived next door and it was always a mystery as to who owned which house. Phyllis, their daughter, was the same age as her aunt, Aunt Annie's daughter, which made her a niece of cousins Penny and Sydney, the youngest children of Fat Aunt Annie. They were all the same age as Albert and I. It was complicated, with Penny's mother being Phyllis's grandmother. I was always confused when we departed.

Aunt Jenny, the widow of Papa's brother, lived in the marital home she had shared with her husband, Alec. Their house on Hutchinson was built on the side of Mount Royal and was quite a climb: two deep steps from the road to the pavement and then several more stone steps until you reached the front door. Always dressed in black, her wispy hair was drawn back into a severe bun, which made her look much older than her years. She made us welcome in her immaculate home and her clear and precise speech gave her an endearing dignity. I had the impression that she was very unhappy and one could not help feeling sorry for her. Her two children, Celia and Harry, fitted into the background and I can't recall ever speaking to them. Strangely enough, many years later, I met my cousin Harry by chance, not knowing who he was, and was surprised to find he was a very pleasant fellow indeed and not at all sombre.

I've never been sure of the actual relationship, but I believe that Uncle Hymie was Papa's uncle. He and Aunt Sophie adored children, but unfortunately couldn't have any. They were a jolly pair, both big people, who seemed to laugh a lot. His clothes were rough tweed, which was scratchy if he came near you, but it seemed to go with his large, fair, handlebar moustache. Aunt Sophie wore dangling jewellery and it would heave up and down on her generous chest. They occasionally came to tea and would spoil us by bringing presents. Their affectionate pinch on the cheek was so hard that it remained bruised for ages. Any attempt to keep at arms' length usually failed.

Papa's two sisters, Aunt Mary and Auntie Fanny and his brother Frank, lived in an alien world to ours and were a disappointment to Papa, who believed in progress. The old part of the city was a small backwater, where time stood still, closed in its ethnic atmosphere. Without the need to learn a new language, one sister didn't bother and the only English I recall hearing her say was, "Dat's nice." The visit I remember to Uncle Frank, who looked just like Papa, was when his tall, fair-haired wife, Nita, had her finger caught by the needle of her sewing machine. It made me cautious to this day of the danger when using my machine.

The highlight of our day after a visit "Downtown" was to stop at Laura Secord, a speciality chocolate shop, on the way home. Albert and I would each be given a nickel and we would choose from the vast selection of handmade chocolates. One special chocolate or a small bag of lump chocolate? Always a difficult decision.

Long, hot summers in the Laurentian Mountains were spent in a glorified version of a "down on the farm" family hotel. We were there from the end of June, when schools broke up for the summer holidays, until September. Trout Lake Hotel was built on a hill by the highway to Ste Agathe, a few miles south of the French-Canadian village, approximately sixty miles from the stifling, humid atmosphere of Montreal. The hotel, in the mode of a log cabin, catered for families with young children. It was set in a clearing in the middle of dense forest terrain, fenced off with barbed wire. We were warned never to stray into the wild areas inhabited by bears, who could crush you to death, and ferocious wolves, who preyed and attacked and whose cries could be heard at night. One could get lost in the wilderness. If someone did stray into the unknown territory, a search party was organized. I remember the anxiety of one such search the previous year when two people had gone hunting and were absent for too long a time.

Across the highway and down a pathway into the valley, was the large expanse of Trout Lake. Clear, ice cold water flowed down from the mountain. An area of the lake was partitioned off for children. A raft with a diving board was further out in a deep part of the lake and rowing boats were situated on the left side of the shore, with canoes on the right. Papa was proud of the fact that he taught himself to swim and felt that for safety's sake, we should know how. He taught us how to swim breast stroke. Mama never went in the water; she sat watching at the water's edge. After swimming in the afternoons, we could watch the cows being milked in the barn behind the kitchen, where the chef would have freshly baked biscuits and glasses of fresh warm milk. Children ate together, supervised by young staff. Sometimes a mother would come in, as was the case of the Miller family: two boys, the same age as Albert and I, and a younger sister.

I was intrigued by the mystery of the Miller family, which no one spoke of openly, but everyone knew. Sly innuendoes would slip out like, "He's making little stones out of big ones."

Their mother nagged the children relentlessly and stood over them at every meal, stating, "Papa sends money for you to be here. EAT."

I wondered how he managed to send money from jail.

Papa and Henry came every Friday evening and spent Saturday and Sunday with us, as was the norm with fathers united with their families every weekend. The hotel organized entertainment at weekends, with music, a bonfire, amateur shows and sporting competitions, that gave the hotel a reputation for being good fun. Even the food was special at weekends.

It was during our third summer at Trout Lake when the fire broke out. Fortunately, it was during the period when most people were out. We were told that the fire started in the kitchen, but the flames took hold of the wooden structure and quickly spread through the hotel. I remember standing with my family on the roadside, watching the flames soaring high into the sky. I wailed that my doll, Kikapoupalis, was in there. Mama tried in vain to console me. Papa came from Montreal to take us home, as did all the other husbands of stranded families.

Everything was lost, but I don't recall any talk of loss of life or severe injury. My tragic loss was Kikapoupalis. Mama gave me another doll and spent sleepless nights knitting clothes, but I mourned for my precious doll and the new one was never the same.

~ *Holiday In Chattanooga, 1932* ~

Albert and I sat down at the dining room table. "What's the meeting about?" I asked.

"Search me," Albert replied, as Henry came in to join us.

"Do you know what the meeting is about, Henry?" I asked.

"Summer holidays," he replied, adding, "I don't think we're going to Trout Lake this year."

We didn't have long to wait for Mama and Papa, who arrived with a large atlas which he put on the table and smilingly said, "Mama and I have planned a different holiday this summer. We're going to close the factory for the month of August and go touring."

I looked at my brothers to see if their reaction was as negative as mine and noted the complete silence as we waited for Papa to continue.

"We need to have a destination in mind and my suggestion is to visit Auntie Yetta and Uncle Ben in Chattanooga." He looked across at Mama, who appeared to be taken by surprise, smiled, and continued, "Mama hasn't seen her sister since she and Uncle Ben left England. Travelling through the eastern states of America will give us a good opportunity to see many interesting historical places."

Papa had obviously given it a lot of thought. No one could fault the idea of a trip which had taken on significance; even Mama became enthusiastic.

We all joined in with discussions about the route, studying maps, while decisions were made about which states and places of interest would be included. Baltimore was added, to visit Mama's brother Max and his family. Albert and I participated, although I'm sure we had little to contribute, but Mama and Papa felt we should be aware of where we were going.

Papa bought a Ford when mass production made the price affordable, and delighted in quoting Henry Ford saying, "You can have any colour as long as it's black."

The motor car had opened up new horizons for Papa, who was easily the world's worst driver; he was really more attuned to the horse and carriage. He was unaware of his shortcomings and derived immense pleasure in touring and seeing new places, but journeys, interesting as they were, meant that we had to tolerate the stench and fumes of his Turkish cigarettes, which he smoked incessantly.

How we fitted into the Ford with all the luggage remains a mystery. Mama did the groundwork in getting everything ready for Papa to do the packing, at which he was a past master. His careful folding of clothes, padding out with others in between, resulted in uncrumpled things to wear.

My favourite doll, Kikapoupalis, lost in the Trout Lake fire, had been replaced by Mama, who gave me a small doll sleeping in a wicker basket. "His name is Moses," she said, adding, "The mother of Moses was Jocheved, your Hebrew name."

"Oh, Mama, he's lovely!" I smiled, cradling my new doll.

At last we were on our way. Going through customs at the border to the United States was my first realization that restrictions were involved, which triggered my pride in being Canadian. We travelled through Vermont, the playground of wealthy Americans featured on films of the period, and found it compared favourably to the Laurentians. Papa regarded the historical status of Boston was a good reason for making it one of our "cities of interest". I remember very little about it except being at the actual place in the harbour and being told:

"This is where the tea was dumped into the sea at the uprising of the Boston Tea Party."

Papa was duly impressed by relevant details which were quoted and explained, but none that I can readily recall.

Atlantic City, however, was memorable. It was the first time I had seen the sea with waves breaking on a sandy beach. We went swimming, enjoying the freshness of salt water, jumping up to be carried in on the tide by the power of the waves propelling bubbling surf on to the shore. We enjoyed two unforgettable days before driving on to New York.

New York was a revelation, with buildings reaching up to the sky, the innovation of the era. The Empire State building and Rockefeller Center were symbolized in the music of George Gershwin, who had made his debut with the Paul Whiteman Orchestra at Carnegie Hall. One could sense the pulsating rhythm of the music while taking in the sights; the clanging, the horns and the pace were exhilarating and exciting. The multitude of theatres on Broadway were mind-boggling, especially compared to Montreal's one His Majesty's Theatre. Walking down Broadway built up an inner excitement which was unforgettable to my young impressionable mind. We took the ferry to Staten Island. Sailing in the shadow of the Statue of Liberty was awe-inspiring, especially coupled with tales of immigration and Ellis Island. We went to Coney Island where the promenade along the seafront seemed to go on forever. On the sandy beach, we had hot dogs in a roll, and chips sold in a paper cone, nothing special today, but revolutionary then.

On to Washington. All I remember is the breathtaking panoramic view of the White House. Looking down at it, I was bewitched by the pure classical proportions of the domed white building encircled by parallel white roads, creating a fairytale image, awesome and inspiring. A sight etched deep in my memory, worthy of being the hub and capital of the United States. It's probably very different now.

Papa was an appalling driver, but he insisted on doing most of the driving, allowing Henry to take the wheel occasionally, so we had to endure Henry's remarks, "Change down, Dad, you're straining the engine," or, "Hey, Dad, you're on the soft shoulder!"

Papa's answer would be one of his black looks that spoke volumes; Papa didn't take kindly to criticism. There would be silence for some time, with Henry staring straight ahead and Mama looking out of the window. Albert and I found it very funny, grinning at each other and stifling our laughter.

Driving through so many states, taking time to see historical towns and cities en route, was a wonderful experience. We travelled south and reached Tennessee, where the landscape became bleak. The heat created a golden haze across the flat cotton fields with ditches either side of the long, peaceful dirt roads, little more than cart tracks.

I found the ditches disconcerting and asked, "Why do they need such deep ditches?"

Henry turned around to explain about drainage.

No one really knew how it happened. Suddenly, the wheels got caught in the side undergrowth and the car veered back and forth, finally rolling over twice, landing in the ditch. Fortunately we weren't killed. Help arrived quickly from out of nowhere and pulled us out of the wreckage.

I shouted, "Moses is still in the car," and the search went on for another child until Albert called out, "It's her doll!" and someone rescued Moses.

Papa was seriously injured with a few broken ribs. I don't remember anything else about the accident. Repairs were made to the car and we continued our journey to Chattanooga, with

Henry driving. My fear of ditches remains and I'm wary of them to this day.

The romantic story was like a fairytale; Auntie Yetta and Uncle Ben fell in love, but they were cousins and permission to marry was refused. They ran away, eloped and emigrated to America. They settled in Chattanooga where Uncle Ben was assured work in his uncle's shop, which he eventually took over.

Auntie Yetta was a few years older than Mama, but not as pretty. She was very much like Mama and had the same gentle way of speaking, with a kind word and ready smile. They spent hours reminiscing about London, singing songs, 'Come and make eyes at me down at the old Bull and Bush' and 'On a bicycle built for two', that brought a sparkle to both of them.

Henry was the same age and with similar interests, as their two sons, Melvin and Erwin and they got on well, showing each other how to play the ukulele and harmonizing songs. They played a lot of tennis, though the heat was stifling. Reah and Sylvia, their daughters, were of similar ages to Albert and me.

Uncle Ben was a very pleasant man who took a delight in showing off his General Store, which was a short stroll from the house. The corner store was built of wood, shielded from the sun by a slanting roof. Two steps led to the veranda, where one could sit and watch what was going on in the street. Screen doors kept the flies out of the shop. Inside, shelves lined the walls behind the substantial counter. Wooden boxes, in which the fruit and vegetables were delivered, were stacked in clumps on the opposite side of the store. Uncle Ben encouraged us to drop in to the store if we were passing and he would ply us with goodies, especially watermelon, which they cut into large slices; it was at the height of its season. They sold pieces of it and you'd see people sitting at the roadside or leaning against walls, eating the thick pink slices and spitting out the flat black pips. I had enough watermelon on that holiday to last me a lifetime.

One day we were taken to visit Uncle Ben's old aunt. Tante Gnesha, a wizened old lady who looked about a hundred, greeted Mama with great excitement and we discovered that she was also Mama's aunt. A tour of her rather large home revealed, to our surprise, an indoor swimming pool. A request from Albert to have a swim was laughingly refused. Later, we discovered that it was a mikvah, where religious women go to immerse themselves, the details of which eluded me. Tante Gnesha was the custodian.

Memories of the deep south around 1932 remain and will remain with me always. One day we boarded a streetcar and suddenly there was a surge as all the passengers in one movement got off. Little did we know that blacks and whites were segregated and we had, inadvertently, entered the black section. Young as I was, it was a sad and bitter experience I shall never forget.

That short visit many years ago created a close family bond, kept alive by letters, between me and my cousin Reah, which has withstood the test of time.

We drove back via Baltimore and that was the one and only time I saw my Uncle Max. It was a complete letdown and a bitter disappointment for Mama. The recognition was cordial but there was no emotion and no warmth. Mama felt her visit was an unwanted imposition on her brother. All I remember was the beautiful veranda of their house and that they called their daughter "Lovey". I'm sure it couldn't have been her real name.

~ Growing Up ~

I don't profess to be a butterfly, but I felt myself shedding the caterpillar skin that kept me cocooned; unexpectedly, I had the sensation that I was emerging.

784 Stuart was the house that marked a change in my life. Coincidentally, it was when Papa began to notice me. I aroused his interest when he considered me intelligent enough to hold a conversation. Could that have triggered my transformation? Be that as it may, that is when I found my identity.

This was a happy period of my life. I was not at ease with people and most of my time was spent in the den, where we had a large gramophone and records, which I enjoyed playing over and over again. Sometimes I would stick paper figures on the record and watch them turn round and round to the music. Mama gave me a cardboard doll with a set of paper dresses. Small tabs on the dresses twisted over the doll to keep them on. Copying the doll, I made another, with an additional wardrobe, which was dancing around when Mama came to see what I was doing.

To my surprise, she called out, "Victor, come and look at what Gwen has done."

They both stood there looking at my doll until the record began to slow down and came to a halt. Papa picked up the doll and to examine the dress. "This is very clever," he said, twisting up the tabs.

"It holds the dress on the doll," I explained. "I like to change their dresses."

"Can we see the other ones?" Mama asked.

I took out the others I had made, and put them on the table.

"It looks like we have another designer in the family," Mama said, smiling at Papa. "Why don't you take her to the factory to show her how you design dresses?"

I don't know whether Papa was just surprised, or shocked, but a slow smile appeared on his face as he asked, "Would you like to come to the factory, Gwennie?"

"Yes, I would. I promise I won't be a nuisance," I replied.

The textile industry in downtown Montreal was a hive of small manufacturing firms, each specializing in their own field, ranging from Men's Wear, which encompassed tailoring of suits and coats, to shirt makers. Furriers abounded, from the purely practical, reasonably-priced, to stylish high fashion, where the sky was the limit.

The Hermes building, behind Saint Catherine Street, was the centre for small manufacturing firms in the rag trade. One such firm was Papa's. Fischel and Klein proved to be the perfect partnership, combining an efficiently run factory with a first-class travelling salesman. Their range consisted of model afternoon dresses, cocktail wear and dinner gowns, with details and workmanship of the highest calibre – ready-to-wear with the finesse of couture garments.

Papa fulfilled his offer to take me to the factory at the weekend, when he began designing the sample range for the new season. Mama packed my drawing paper and crayons and Papa settled me in the reception office. The little office without a window was dreary, and after a while, I wandered out to where Papa was at work. He glanced up and continued with what he was doing; I found it fascinating.

"Do you mind if I watch?" I asked.

"No, of course not. I'll try to explain what I'm doing, if I can," he replied.

He patiently demonstrated how he went about making patterns, showing how the style in the sketch was interpreted onto the pattern. He explained how to attain a third dimension while working on a flat surface, as well as explanations of matching seams and coding that made directions clear for machinists to sew garments together. His methods intrigued me; I absorbed it all like a sponge. He took pleasure in explaining everything, including the procedures, as work progressed through each stage of manufacture. He explained in detail the importance of the layout of the pattern on material before cutting it out: whether the arrow on each piece was positioned on the straight or bias and care in matching patterns of fabrics with designs, especially stripes. I gained so much from his pleasure in doing something really well. He was a perfectionist and he instilled in me the importance of doing things the right way.

I remember the large open factory area and yet it wasn't really open. A garment had to progress through every stage, which was strategically placed so that there was no waste of space, or time, in going from one stage to another. The finished dress was identical to the original drawing.

The clarity of Papa's teaching was so comprehensive that it has remained with me ever since. As a teacher, he was the best. Little did I know that this lesson was to play a large part in my later life.

My brother Henry, and cousin Mel, both worked in the business, adding a younger approach to the production and working processes. Henry by this time was also an excellent pattern-maker and, I might add, a wonderful brother. He noted my "Oohing and ahing" about certain designs and made miniatures of them just for me, as a birthday present. That year I was the best-dressed girl in Montreal.

One could not help being aware of the Depression invading everyday life. Soup kitchens were opening up in the poorer areas. Shops were closing down as they went out of business and hungry men begging for a crust of bread was not an unusual sight. The tenor of the country reflected in the song, 'Brother, can you spare a dime?' Despair was in the air.

Mama was an avid charity worker, both on committees and by physically helping the needy. Bridge parties were held regularly in our home to raise funds. Every so often she would say, "Sort out any toys and games you've grown out of," as well as, "Put any of the things you don't use in this pile."

Clothes slightly outgrown were bundled together ready to take to the East End.

We lived in a more affluent area, sheltered from the sight of beggars, but we couldn't help being aware of the situation. Mama spent time each week at the soup kitchen in the East End and came home disturbed about the conditions people were having to contend with. Even radio programmes echoed the plight of families.

On Sundays, Albert and I were allowed to listen to Eddie Cantor on the radio, giving our hair time to dry after the hair-washing session. I remember being heartbroken when he sang, 'He's the little boy that Santa Claus forgot.' It brought home to me what the Depression was all about.

It hadn't been obvious to Albert and me that the Depression was affecting Papa's business, but that summer we did not go to the Laurentians. Instead, we toured to Ontario, visiting relations in Hamilton, Toronto and Port Colborn. The trip culminated at Niagara Falls, one of the memorable wonders of the world. It was an historic period of the Falls, when they first introduced the lighting, and tightrope walkers risked their lives walking across the wide expanse. It remains the same today as it was over sixty years ago, with the Maid-of-the-Mist sailing below the Falls, and people donning raincoats and wellies to walk underneath.

With hindsight, I now understand why certain events took place. At the time, I thought our trips to Chattanooga and Ontario were just holidays, but later I realized that Mama and Papa were looking to see whether there were better prospects further afield.

Shortly after our trip to Ontario, Papa left for England to investigate the rumours that there were good prospects for craftsmen experienced in ready-to-wear and mass production. For years, Mama had harboured a yearning to return to London, where she had been really happy and so the prospect of returning to England appealed to her. Papa, on the other hand, was ready for a new challenge. It was a brave move to make, but with nil prospects in Canada, he felt it worth a try.

We moved from our lovely home at 784 Stuart to an adequate apartment in Davaar. The rooms and layout were nothing special; the only unusual feature worth a mention was a rubbish chute, never before and never since experienced. One emptied rubbish into the opening in the wall; the rubbish slipped down into the fire burning in the basement furnace. A clever idea, but one I would have thought dangerous if combustible items were inserted.

It was a much longer walk to school. Albert and I had always gone together, but that year Albert moved up from Guy Drummond to Strathcona Academy, not the same direction. Mama arranged for me to walk to school with two girls my own age, who lived next door. They made it obvious that they did it under duress from their parents. Bluma and Matte allowed me to tag along while they chatted and giggled. It did little to build up my morale, but the experience was a good lesson on how to cope with life. It taught me that often people are very hurtful for no reason, especially if that person is shy.

Mama kept busy, getting things ready for a move, but she had a lot of time on her hands and when my cousin Queenie had her appendix removed, Mama insisted that she recuperate in our home.

Queenie was high-spirited and always getting herself into trouble. Mama insisted that there was to be no nonsense under her roof and Queenie agreed. Nelson, Queenie's husband, a handsome travelling salesman, sent flowers, with apologies that he would be away part of the time. That's when things got out of control. Morrie, her husband's best friend arrived to visit.

Mama knew Morrie and as she took him in to see Queenie, remarked, "How nice of you to visit. That's what friends are for."

She went to make tea, when Albert came running in to tell Queenie that Nelson was just parking his car.

"Oh my God!" shrieked Queenie.

Morrie jumped up, grabbing his coat and turning to Mama implored, "Where can I hide?"

Mama now sensed the situation. "Albert, go downstairs and ask Nelson to show you the car. When he's shown you the engine, ask to look at the lights, then the wheels. Anything to keep him downstairs. Maybe go for a ride around the block."

"OK, Mama," he called as he ran downstairs.

Mama returned to the bedroom and led Morrie, who by this time was panic-stricken, to the fire escape by the kitchen door.

"What if he recognises my car?" Morrie muttered.

"You'll have to work that one out yourself. As far as I'm concerned, I haven't seen you."

Returning to the bedroom, Mama took away the gift Morrie had brought and shaking her head to control her temper, admonished Queenie with all the control she could muster, saying, "You stupid girl!"

By the time Nelson came up, all was serene.

That winter I do remember, with joy, playing outside in the snow. The park near our home had a natural slope and every year, a toboggan slide was put up. The steep slide, packed with ice, made a run from the top of the park to the edge of the skating rink at the bottom. Albert and I each had our own toboggan and we spent hours trudging up to the top, to enjoy the exhilarating steep surge down. Other times we would skate on the ice rink. After a fresh snowfall, the neighbouring children joined together building an igloo large enough for all of us to sit in. It remained throughout the winter and formed a meeting-place until the spring sun melted it.

Spring brings back the memory of my first day on my bicycle. The bike was fitted with pedal brakes. To stop, you had to push the pedals backwards, but first I had to master the art of balance. Henry volunteered to hold the bike and run along by my side until I gained my confidence. As I mastered the art, he let me go. I was getting near to the end of the road when I found that I couldn't master the brakes. I screamed,
"Stop me, Henry! The brakes don't work," but he was too far away.

I went headfirst down a ten-foot ditch filled with broken glass and rubble, cut my face to pieces and wrecked the bike.

He consoled me by saying, "Isn't it great that you can balance yourself on the bike?"

I grudgingly gave him a wry smile and said, "I suppose so."

Whenever I want to think of something wonderful, I think of the Laurentians. Summer in Montreal usually provokes an exodus to the mountains to avoid the intense heat of the city. Family hotels are simple log cabins by a lake. This time we stayed at the Hotel des Monde, on a delta at the edge of Ste Agathe, a French village. It was one of the most enjoyable holidays of my life, canoeing through the rapids, toasting marshmallows round the bonfire, and joining in the games. They had an amateur concert towards the end of the holiday. All the children took part in it, including me. Imagine my surprise when I won first prize for singing 'Shanty Town'. ME ! The little dummy!

Indeed, I felt like the ugly duckling who turned into a swan. It was a bit like being a butterfly. I had reached a turning point and looked forward to the future, maybe in England.

~ Our Move To England ~

The doorbell rang. There was a telegram. Mama turned it over and over in her hand, not knowing what to expect. In those days, the rare delivery of a telegram usually brought bad news. Mostly, news of a death. Mama hesitated, trembling, staring at the unopened envelope.

Henry gently put his arm around Mama. "I'll open it, Mama," he said as he took the envelope from her trembling hand. Deftly slitting the envelope open, he opened the telegram; a large smile suddenly lit up his face.

"Mama, it's good news! Everything is all set for us to pack up and leave. Oh! Mama, everything is wonderful."

He put his arms around Mama giving her a big hug. We all joined in, elated and he read out the telegram, so we would all know what it said: "Everything ready for you to join me. Let me know what arrangements you can make. Letter following. Victor."

Good news! The rumours had been right. There was a whole new world, just waiting to be nurtured into the mass production market. Mama was very excited. For years, she had harboured a yearning to return to London and was looking forward to the prospect of going to England, where she had been really happy.

Papa found that the clothing industry, at that time, consisted of handmade tailoring and made-to-measure dressmaking. The industry was crying out for experienced craftsmen in ready-to-wear and mass production. To his delight he secured a position to set up a ready-to-wear factory in Nottingham. The entrepreneur was an established lace manufacturer who had several factories. A large factory was put at Papa's disposal, with every assistance in setting up this new project. Papa wanted to get everything under control before sending for us; now he was satisfied that all was going well. It was time for us to join him.

Mama began organizing our move, a mammoth task, the extent of which I didn't realize until now. She had to be discerning about everything to be included in the move. Packing and storage were costly and had to be worth the expense. Furniture included the grand piano, books, toys, all the furnishings such as curtains and linen, all the additional clothes we couldn't take with us, even white elephants. Everything was to be put into storage until we had a home to which it could be sent.

For our clothes, and to tide us over until our things arrived from storage, Mama arranged for us to have two cabin trunks. The mini-wardrobes stood on end, opening in the centre to reveal four drawers on one side and on the other, special flat hangers to facilitate hanging clothes. Mama and I shared one and Henry and Albert shared the other. They were to be sent on in advance to the ship. Hand luggage would travel with us.

It wasn't until the removers came and emptied the house that the impact of the situation hit home. The actual departure from Montreal was traumatic. Mama had so many friends; she was loved by everyone who knew her. Coupled with that was her involvement with charity work and the large circle of friends who sought her advice. The sanatorium at Ste Agathe gave her a symbolic Indian totem pole, together with a silver salver inscribed with their appreciation. Another committee gave a silver dressing-table set. Everyone came to see us off, not just family, but whole committees of the charities she supported. It must have been a tremendous wrench for

We travelled by train to New York. In the long Pullman car we had upper and lower berth sleepers, each large enough for two. I shared the lower one with Mama, envying Albert having to climb up. I don't think any of us actually slept, but it certainly was exciting. We were met at the station by relatives. Cousin Queenie, – another one – was living in New York with her husband Henry and son Leslie. Dr Aaron Goldblatt, Uncle Nechemya's son, came to see us – luckily, as we had all developed sniffles. Mama was worried in case Albert had developed a contagious illness and feared that if that was so, we would possibly have to postpone our trip. Dr Goldblatt prescribed medication and assured Mama there was nothing to worry about. We spent an enjoyable few days in New York.

Albert and I remember the Automat. It was an amazing restaurant, all steel and circular glass. Individual compartments each displayed its contents. You inserted a coin into a slot by the sideband the door flew open, enabling you to take out the dish. The epitome of the Deco era. But we remember it for an even better reason. Albert created chaos by bringing the entire cutlery tray crashing down on to thc marble floor. Following the tremendous crash and an astonished hush, everything came to a standstill. There was complete silence as everyone watched the staff scurrying round retrieving the pieces from all over the floor and setting up replacements.

The family came to give us a good send-off at the docks. The crisp white ship, proudly displaying the name *Samaria* looked impressive. There were three gangways and it was thrilling to walk up, stepping onto the deck. We were immediately greeted and shown to our staterooms. We wasted no time staying there, but hurried back to the deck to watch as the ship set out to sea. It was fascinating to see the small pilot ship lead us out and then to feel the fresh sea breeze on our cheeks, echoed by the clamour of seagulls, wishing us well on our way.

There were three classes of travel. First class was the roped-off top deck. Tourist, the middle class, was the middle of the ship and Third Class was practically in the hold. They were all clearly designated. We travelled tourist class which was very pleasant.

To us the ship was a moving city, but it must have been a small ship because it took ten days from New York to Liverpool. How well I remember that trip. Ten days of fun. The playroom had the first motorised animals I had seen and I enjoyed riding the camel. It had a circular motion and the aim was not to slip off. The coach in charge of the adjoining sports room, kept a watchful eye on us as we wandered in. The mesh masks and long pointed swords hanging on the wall aroused my interest.

"What are these for?" I asked, pointing to them.

"They are used in fencing," he replied.

"Where is the fence?" I asked, looking around.

He roared with laughter and explained, "Fencing is a sport of bygone days when noblemen used to fight duels. It's the art of fighting with swords."

His offer to show us how it was done was eagerly accepted. Albert and I put on the masks and he demonstrated how to stand and hold the sword, which he referred to as a foil.

"Hold your left hand up, behind, to balance yourself," he instructed.

We followed his movements which progressed from thrust and parry to how to combat your opponent in a duel. By the end of the voyage we were quite good. Watching a duel on film is enjoyable, knowing and recognising the movements.

On deck there was shuffleboard and shuttlecock and quoits, but the wintry weather did not merit much outdoor activity. The evenings were more special, with concerts, games and the inevitable Fancy Dress. So much more is stored in the memory of that trip, mainly the camaraderie of the passengers, the fresh smell of the sea, and the spray of the waves on your cheeks when walking the decks, watching and listening to the seagulls following the ship.

Sadly, Mama was a bad sailor. No matter what was done, she could not overcome being seasick. The attentive steward kept trying known methods, but nothing did any good. She spent most of the voyage in her cabin eating cream crackers, which were supposed to help.

She would give me a wan smile and say, "Go and enjoy yourself. I'm better just being left alone."

With hindsight, it was a rough crossing, although my brothers and I didn't appear to be affected. But coming into the dining room one morning, we were surprised to see that the edges of the tables were raised and tablecloths were dampened. The steward amusingly told us, "It's to stop the dishes from slipping off if the ship suddenly lurches."

It was not unusual to find the dining room not filled to capacity on those days. Walking through the corridors, one had to hold on to the brass rails as the ship would suddenly veer from side to side.

It was sheer bravado that had Albert saying, "It doesn't bother me," with my response, "Nor me."

We found it amusing and it made the trip memorable.

It took a long time to dock; we watched the pilot manoeuvre us in. Liverpool was a very important shipping centre at that time and the docks were enormous. Some things seemed miniature by American standards; trains were tiny in comparison and cars were smaller.

Now we could see the people waiting on the dock and there at the front was Papa. We waved madly to attract his attention. And then we could see that he had spotted us and was waving back.

We watched excitedly as the sailors threw their ropes over and secured them and heard the clang, clang of the anchor going down and the gangways being put in place. And at last, the thrill of walking down the gangway to a strange new country. We were in England.

~ *Arrival In Liverpool and Nottingham* ~

Papa pushed his way through the waiting crowd to meet us as we made our way down the gangway. He looked wonderful, a broad smile on his face, and we descended on him like a swarm of locusts, throwing our arms around him, each one in turn. It was great for us all to be together again. Henry was in charge of finding all the luggage. Mama and Papa had much talking to do, while Albert and I looked around Liverpool.

So this was England! We looked at the small, shabby, terraced cottages, the cobbled roads with barrows and horse-drawn carts and a few small cars. Everything was so primitive. Albert and I just looked at each other, shrugging our shoulders, without saying a word.

We went by train to Nottingham. The train and rails were miniature compared to those in Canada, but we soon adapted to the fact that this was just a small country. The steam engine was beautifully painted and embellished with a lot of polished brass. Carriages were not interconnecting, but divided into compartments, each having its own door to the platform. We had one all to ourselves, comfortably upholstered, with brass luggage racks above and pretty, brass and glass-shaded lights above each seat.

Papa explained, en route, what arrangements he had made. He was anxious to tell us that life here was a little different from that in Canada. There was much more tradition and we would, perhaps, find some of the customs a little old-fashioned and more formal.

He went on to explain, "Instead of saying 'hello' when you greet someone, you say 'good-morning' or 'how-do-you-do'."

He laughed at our concern and added, "You'll soon get used to it."

We arrived in Nottingham, delighted to see that it wasn't at all like Liverpool. Everything looked beautiful: impressive buildings, paved squares filled with flowers and towering above, dominating the city, Nottingham Castle.

Settling down in Nottingham was an adventure and a different world. Papa had organised furnished accommodation and we soon settled down. He was full of enthusiasm and delighted with his new world. Nottingham was small compared to Montreal, but it was a pretty city. Mama's first concern was to get us settled in school. That would really determine where we would live.

The educational system was very different from Canada's, and Mama and Papa were confused that one had to pay for the public school near the city centre, which appeared to be old and primitive. An associate from Papa's firm told him about a modern school with superb amenities in the process of being completed in West Bridgford, where he lived. Mama was impressed, and Albert and I were taken to a large Victorian building, to be interviewed by the Headmaster, Mr Holmes. We found ourselves in the midst of a Dickensian world. Above the two entrance

doors, clearly carved in the stone lintel, were: GIRLS and BOYS. Albert and I, a little confused, entered the appropriate entrances and found ourselves at the beginning of a long bleak corridor, which parted to make way for a double staircase. Suddenly a bell rang and the empty space was seething with young bodies going in every direction.

A tall man, with a mortar board, his long black gown trailing in the breeze, approached and enquired, "Can I help you?"

To which Albert replied, "We have an appointment to see Mr Holmes."

"Follow me, I'm going that way."

We trailed behind, amused at having to keep our distance from his billowing gown. He stopped at an imposing panelled door with HEADMASTER engraved in large letters on the brass sign.

"Good luck," he said as he hurried off.

Mr Holmes was a quiet man who automatically commanded respect, while having the ability to make one feel at ease. He explained that they were still in the old school, pending the completion of the new building and said he would understand our disliking it. However, the new school would offer students facilities of the highest calibre and would be the best available. It was worth waiting for. We were very impressed and made it our first choice, a co-educational school with five hundred pupils.

Mr Holmes was wrong, however, about my not liking the old school. For me, it had a sort of magic. The ghosts of bygone days seemed to ooze out of the walls, to create an aura. The large assembly hall, with its vaulted roof and long large windows either side, where the whole school gathered each morning for prayers, had a dignity of its own. The teachers, each in their own particular gown which denoted the source of their degree, would gather on the rostrum, and all the school would be at attention, awaiting the Headmaster. Hymns were followed by the Lord's Prayer. This was traditional England. In fact, attending prayers was something I chose to do. By rights, being Jewish, I didn't have to attend, but I liked belonging.

I loved school and I would go so far as to say that it was one of the happiest periods of my life. I made wonderful friends and gained a confidence I had not known before. Probably the same could be said for Albert.

The furnished accommodation, a Victorian house at 91 Melton Road, was very near the school and an acceptable stopgap until a suitable permanent house was found.

That first house in England remains deep in my memory. Mainly it was the cold. We were used to central heating, but here we had to contend with a coal fire in the living room. The bedrooms were like an icebox and the cold and damp seemed to penetrate into our bones. The boiler in the kitchen heated the hot water and took some getting used to, until we mastered the art of not letting it go out. The front step needed to be whitened daily with white chalk, and the red quarry tiled entrance floor and scullery floor, required red cardinal paste to be applied and polished regularly. The step and floors were assigned to me until we managed to get a helper.

Mama set about house-hunting; a considerable task, taking into account the size of the furniture we had in storage. Eventually, Mama and Papa decided on a double-fronted house with an arched entrance to the front door. Our things were taken out of storage and in no time at all, our home looked like a palace. In Montreal we had always lived in a flat. 19 Stamford Road was our detached house and garden. It was modern compared to Melton Road and within cycling distance of the school. It was also at the end of the bus route which took Papa into town. The bus driver waited for him outside the house every morning, with the conductor occasionally calling out, "Come on, Mr Klein."

The system of teaching in set classrooms, with a timetable of teachers coming and going for different subjects, took a little getting used to. No sooner had I done so, than we moved schools and the system changed. Instead of the teachers changing classes, students did the moving.

The new school building lived up to and surpassed all expectations. Form rooms with large windows overlooked spacious playing fields. Each of the sciences – Chemistry, Physics and Biology – had a laboratory, with facilities for students to do experiments in pairs. A fully equipped gymnasium, with ladder-lined walls, catered for all forms of physical development.

The teachers were strict but fair and most of them memorable. In Chemistry, there was one Bunsen burner between two students doing experiments. Mr Fuller was a very thin man. In class he always wore his gown and mortar board, but walked out with a bowler hat perched on his head, carrying a rolled up black umbrella which matched his suit. We called him Mr Gamp.

Our Physics teacher was the typical absent-minded professor. He dressed in tweeds and looked messy, with his gown just about hanging on to his shoulders. His straight fair hair tumbled over his troubled face. Every experiment he set up went wrong. We were not allowed to laugh and we would watch in silence as he got himself into even more dire straits. Most lessons were spent waiting for him to sort himself out. He was a nice man.

The maths teacher was a toughie. His nickname, Spike, describes him perfectly. No one messed around in his class, be it Arithmetic, Algebra, Geometry or Trigonometry, using simple brain power. He was stern, but a good teacher.

Mr Chambers, the Art teacher, was a portly man. His large round face was always red and smiling. He was gushing in his praise. The Art Department was well appointed and Mr Chambers was a good, dedicated teacher. He admired my talent and there was never any doubt that I would follow a career in the art world.

One subject, 'Housewifery', disappeared altogether. Miss Forbes, the housekeeper, matron and caterer, lived in the caretaker's cottage at the side of the old Victorian building. One half day a week, we reported there to do Housewifery. We learnt how to dust, polish furniture, polish silver, clean carpets (by hand), and scrub floors. We were taught the rudiments of washing clothes, using bar soap on a scrubbing board or manoeuvring it with a three-legged dolly, boiling and blueing whites, and starching. There was a mangle for wringing the clothes and we learned the proper way to hang washing on a line with clothes' pegs, using a prop to secure the best breeze. The sequence of ironing various types of materials and articles, was followed through. We learnt how to darn, patch and make French seams, as well as a variety of embroidery stitches. Today, we live in a throwaway society, and so even the mention of the subject belongs in a museum. 'Housewifery' was replaced by Domestic Science, which encompassed learning about nutritional values, basic cooking and hygiene.

In our form room we had typical students' double desks, with a lift up top, an inkwell in the right corner and fixed seats. I had reason to remember that I shared mine with a spirited girl called Joyce. In form lessons, she used to change places with one of the boys, who would come and sit next to me, much to my embarrassment. The class were in hysterics. Although I was in the front row, it was several weeks before the teacher noticed. Everyone thought it was hilarious, but I wanted the floor to open up and swallow me.

Joyce was my best friend. We were a strange alliance; I was Jewish and her family were in the Salvation Army. Her father was the head of the community in a small town near Nottingham. Many of the members lived with them in their home. Others lived in the centre. I would stay with them for an occasional weekend or she would spend a weekend in our home. I loved the atmosphere of everyone gathered around their scrubbed table in the kitchen for meals and following the band as they sallied forth to spread the word of the Lord. Perhaps they thought they had a convert in me when they saw me singing the hymns. Joyce knew differently. Joyce loved the relative quiet of our house and we used to laugh at the contrast. She was my opposite, gregarious and full of fun.

She would draw me out and through her I began to be less inhibited.

Joyce would say, "If people laugh with you, they don't laugh at you."

Cynthia Jones was another influence in my life. Her father was a high-ranking military man, who had been stationed nearby. She joined the school in my last year. A winner, with short fair curly hair and deep blue eyes in a delicately chiselled face. Whatever she did, she had to be first or she would think she had failed. In sports she had the same conviction, to the extent that she would push herself to her maximum and then collapse with exhaustion. I'd never met anyone before with such determination.

One relay race remains in my memory, when we ran in the same team.

"Try to win," she implored; and I did.

When not competing, Cynthia was a wonderful, thoughtful person and we became good friends, laughing at our contrasts, because I never wanted to win. It meant nothing to me and so much to my competitors.

Pat Leonard was my first friend. She was more like me, laid-back and artistic, extremely pretty and softly-spoken. Years later, when I returned to England, I was sure she had become a film star. Whenever I saw Patricia Roc on the screen, I thought of Pat. I never followed it through and always regretted not trying.

There were others, but these three girls remain in my memory and my heart as the best friends I ever had.

Albert was the shining star of the school. He was always top of his class in everything and he was truly every teacher's pet. He was made a prefect and then became Head Boy. He was the head of the debating society as he was always ready to speak for the opposition and he duly became school spokesman. I was known mainly as Albert's sister and lived in his shadow, except in Art, in which I shone. Occasionally a teacher would corner me in a corridor and tell me that I too could do as well as Albert if I tried.

"Thank you, sir. I'll try to work harder," I would reply. It was nice to know they didn't consider me a complete loss.

Albert and I were serious chess players and represented the school in the Inter-County Championships. Albert was knocked out, but I went on to become runner-up.

My exaltation was short-lived. Papa brought me down to earth, saying, "You were lucky. Albert is a better player."

~ England: Late 30s ~

"I'm going to fly to Paris for the Couture Fashion week." Papa's announcement took us all by surprise; air travel was still in its infancy and mainly regarded as a sport.

"In an aeroplane?" Albert's remark echoed our surprise.

"How else? I haven't grown wings," was Papa's dry response.

We all travelled down to watch Papa's plane take off at Croydon, London's First Airport. The plane looked as if it was made of tissue paper and it had the delicacy of an oversized butterfly. We watched him climb in and he waved as the plane careered along the runway and slowly rose into the air. I don't know how long we remained on the roof of the building, staring into space, but eventually we made our way to London and spent the week there with Henry.

Henry had moved to London where he was successful in establishing himself. Young, good looking and clever, Henry was in his element. This was his field: fashion for the younger generation. He was good and his flair was sought after by the big progressive firms. There was no competition between Papa and Henry. They were at contrasting ends of the fashion market. Papa's world was haute couture ready-to-wear of original models, while Henry's field was reasonably priced copy-cat. I remember a sense of pride in seeing the Guinea Dresses displayed in shop windows all over the country. A really well-made dress, beautifully styled, for only twenty-one shillings. The Guinea Dress was Henry's creation. It was the period of the Fifty Shilling Tailors, when a man could get a made-to-measure suit, in the material and style of his choice, for just £2.10. So too, became the popularity of the Guinea Dress. The range included every type of style, from tailored conservative designs to sophisticated 30s, in tune with the Charleston era. The quality was high and the value indisputable.

London was the world Mama remembered as a young girl and where she had hoped to return. Henry had found accommodation for us in Dalston, near to where he was working in the East End, which pleased Mama, as she absorbed the atmosphere and camaraderie of London, in search of past memories.

"It's just the same as when I was a girl," Mama enthused as we walked between market stalls of Petticoat Lane, teeming with stall-holders selling anything and everything, tempting customers with double-talk of offers. Food shops and stalls competed with each other. It was wonderfully exciting.

"The food reminds me of Moishe's in Montreal," I remarked.

"Yes, Jewish food is the same all over the world," she said, smiling, as if the thought of the whole world brought back more memories and added, "I'll show you where we used to live." She quickened her pace and we had to hurry to keep up with her. The short walk took us to Brady Street, where the large grey brick building, with BRADY STREET BUILDING carved in stone on the front, took up the whole street. Another walk to Gardiner's Corner awoke more nostalgia. "This is where I used to meet my friends."

In Mama's search for memories of the past, she actually found an old school-friend. Theirs was mutual joy as they rolled back the years and shared past experiences of their lives. They continued to keep in touch and we were invited to the wedding of her daughter, Tilly. It was a strictly orthodox occasion and I still recall the water-ice interval in the middle of the seven-course dinner.

Other days were filled with visiting museums. The Science Museum in Kensington had installed a 'seeing eye', a beam which, when broken, opened a gate. Albert and I took turns going through, which kept us busy for a considerable time. I did sketching of period costumes and gathered data at the Victoria and Albert Museum.

In the evenings Henry took us to places like the Lyons' Corner House. I particularly liked the Brassiere, with its red checked tablecloths and live music. The menus, with each dish beautifully illustrated, were fascinating. Henry was well-known to the musicians and his "give my kid sister a treat" resulted in the violinist strolling round and playing over my shoulder, to my embarrassment. As if that wasn't enough, the Street Singer, who was appearing there at the time, serenaded me. The ground didn't open up and swallow me and pleasant memories remain.

Watching the return of Papa's plane from Paris was just as exciting as the take-off. It had been an interesting week and now we were on our way back to Nottingham.

Papa had difficulty choosing a car. Most of the cars of the period were aimed at car buffs, who could tinker away and keep an engine in tune. Papa was definitely not of that ilk. His total commitment was to check the water in the radiator and keep it topped up, insert the dipstick in the slot provided, to check the level of oil and use the pressure gauge for the tyres. He considered the Riley, Wolsely and Alvis were sports cars, not family cars, and the Morris very cramped. It was fortuitous that Henry Ford's Ford Prefect appeared on the market. That was it, a small family car, black, of course.

Our first trip, the long-awaited visit to Sherwood Forest, on the edge of Nottingham, lived up to our expectations. Large oak trees, their trunks spanning several feet, stood majestically on guard. It was both open country and sheltered copse spread across the landscape. One felt the mystery of Robin Hood and the myth seemed real. It wouldn't have been surprising to come across Friar Tuck or to see Little John striding out.

Sunday picnics became the norm. The picnic-set had inset metal legs on one side which kept it well off the ground, away from ants. Inside were a methylated heater on a stand, a tin kettle, a bottle with water, and milk and sugar. Plastic cups and saucers completed the tea things, with two boxes for sandwiches and biscuits. The plastic cups made the tea taste terrible. The trips were usually to villages around Nottingham. Some were interesting, others were abysmal, but the countryside was always worth looking at, like a patchwork quilt, small stone walls between colourful crops blowing in the wind. Occasionally, we'd come across a village green with stocks from a bygone age, or a rough stone wall edging a humped bridge over a stream with a working mill by the side. If an open space didn't present itself, Papa would pull into a roadway in a field and we'd set the picnic up near the hedge behind the car, Mama and Papa seated in their folding chairs and Albert and I hovering between tractor ruts and nettles.

Papa had been told that the beaches in Wales were the best, so for our summer holiday we drove through the beautiful countryside of North Wales, stopping at Ruthin to wander around the castle and small, hilly village and through Betws-y-Coed in Snowdonia to Llandudno, which was our destination.

Our first impression of Llandudno was disappointing. Grandiose Victorian hotels, all in line on the road facing the strip of sandy beach, hardly fulfilled our impression of a seaside holiday resort.

How well I remember the beach and sea at Llandudno. I was at the in-between age, not child, not adult and very conscious of my developing body. Mama had been understanding, patiently knitting a two piece swimsuit for me, not too big, not too little, but just right.

It was a glorious day; the golden sand stretched for miles, with the shallow water lapping up and ebbing away. I made my way down the crowded beach and plunged into the clear seawater. Suddenly, I realized that my shorts were no longer short, nor clinging to my body, but were somewhere around my knees. Fortunately, the elastic held the top of the shorts around my waist; the fitted top fell in deep folds down to it. Looking around, I could see the tide going out and as my eyes took in the long, crowded stretch of beach, I began to panic. To this day, I don't know how I made it.

It was ironic that the one person who had instigated the move to England, fared the worst. Papa, Albert and I were experiencing new interests, but not so Mama. West Bridgford was a relatively new suburb of Nottingham, with no local social activities, as far as Mama was concerned. We didn't belong to, or go to the synagogue, which was in another part of the town, where she could have met people with similar interests. It gave Mama little opportunity to get to know members of the Jewish community. Mama had no friends to talk to, except the occasional shopkeeper, which wasn't conducive to holding a conversation of any relevance. But I can't recall Mama ever complaining.

In the spring of 1938, Mama considered us capable of looking after ourselves and went back to Canada for a well-deserved holiday. We all went to Southampton to see Mama on her way in the French Flagship, *Normandy*, the prime ocean liner of the era. It crossed the Atlantic in five days, a major consideration for Mama, who became seasick at the thought of boarding a ship. We were able to go aboard and look around the ship before it sailed. It was magnificent.

The house without Mama was like a day without sunshine. Home wasn't home without Mama. I'm sure Papa felt the same loss. It was the first time Papa took me out and my first experience of going to the theatre, front row stalls to see *Madame Butterfly*, an evening I shall never forget. The second week we went to a play of great interest to Papa. *The Wandering Jew* was a translation of a Jewish story by the writer *Sholom Aleichem*, one of Papa's revered writers. It was very moving, especially with Papa's comments about the script.

Mama returned on the *Queen Mary* and we were there to greet her. For me, there was no better sight than to see Mama waving from the deck and then walking down the gangway. It was good to have Mama home.

Holiday trips were mainly planned by Papa. He was eager to see Land's End. It conjured up a picture of everything suddenly dropping off. We stayed in all types of places through Devon and Cornwall, sometimes on a farm, other times in villages, usually bed and breakfast, one or two nights in each place. The wet weather meant we were confined to the car or sheltering, which rather put a damper on the trip. The highlight of our holiday was the few days we stayed at Forde House, a remote, rambling Manor House in Cornwall, where we sought bed and breakfast accommodation. It was a contrast to the places we had been staying at, but the weather was bad and Mama had tried a few places, unsuccessfully, for shelter. This was a step into the world of landed gentry, and even though everything was understated, the finesse was unmistakable. It wasn't just the furniture that made an impression on me, but the complete structure of the house. Beautiful large rooms, their high ceilings moulded with decorative cornice. Tall narrow windows, with just a whisper of wood holding the panes of glass together, flanked by panelled shutters which closed over the windows, adding both warmth and shelter from storms. There were open fireplaces with carved overmantles in each room, their guarded hearths stacked with additional logs ready to add to the fire. Family portraits hung on the wall of the wide staircase. The handrail above the turned twisted balusters gleamed with the patina of age. Forde House was obviously a family home. The proprietors, Mr and Mrs Browne, made us very welcome, sharing their stories with us, proud of the house which dated back to the 16th century. Additions had been added and the house was modernised mid-19th century. We were experiencing a sense of history at its source. They delighted in giving us the run of the house, revealing secret corridors and staircases to Albert and me, with tales of ghosts, which made it eerie and memorable.

We went to Scotland in the summer of 1939 for the Edinburgh Festival. We just happened, by chance, to be by the drive to Balmoral when a crowd gathered. Papa asked one of them, "What are you waiting for?"

"The royal car will be passing with the King and Queen," he replied.

I stood with my camera on the ready and suddenly there they were in an open car: King George VI, Queen Elizabeth and the two Princesses, all waving. Sadly, my photo was not a success, but I had an interesting print of the rear bumper of their car.

From Edinburgh we went to Inverness, where a Scotsman, probably drunk, gave us a lesson in Scottish, for what it's worth: "It's a brae bricht moonlit nicht t'nicht." Up to now, I've not had need for it.

Loch Ness was our last stop. We watched the lake for a considerable time, but the Monster didn't appear.

Not long after we returned home, war with Germany was declared.

~ September, 1939 ~

We were at war with Germany! It was not entirely unexpected. Neville Chamberlain's white piece of paper "Peace in our time" had convinced only a few pacifists. The blinkered nation had a rude awakening, but rallied to the call of the new Prime Minister. At the helm, Winston Churchill, whose prediction had proved right, formed a Coalition Government, emphasising that this was no time for party politics. Peaceful, rural England became a war machine.

Almost immediately, we were inundated with instructions. Identity cards, which had to be carried at all times, were issued to each person. The country was put on Full Alert by signs in public places: Walls Have Ears warned to watch for strangers, hinting that enemy agents could cause havoc by sabotage. Suspected enemy aliens were rounded up and interned.

The Government considered gas poisoning to be a real threat and gas masks were distributed to each person. Blackout requirements and instructions to seal windows with tape crisscrossed to prevent glass splintering, were included in the advice about precautions to take in case of an air raid. Air raid shelters were supplied to those who wanted one. An Anderson shelter was a corrugated steel arch which had to be set in a hole dug out in the garden, to provide shelter during an air raid. Papa was not convinced of the safety of the Anderson shelter and was reluctant to have the garden dug up. Mama said she wouldn't go in it anyway and it was ruled out. Alternatively, square-shaped shelters were issued for use on the ground floor of a house. If the house collapsed during a raid, survivors could still be rescued. Mama and Papa decided that we would shelter under the substantial dining-room table.

It didn't take long for the reality of the situation to sink in. Within the first day, the sound of the air raid siren filled the air. The wavering, droning whine seemed to creep into each sinew of brain and body and struck indescribable fear. Only the comfort of the steady All Clear brought relief. But after the initial shock, everyone took things in their stride and it just became another way of life.

Suddenly the whole country was on the move. There was mobilisation of men into the Army, Navy and Air Force, and of those with industrial priority occupations, to produce equipment for the war effort. Women, too, were called up. Land Girls worked on farms; others worked in factories which sprang up everywhere to cater for the needs of war. Alternatively, they could volunteer for the armed services: the Army, Air Force or Navy. Children were evacuated from cities to foster-homes in rural areas and all who could arranged to leave vulnerable targets.

Papa joined the Home Guard and was an early recruit for "Dad's Army" as we now know it. Night-time would find him fire-watching on the roof of the factory where he worked in the centre of Nottingham.

All foreign nationals were advised to return to their own country. Papa refused to leave, saying, "The war will soon be over." Mama booked passage to take Albert and me back to Canada to continue our education. She was told, "It is a dangerous period, with German U-boats waiting to attack all cargo ships coming and going from every harbour. You will have to wait till late spring, to go in a convoy".

It came as quite a surprise to us when Henry announced that he was getting married. He brought Eileen to Nottingham to meet us. She was not really pretty, but with her fair hair, light-blue eyes and high cheekbones, she had a cool elegance. Her complexion was almost translucent except for the few freckles on her nose. Her slow smile hid an almost silent laugh.

The small wedding took place in London, on October 2nd, with just a few friends and family. Eileen looked beautiful in a pale-grey suit with fox fur cuffs and matching pillbox hat, swathed in veiling, tilting over her forehead. She carried a trailing bouquet of ivory roses which linked with the simple pearl necklet. She was the epitome of an English rose, and Henry, in a grey morning suit, completed the picture. The ceremony was followed by tea in her parents' home, an imposing Victorian house in Brondesbury.

Eileen's parents struck me as being very odd. Mrs Marshall was the matriarch who took her place of honour while Eileen and Sarah, her sister, made and served the tea. Mr Marshall seemed oblivious to his guests and the fact that it was his daughter's wedding.

In the evening Albert and I were taken out to the Trocadero with a few of Henry and Eileen's close friends. The only ones we knew were Sarah, Eileen's sister and Frank Smith, who was unofficially best man, inasmuch as he looked after all the details of the wedding, although Albert was given the honour of standing by Henry's side. I had a secret crush on Frank. He was tall, good-looking, debonair and a fantastic dancer. That evening was a special treat for me.

Mama had a meeting with Mr Holmes, our Headmaster, to tell him of our plans to return to Canada. He was very understanding, realising that these were crucial, formative years in our lives and should be given every consideration. Albert was in his final year and would be taking his matriculation. There was no doubt in their minds that he would do well and be prepared to go straight into McGill University. He held Albert in high regard. He was Head Boy and school spokesman and would receive a good recommendation.

My situation was somewhat different. I would be only halfway through a two-year course. After some discussion, they concluded that there was no doubt that I would follow a career in the art world. Following that meeting, Mr Holmes made a special recommendation to the Nottingham Royal College of Art for me to be assessed to see if my standard was high enough for entrance. The college sent a registration card for me to begin the following week. I hadn't realized until then that it was a branch of the Royal College of Art in London and as such, would be a first-rate reference. I was accepted into the first year, ready to absorb all they offered me.

The Art College was on the other side of Nottingham, and every morning, I travelled with Papa on the bus to the square in the centre of Nottingham, each going our own way from there. Mine was a long climb up a steep road. At the end of the day, I would meet Papa at his factory and we would travel home together, except for the nights he did fire watching for the Home Guard.

I enjoyed the teaching, but being at the college was not without a slight problem. I had no friends. I was an immature fifteen-year-old, whereas the average age of my fellow pupils was eighteen-plus. But I made good progress with my work and to my surprise, in the spring term, I moved up into the second-year-class. In my final term, I moved up again. In other words, I was basically given the entire course, not allowing for repetition, so that I would know, when I arrived in Canada, which branch of art I wanted to concentrate on. By the time I left, I had a very comprehensive portfolio, to put me in good stead to continue at Beaux Arts in Montreal.

Bill was a third-year student, very talented and conscientious. He had won a scholarship to the college and came from a farm near Grantham. We were both drawing the same model and during her rest period, Bill came across to see how I was getting on. His modest "Pretty good" was music to my ears and I smiled with my appreciative "Thank you". At the end of the lesson, he caught up with me as I hurriedly left the classroom. Imagine my surprise when he asked, "Would you come to the pictures with me one day?"

Completely taken by surprise, I replied, "After school?"

"Yes, of course after school!" he exclaimed.

"I couldn't go home alone at night," was my reluctant reply.

"Of course not! I would see you home to your door."

"Well then, yes. I would love to go to the pictures with you." I had been asked out on my first date!

Mama and Papa wanted to know all about him and gave their consent.

The following Thursday, Papa's day for fire-watching, Bill and I left the college together. We went to a café and had high tea. He was a quiet boy and as he spoke about the farm and his family, I could see that he was as shy as I was. I told him about Canada and that I would soon be going there.

By then it was time to go to the cinema. Reginald Forte was playing the organ which was being broadcast on the BBC. Then came the major film, *Snow White and the Seven Dwarfs.* It may seem a strange film for a first date, but we were both art students and for that reason, interested.

Slowly walking back to the square, we discovered that we had missed the last bus to West Bridgford. It was a long walk to my home. Hours, in fact. When we finally did get there, my parents were waiting on the doorstep. Poor Bill ! He felt the force of Papa's temper although I pleaded that it wasn't Bill's fault. Bill had to walk back to Nottingham, probably too late for the train to Grantham. He wasn't in school the next day. That first date was enough to put me off dates for life.

The army officer stood to attention and saluted as Mama opened the front door.

"Is this a military operation?" Mama asked.

"No, it's my greeting to say 'hello' to you," said the soldier.

"Thank you," Mama replied.

The soldier laughed, adding, "Don't you recognize me? I'm Frank, Henry's friend from London."

Mama was stunned! Her troubled look turned into a smile as she admonished, "You naughty boy! You scared the living daylights out of me. What are you doing here?"

Frank had joined the army and was stationed near Nottingham. Thereafter, he stayed with us when he had a short leave with insufficient time to go to London. He looked even more handsome in his officer's uniform and I still thought he was fantastic. I admit to being jealous that he was in love with, and spoke constantly of, Della.

The year passed quickly and it was June when we got our passage to Canada on a ship called the *Arcadia*. We sailed from Liverpool in a convoy of ten ships. The ships kept in fairly close proximity, each one zigzagging on its own course.

The atmosphere aboard ship was tense; the main interests were watching the ships alongside. Counting them appeared to be quite a joke until one ship disappeared. It was during the night and news travelled quickly through the ship confirming that it had been sunk by a German U-boat. If anyone had allowed themselves to become complacent, they were now brought back to reality.

Many of the passengers had no real plans or knowledge of what the future held for them; their only hope was to arrive safely. We chummed up with two boys, Shirlea and Glenn, who had been studying at university and had cut short their course, to return home to mid-America and we compared our aims and prospects.

The sea was rough and the weather mainly raining. Tables in the dining rooms had raised edges and dampened tablecloths to stop dishes from slipping off. The rough crossing had dire effects on Mama, who suffered abysmal seasickness, not venturing out of her cabin.

She was pleased when I told her, "We met two American students, Glenn and Shirlea, who have been waiting, like us, to go back home. They're very nice".

Albert and I spent a lot of time with Shirlea and Glenn and when Mama asked, "What have you been doing?" my usual reply was, "I was with Shirlea," and Mama would smile with approval.

We could see land! Newfoundland. The worst was over. The convoy seemed to disperse and we found our journey was making its way up the St Lawrence, with land on either side. A beautiful sight, especially when we could see the large cross at the top of Mount Royal. It seemed to beckon to us and one could sense the joy of the Pilgrim Fathers and early settlers.

The slightly gloomy atmosphere of the passengers turned to elation and even Mama managed to leave her cabin and come on deck to watch the intricate manoeuvring as we approached the harbour. For a moment the reason for the return was forgotten. Thoughts of war were pushed aside. There was just thankfulness that we were safe.

I could see Glenn and Shirela wending their way through the people on deck, coming towards us. I waved and turned to Mama, saying, "Look, Shirlea and Glenn are coming to say goodbye."

Mama's eyes took in the two six-footers. "Where's Shirley?" she asked.

"The tall one on the right," I replied.

Mama's astonishment was obvious as she said, "I thought Shirley was a *girl!*"

If Mama suspected a shipboard romance, she was wrong. I was so naive that if one of them had made a pass, I wouldn't have recognised it.

Montreal was more beautiful than I had remembered. I left it as a child and now I felt it welcoming me back.

~ 1940: Wartime in Montreal ~

The war was responsible for the change of circumstances in which I was thrust from a sheltered childhood into an adult world, forced to grow up quickly and accept responsibility.

Our arrival in Montreal was a warm homecoming as we were welcomed back by cousins Mel and Queenie. Mama was the first to see them as we watched the gangway being put in place.

"Look, the girl in the red dress is Queenie!" she said, as she began waving, adding, "and that's Mel beside her. How nice of them to come."

Queenie began waving back, calling out, "Aunt Mary."

I recognized the voice and began waving, too.

After an emotional reunion, they helped collect the luggage, which was put on a trolley and wheeled to Mel's car and we all piled in.

"Ma told me that you'll be staying with her until you get settled," he said as he drove towards her home.

Auntie Annie, Mama's eldest sister, struggled as a young widow to bring up a family. Mel and Queenie, two of her children, spent much of their formative years in our home in the years before we went to England, with Mama and Papa playing a large part in their upbringing.

Mel pulled up in front of a shop. He looked at our surprised faces and explained, “This is Ma’s store; she lives in the apartment at the back.”

Aunt Annie was waiting in the doorway. She looked different. Could this be the troubled sister who struggled to make ends meet? I took in the groomed silver hair and confident warm smile as she greeted us with outstretched arms. She threw her arms around Mama; Albert and I watched as they remained locked in an embrace, making up for the years they were apart.

Aunt Annie looked around, still holding Mama and said, “My, aren’t the children grown up?” and gave us each an affectionate hug. “Come inside. The place is small, but we’ll manage,” she said as she propelled us forward.

We followed Aunt Annie through the small shop to where a smiling girl was waiting.

“Pearl, come say hello to Aunt Mary, Albert and Gwen,” she instructed; and turning to us, added, “Pearl’s been getting everything ready.”

Cousin Pearl was the youngest daughter, just three or four years older than I, a comparative stranger, as we didn’t have much contact before we went to England.

To the right of the passageway leading to the kitchen was the sitting room. The kitchen was quite large, old-fashioned but basic, with a large table in the middle. The bedrooms led off from the kitchen. Though there were only two bedrooms, Auntie Annie made room for us until we could find suitable accommodation. It had a pleasant, welcoming atmosphere and it was nice to be back with the family.

Auntie Annie ran a successful delicatessen shop in Outremont, a suburb of Montreal. We spent time settling down in the comfortable flat behind the shop and found it amusing when the occasional customer would engage the dangling bell, put there for regular customers, who knew that the shop was open all hours.

Mama enjoyed helping Auntie Annie in the shop. She loved chatting to the customers, most of whom were regulars and she bubbled with the pleasure of doing something useful. Slicing smoked salmon, making sandwiches, suggesting additional accompaniments like coleslaw and cucumbers, all came to her naturally. She had a fantastic personal approach which the customers appreciated. It brought back her vitality after the years of comparative solitude in Nottingham.

Pearl was fascinating. She was the epitome of the smart young sophisticated woman of the 30s and 40s. Immaculate make-up, coiffured hair and red lips, she was obsessed with her appearance. Her main occupation was looking in the mirror or polishing her nails. If Miss World contests had existed at that time, Pearl would have been a suitable contender. However, she had achieved one goal with her beautiful hands: she was a hand model. Hers were the beautiful hands holding a bar of soap or any commodity in an advert. Long, tapered fingers ending in delicate, long oval nails, always beautifully lacquered.

One day she held out her hands showing a letter on each nail that read PEARL SACKS. It was her way of distancing herself from the shop, which she loathed. I could see her point when she confided:

"I feel the smell of the shop clinging to me always. It's Mama's life, but I hate it".

Albert lived up to expectations and was welcomed at McGill University. Beaux Arts College were impressed with my portfolio and the standard I had attained in England. In their opinion I was ready for the commercial world, suggesting that I should try to get into a good design firm or gain experience by freelancing. My first reaction was disappointment, but I realized that it was a commendation of my work.

I loved being in the city with wide, clean streets and clanging streetcars. Everything began early in the warm, balmy mornings, before the day got too hot. Lunch in a drugstore on a high stool by the counter, always the same toasted tomato and lettuce sandwich and chocolate milkshake.

I found it easy to get work sketching for the small dress firms who needed sketches of their samples. One firm recommended another and occasionally, I'd meet someone who knew Papa, and they would greet me like a long-lost cousin. I sketched handbags for a manufacturer who offered to teach me how to make patterns for the designs, in lieu of payment, and another firm who made slightly naughty lingerie. Pearl introduced me to the photographers and they occasionally gave me work retouching photographs and taught me how to use an air brush. It was my introduction to working in the commercial world and I loved it, but sadly, the pay was insufficient.

Until then I had no idea that our financial position was critical. It only came to light when Mama took a position in a shop. We thought it was good for her to be occupied, but one day I noticed that she had difficulty in lifting the heavy coats. It was then that I discovered that she had a serious heart condition. Our relationship changed and our roles were reversed. We were no longer just parent and child, but colleagues, friends and partners. After that I left no stone unturned to find work, but sadly, I wasn't earning enough.

The bombshell came when Mama informed us that we were taking over the shop. Auntie Annie had been offered a concession booth in the city. With shorter hours, she could manage without Pearl. Mama pointed out that we would have a nice home behind the shop and an added income, which we desperately needed. Surviving the shock, we accepted the situation, which proved to be quite an experience and a very interesting interlude in our lives. I look back at it with very pleasant memories.

The tiny shop was little larger than an average room. DELICATESSEN was painted in simple lettering across the large plate-glass window. The entrance door on the right brought you straight into the shop. Two small tables by the right wall accommodated the occasional hungry customer, but it was in no way a restaurant. The counter to the left was glass-fronted, with perishable foods clearly displayed and everything within easy reach.

The back wall, lined with shelves, held all types of groceries: tinned fruit, cereals and packaged, non-perishable food. The sale of these were prohibited out of normal shop hours. These had to be inaccessible. The contraption we acquired from Auntie Annie was effective, but had to be seen to be believed: wire netting, as used for fences, held to ceiling height by sturdy wood batons, a few feet apart. During the day the rolled-up netting stood in a corner. Each evening it had to be unrolled, stretched across the front of the shelves and padlocked. At first we thought it was by coincidence, but then discovered that the local policeman on his beat made a point of passing by the shop just then, and would come in and do it.

We planned to get the bedrooms redecorated and so to give myself a little practice in life drawing, I drew life-sized nude figures all over the walls. It caught the eye of a plodding policeman, who passed the word around and it became the haunt of peeping Toms. The decorating was postponed for a long while, much to my embarrassment.

One really cannot comprehend the complexities of retailing and catering unless born into it. Mama took to it as to the manner born. She was marvellous with the customers and enjoyed being in control. The advantage was that Auntie Annie had done it for years and had, with experience, organised a very efficient, workable shop. I, too, soon became a dab hand at slicing salmon, making sandwiches and explaining the various types of salami. There were two items I detested: the pickled cucumbers and the schmaltz herrings. They had to be picked by hand out of the barrel; a fork would tear them to pieces and tongs or rubber gloves had not yet been invented. For me, the worst factors were the odours which seemed to linger in my hands and hair: the fishy smell of smoked salmon, the garlic in the salami and the spices of pickled cucumbers and herring. I now realized what Pearl had complained about, and I fully endorsed her grievance.

I shared the work with Mama, making the occasional excursion to do art work when the opportunity arose. Strangely enough, I liked working in the shop. My inhibitions gave way to making suggestions to customers, which rid me of my acute shyness. Albert was at McGill, so he got let off working in the shop, but he did sometimes help out.

My greatest joy was being with Mama. Working with her brought us closer. To me she was very special, glowing with kindness with a wonderful, imaginative mind. She filled my heart with so much love that every thought of her makes me burst with joy. I wasn't alone in admiration of Mama; she was revered by all who knew her.

Albert had settled in well at McGill and seemed to be enjoying himself. I shared his fun and revelled in the antics he got up to. I remember the time he had to clean a section of street-car rails with a toothbrush to gain admittance to a fraternity. He did it and was accepted as a fellow.

Mama was concerned that I hadn't any opportunity for making friends in my isolated existence. It bothered her. When Albert suggested that he would be going to the annual McGill black-tie dance, Mama insisted that he would have to take me unless he found a personable friend to escort me. He sorted out a nice, tall, good-looking boy and I must admit that I was chuffed. Mama was right. I was missing out on a social life. I did enjoy going to the ball and I'm sure Cinderella couldn't have been more pleased.

However, a smooth, uncomplicated life is not for me; the next day found me desperately ill with pneumonia. The doctor reassured Mama that it wasn't serious and the new M and B drug would rid me of it in a couple of days. Little did he know that he would experience his first adverse reaction to the drug. It was also the first indication of my allergic reaction to drugs, a problem I would learn more about in time to come. I lingered at death's door for two long weeks, but thankfully my name was not on the list.

Incidentally, I cannot recall the name of the boy who took me to the dance, nor did I ever see or hear from him again. I resigned myself to the fact that I wasn't a social butterfly. To be a good mixer you have to talk a lot without saying much and I wasn't very good at it.

It did, however, convince Mama that I should look for work in my own field, which would give me an opportunity to make young friends.

~ *Lac Brulée* ~

"I've arranged for you to recuperate in the Laurentians."

The words came as a surprise, as I shuffled around the apartment, feeling the strength returning to my wobbly legs.

I turned and stared at my mother. "What, alone?" I asked.

"Well, I can't just leave the shop with no one here," was her logical reply.

"You need the holiday more than me," I countered. "You're worn out."

"When you come back fit and strong, I'll go away for a few days." Her words weren't very convincing.

"Promise?" I said, doubting her.

"Yes," she replied, putting her arms around me and kissing my cheek.

And so I reluctantly agreed to go. I was apprehensive about going to a hotel alone but fate stepped in, in the guise of one of my many cousins, namely Queenie. Her proper name was Gwen, the same as mine, but though she requested it, her nickname stood. Queenie's sister-in-law, Anne, had a hotel at Lac Brulée. When she heard about me, she phoned and invited me to stay with her in her log cabin by the hotel. She said she would be pleased to have the company as she lived alone and though she mixed with guests at the hotel, she enjoyed having an occasional friend to stay. As it happened, her nephew was coming down and he could bring me with him. That changed the whole situation and I allowed myself to get excited.

Two days later found me sitting in the lounge, my bag packed, nervously awaiting the nephew. I didn't even know his name, but he was, so to speak, family and so obviously all right. I also knew Mama wouldn't be throwing me to the wolves.

I looked up in surprise as a golden baritone voice rang out. "Hello, I'm Eddie. Are you ready?"

I wasn't prepared for what I saw as I looked up, for standing there before me was the most handsome man I had ever seen. He smiled a warm, broad smile that stunned me even more.

"Are you Queenie's nephew?" I asked. "She didn't tell me your name."

"Guilty, I'm afraid," he replied. "I wasn't told your name either. My Aunt Anne just asked me to pick up Queenie's cousin."

"Well, thank you very much. I'm very grateful. I'm Gwen and yes, I'm ready."

As I picked up my case, he reached over, taking it from my hand saying, "OK, let's go."

I turned to him as we walked through the shop and said, "I'll be with you in a minute. I must just say goodbye."

He nodded, understanding. "I'll put this in the car and wait for you."

I was near to tears as I put my arms around Mama and walked to the door with her. She stood there waving as we pulled away. She probably found the parting as difficult as I did. I was growing up and this was my first flight from the nest.

As we set off, I stole a look to see what Eddie was really like. The introduction had been very quick and offhand. Yes, he was nice.

He seemed to feel my eyes on him, because he looked around and smiled. "I hear you come from England."

"Yes," I replied, "but I only lived there a few years. I was born here. I used to spend the summers at Trout Lake, so this holiday should bring back a lot of memories."

"Well, tell me if you want to stop anywhere to have an extra look."

Thanking him, I eagerly took in the sights. The drive to the Laurentians was even more beautiful than I had remembered. I recognised the small villages and laughed when we came to the very steep incline at Saint Moraine and couldn't help but remark, "My Dad always had trouble with this steep hill, both going up and going down. It drove my elder brother nuts."

"Funny, my Dad had the same trouble." And we both laughed at the coincidence, then he added, "Mind you, the cars were much harder to drive then. You had to double-declutch and that was tricky." I nodded, regretting making the critical remark.

As we approached Trout Lake, he pointed to the hotel, which looked much bigger than I remembered. I told him about the fire when the original hotel had been burnt to the ground one summer when we had been staying there, and the trauma of losing everything, including my favourite doll, Kikapoupalis, so-named by my eldest brother.

We came to Ste Agathe. I was choked with memories going back so many years and asked if the Hotel des Monde was still there. It was and Eddie promised to take me to see it one day. He was surprised, because it wasn't very popular, but I explained about winning first prize at the amateur concert.

"So you sing as well. You're very accomplished."

"I was just ten, and it was an amateur contest. There probably wasn't much choice."

Lac Brulée was a short way further north, and as we approached, he pointed out the hotel on the top of the hill. A traditional log cabin stretched out with a backing of fir trees sheltering it from the wind. It had the edge on the older hotels, perched high on a mountain, unspoilt by surrounding houses and cottages.

"What a wonderful setting!" I exclaimed.

I must say I was overwhelmed by the sight. Eddie smiled appreciatively. He was obviously very proud of the place, remarking, "I agree with you. I love it here."

As we drew closer he pointed to a small cabin by the side. "That's Anne's cottage. You'll be staying there with her."

I liked Anne the minute we met. She was much younger than I had expected and very attractive. The small cabin was wonderful, typical of a country home, with a fur rug in front of the large, open, log fireplace. There were comfortable settees and chairs and chintz curtains on the windows. Two bedrooms were beautifully appointed and comfortable. The only really unusual item was the water pump by the sink in the kitchen.

After we settled down, Anne suggested that Eddie should give me a tour round the hotel and grounds, to get me acquainted with the place. The countryside around the hotel was completely unspoiled. A small path led to the very calm lake sheltered by trees. We walked upstream to where the source of water came down the hills, tumbling over rocks which formed small rapids, the water so clear that you could see swarms of fish splashing about close to the surface, in such abundance that I felt I could reach in and just pull one out.

In the evening, at dinner, sitting opposite him, I was able to take in his features. The first glance had kindled a spark in me. Now I could take a closer look. Wide-set blue eyes with dark curling lashes deep-set in a square strong forehead, brushed by casual waves of dark brown hair. An aquiline nose above a well-defined mouth, which curled up at the corners when he smiled, and added a mischievous twinkle to his eyes. Each time I looked at him, my heart skipped a beat. I was mesmerised. I had never experienced such a feeling.

That evening I took a close look in the mirror and my heart sank. I was no beauty and I was far from sophisticated. My eyes were all right and my nose not bad, but I was plain. I had tried make-up but it made me look like a clown and my dark brown hair had a will of its own. Years before I had tried having a perm, but it was a disaster. Now my hair told me what it wanted to do and that was to hang down around my shoulders, in soft waves. I looked at my figure and frowned at the curves above and below my twenty-three inch waist. The fashion of the moment was flat-chested with minute hips. I was stuck with what nature had provided. I couldn't imagine that anyone would notice me. I was like a mouse, but tried to think positively. When I got back to Montreal I would be looking for a job and aiming for a career.

I couldn't sleep. I couldn't explain my feelings, but meeting Eddie had taken me off my guard. I usually didn't like good-looking men and he was exceptionally handsome. But he was slightly shy and had a modest charm that I found irresistible. He was the answer to a prayer. I realized that I was smitten and it scared me. All my thoughts centred around the Adonis who filled my heart with romantic dreams

The air was fresh when I woke up in the morning with the sun telling me it was the start of a lovely day.

Anne was in the kitchen making breakfast. She gave a broad smile. "I'm so pleased you're an early riser. I always get up early and worry about disturbing guests. It's going to be a lovely day. Is there anything special you'd like to do?" she asked.

I shook my head. "No, I haven't given it any thought. What would you suggest?"

She seemed to think a minute. “I think Eddie should decide. He knows the place better than anybody. He’ll come up with something.”

“I don’t want to be a burden, or for him to feel obligated.”

“Nonsense! It was he who suggested that he’d like to show you round and believe me, you couldn’t get a better guide. Come.” She pointed to a chair by the table laden with an assortment of dishes. “Tuck into your breakfast.”

We were still eating when Eddie arrived,

“Would you like some coffee?” Anne asked.

“No thanks, Anne,” he replied. “I had breakfast in the hotel.” He sat down at the table and looking straight at me asked, “What would you like to do this morning?”

“I’m in your hands.” I smiled. “I know I’d like anything you suggest.”

He planned something different every day, sometimes taking a picnic and going north through the small French villages, every one with a beautiful church. He spoke fluent French and seemed to know a lot of local people. Other days we’d spend fishing on the lake or swimming in the beautifully clear water. The lake was very deep with a springboard on the raft in the centre. Not for me though. I can swim but I hate getting my head under water. I learnt how to tack, to catch the wind in the small sailing boats, or the calm of sitting in a boat in the middle of a lake, dangling a line to tempt a fish to have a nibble, or wading in the water by the rocks, fishing in the fast-flowing stream. But by far the most exciting memory was going through the rapids in a canoe. We revisited the places I remembered as a child and found they hadn’t changed much.

We spent hours talking about our dreams and aspirations. He told me about the agricultural course he was taking and his plans for cultivating the land around the hotel, which in part belonged to his father. He explained how he really planned to make this place his life and home.

He endured my chatter about art and the ambition I had about finding the right field of commercial art to follow. He laughed, saying it was a world he didn't understand, but nevertheless he was interested. He was great company and I was glad that he was staying at the hotel. He loved and felt very much at home in the country, whereas I was very much a city girl. We talked a lot and discovered that we did have a lot of mutual interests.

By now I was madly in love, young innocent love, that fills the world with sunshine and in turn draws one deep into the depths of despair. The pangs of first love. The touch of his hand sent shivers down my spine, but he was unaware of the magic hold he had over me. Anne was amused to watch us and in her quiet way she was really the fairy godmother who threw us together.

I well remember the day he arrived early, in high spirits, saying he'd ordered a picnic.

"What have you mapped out for today?" Anne asked

"Something special. It's a surprise," Eddie replied, with one of his beaming smiles, eyes twinkling, as if he wanted to say, but wouldn't.

"Shall I take anything special?" I asked.

"Comfortable shoes," he answered.

He joined us at the table and no more mention was made of the destination, but we were all amused. Eventually we set off. I was excited at the thought of a mystery ride.

"Are you going to tell me now where we're going?" I asked.

He smiled and replied, "I'm going to show you the estate of Lac Brulée."

"What does that mean?" I was puzzled.

"All our land," was his simple reply.

"Oh," I answered, still confused, but said no more.

I'd always loved the Laurentians. Trees, especially the maple with their leaves turning colour in the autumn, making the countryside a blaze of reds and yellow. We pulled up on the crest of a hill, south facing, looking down over a broad panorama, a clump of trees behind shielding the area from the north wind. I was surprised at the size of the estate

"Is this where we're going to picnic?" I asked.

"Yes, do you like the view?"

"How could anyone not like the view!"

He put his arm around me and pointed in each direction, explaining the location and then he modestly said, "This is where I plan to build my house. Do you think you'd like it?"

"Surely the most important thing is that you like it. What difference if I do or don't?"

"I didn't put it the right way." He seemed to hesitate and continued, "I really meant would you like to live here with me?"

Confused by this bolt out of the blue, I asked, "Is this a proposal?"

"Yes! What else did you think?"

"Is living here a condition?"

"No, I just wanted to know how you felt about it."

I hesitated. Was I being silly? But I had to tell him how I felt. "I'm not sure about the house, but I'd marry you because you love me and because I think I'm in love with you. I'd go to the ends of the world for that."

"That's good enough for me," he said as he took me in his arms and kissed me for the first time, sealing our fate for a future together, wherever it would be.

It's not every day that one receives a proposal of marriage from a comparative stranger and doubly unusual if there's an affirmative response. I had so much to tell Mama, but my pleasure suddenly dimmed when I saw how ill she looked. I experienced an extreme sense of guilt for leaving her with all the work. In my consternation, I decided not to say anything about Eddie's proposal, but to wait for the right moment. When I finally told Mama, she was taken by surprise and wanted to know more about him. Eddie's parents had a similar reaction, considering us too young to contemplate marriage. We dispensed with the formality of getting engaged and were happy to be "going steady".

First love never dies. It's a fairy tale that really happened. Time cannot erase those magic moments and precious memories. One should treasure what they were, like the first flowers of spring or the first flakes of snow.

~ *Nordyn and Royal Victoria* ~

It was time for a change. It was obvious that the hard work and long hours were too much for Mama; the shop, no longer a viable proposition, had only been meant for a stopover.

Mama had cared for cousins Mel and Queenie when they were young; now they were concerned and determined to look after Mama.

Mel arrived to take Mama to the hotel at Lac Brulée and consoled her, saying, "You're going to have a holiday, Aunt Mary, and we're going to take care of everything. You just concentrate on getting well."

Mel's wife, Mollie, found a suitable apartment near to their own and together with Queenie, made it ready to move into. Everyone helped in the shop until it was disposed of. Mama missed the shop at first, but by now she was not well and she could no longer protest. Having her sisters and especially her nieces, close by, was a blessing. Not long after we moved, Mollie had a son called Morty; Queenie had a daughter called Natalie; and Henry and Eileen presented Mama with her first grandson, Peter.

Mama had been compiling a book for Papa: *Principles of Dress Designing and Pattern Making*. She had started writing it in Nottingham and now she concentrated on completing it.

I began looking for work. I replied to an advertisement for a draftsman or tracer at Nordyn Aviation, an aircraft plant on the outskirts of Montreal. They were surprised to have a girl apply for a position in what was considered masculine territory, but they offered me a trial period as tracer. It involved tracing detailed drawings which had to be included in the specification of a larger project. The work was precise and details had to be accurate.

I advanced to doing small drawings. As I gained experience, projects became larger. With each increase of responsibility, my drawing board would be moved to a more advantageous position, closer to the window and natural light. I was now earning a good salary.

I progressed well in the drawing office, making drawings which were intricate and more detailed. They discovered my potential as I worked my way up the scale. Cliff, the Head of Department, recognized that I, as a woman, was more attuned to getting details of the interiors accurately placed; thereafter, interiors were considered my field. I worked closely with Cliff and became a Senior Draughtsman.

Nordyn Aviation produced the *Norseman*, a large, rather clumsy-looking cargo plane, able to carry vast amounts of freight. Demand for the planes increased as Canada became involved with transporting supplies to the war zones. The format for handling the interior plans for these airships were modified as time became the decisive element. The engineer on the floor would be given a pilot sample of a shipment order. He would work out the most suitable storage position of each item and the method of keeping them secured in flight. This could vary from retaining straps to fixed partitions. They would be tested for their stability in flight by the test pilot. When they were completely satisfied, my job was to make an accurate drawing for the assembly line. Each fitting and measurement was crucial and accuracy was vital. Both the plane and crew could be at risk if the cargo shifted in flight, which could result in improperly distributed balance of weight. Detailing every nut, bolt, strap or partition, became my main task.

Taking measurements in the factory was embarrassing at first: I had to endure the chorus of wolf-whistles and catcalls by workmen on the shop floor. They eventually got used to me and the novelty wore off; they even became helpful. My promotion was rewarded with gaining an assistant, which made it easier to double-check everything.

The journey to Nordyn was particularly difficult during the winter months. The streetcar – tram, really – took us from Montreal to a pick-up point about ten miles away, where a company bus would be waiting to take us to the plant. Exposure to the elements in the severe arctic conditions was hazardous. One employee, who walked the distance instead of waiting for the bus, suffered severe frostbite, which, I believe, proved fatal. After that episode, no one took chances, but sensibly bundled up.

As the plant grew, so too did the Administration Department. It was quite a revelation to find female staff filtering into the canteen for lunch. I felt more comfortable having two friends of my own gender to chat to. Shirley and June soon became good friends and we took to travelling together to and from Montreal and meeting daily during lunch breaks.

The year was passing quickly. News of the war was not good. Canada was getting more and more involved, especially with reference to the Air Force. As well as building planes, young, potential airmen were being sent to Canada to learn to fly. When they had flown sufficient hours, or had the required training, they were sent overseas to the war zones. Daily the numbers of military in the streets were growing. Young men of military age felt compelled to enlist.

And so it was not too surprising to see Eddie arrive in uniform one day. He had joined the Air Force. Following that, Albert, too, enlisted in the Air Force. They both became wireless operators.

Eddie was sent to England, Albert to Ontario as an instructor. We had not avoided the war by evacuating; it was here on our doorstep.

Mama was upset that Albert had not waited to get his degree before joining the Air Force. He hadn't long to go and was still under-age for enlisting, but she had to accept it. Eddie's departure was a sad experience for me and I wore his wings as a symbol of my commitment.

Mama's health seemed to be going downhill, until in desperation, I called the doctor. She was indeed ill. He immediately took her into hospital with pneumonia, pleurisy and a very rickety heart.

The Royal Victoria was a large Victorian hospital stretching across the side of the mountain in downtown Montreal. Each evening after work, I made my way to the city centre and climbed up the hill to the room in intensive care, where they kept a close eye on Mama. The pleurisy was causing problems with her heart and her condition was critical. I went daily, helplessly watching her struggle for breath, but she never complained, always more worried about me and whether I was eating properly

Mama had been in hospital about five weeks when I began getting very sharp pains in my side. I ignored it at first, thinking that it was due to trudging up the steep hill to the hospital, but it was getting worse. One day, when the pain was severe, I mentioned it to the Matron as I made my way to Mama. Before I knew what was happening, she trundled me into another room and contacted the house doctor. He diagnosed that it was my appendix, which could be very serious if neglected. I was in a quandary, but Matron said she would arrange for me to be seen by the senior surgeon. I told her that on no account was she to say anything to Mama.

The next day I was ushered into an examining room by Matron, who stood watch over me, probably suspecting my urge to run away.

In walked a large bearded man, who bellowed out in a brusque manner, “Hmmmm, so this is the child you want me to see, hmmmm . . .”

His fingers tenderly touched my tummy, his manner surprisingly gentle and serious as he did his examination.

The silence was broken as his booming voice rang out: “Quite right, Matron, the appendix has to come out. Fit it in this week.”

He had not bothered to speak to me and was taken unawares as I said, “I can’t have it done now. My mother is too ill. The shock may kill her.”

“Nonsense, child. We’ll put you in with her.”

“Not until she’s out of danger,” I insisted.

“Listen, child. You are in danger if your appendix bursts. Peritonitis is very serious.”

He made to leave and I added, “I’ll have to take that chance. I’ll wait until her doctor says she is strong enough to take a shock. I’m all she has to cling to.”

He didn’t argue with me, but agreed to speak to her cardiologist, who confirmed that what I had said was true. I was put on a strict regime. I was to carry an emergency phone number; my temperature had to be taken three times a day and if it exceeded 100, I had to phone and come right in. No solid food was to be taken; I was allowed baby cereals and strained baby foods. No fruit and nothing but bland pap and I was not to do anything strenuous.

I kept up this regime for seven weeks. My days consisted of going to work and then to the hospital. I was getting very thin, but Mama didn’t seem to notice.

It was pathetic to watch her lying there so weak and ill. “Wind up my bed, dear,” she would say and I’d carefully crank the handle at the end of the bed. “No, please put it down, just a little.”

I’d reach for the crank, praying it wouldn’t be too much strain.

I had been staying alone when my brother Henry suggested I should stay with them. I did, for a short time, but Eileen was suffering with postnatal depression and there wasn't really room for me, so I moved back home. The mother of my friend Beatie persuaded me to stay with them in case I became ill in the night, insisting that it was dangerous for me to be alone.

At last the two doctors agreed that Mama was sufficiently out of danger and could take the news about my impending appendix operation. In fact she found the idea of me sharing her room very amusing.

The date was set; I booked into the hospital as a patient and they put another bed in beside Mama. It was reassuring to be by her side.

Dr Dubois strode in, his voice booming out, "Well you survived the long wait without an emergency, good girl!" He gazed at my chart. Turning to Mama, he continued, "How do you do, Mrs Klein. You have a plucky daughter who is determined and not easily swayed. She had two departments keeping a check on both of you. I'm pleased to hear you're making good progress and now we'll concentrate on her."

Mama looked surprised. She was unaware of the long build-up to this day. I had some explaining to do!

Dr Dubois, turned back to me. "I have a suggestion to make to you. We have a new form of anaesthetic called a 'spinal', which is given by injection. It's considered preferable to the conventional anaesthetic, which usually causes the patient to be sick after the operation. If you are agreeable, we'll give you the spinal injection."

"I'm in your hands and if you consider it best, I agree to it," I replied.

"Good," he said in his matter-of-fact way, "I'll see you in the operating theatre," and with a "Don't worry, she'll be all right" to Mama, he departed.

I smiled at Mama in reassurance, adding, "Matron recommended him and says he's a brilliant surgeon."

My brother Henry came in to stay with Mama while I was being operated on. I'm sure they were more anxious than I was as the porters arrived with the trolley and wheeled me out.

I was wide awake as we entered the operating theatre. I had expected to see a sparse room, hygienically disinfected, with the doctor's gloved hands held up over his head ready to spring into action. Not so! I was wheeled into the centre of an amphitheatre and it would appear I was the star. It was crammed to capacity with doctors and medical students, in animated chatter. There was a hush as I was wheeled into the centre.

One of the more senior-looking doctors greeted me and said, "Dr Dubois will be in shortly to give you the injection. It is a new procedure and all the doctors are interested to watch."

I hadn't expected an audience, but somehow it didn't seem to matter.

The calm was broken as Dr Dubois strode in, his strong voice booming out, "Good morning, gentlemen." Peering down at me, he smiled and added, " . . . and lady."

His head was swathed in white and an apron was stretched across his corpulent frame, emphasizing his pouch. His hands were held up in front of him, ready to make a start. He nodded to the doctors around the table as they busied themselves; then gazing at the large gathering, remarked, "It's reassuring to see so many of you interested to see this new spinal injection."

He gave a running commentary as he worked. "This is a new stride to help improve our work. There is no sensation and she cannot experience any pain in her lower body. Now let us get on with the operation."

He proceeded to question the group of student doctors surrounding me. "Good! Now who can tell me which side to make my incision? Speak up, we haven't got all day."

A feeble voice suggested, "Right side, sir."

"Well, one person knows which side the appendix is on! Here we go, a nice clean cut on the right side." He stopped talking for a minute, as if in thought, then continued, "It's rather a long incision. Does anyone know why?" He waited, then continued, "No, you don't! I'll tell you. This young lady has been walking around with an inflamed appendix for about two months, due to personal circumstances. What could have happened if it had ruptured?"

"Peritonitis, sir?"

"Yes, and that is why we'll have to handle it with utmost care."

They watched him silently,

"There it is, twisted, just as I thought." Then directing his voice in my direction, said, "Good thing this is coming out, my girl. Would you like to see it?"

"No, thank you. It was bad enough hearing about it."

He chuckled at my reaction. "All right, let's put her together with nice neat stitches. That should do it." He seemed to heave a sigh of relief. Then, "Hold on!" he called out, "It's still bleeding!"

There was a complete hush.

He leaned his head close to mine, "Do you always bleed like this?" he enquired.

"I don't know," I replied.

Calling out instructions, he shouted, "Double up with clips. Quick now. Yes, that should do it." He leaned his head close to me again. "Don't worry. We're in control."

He called out further instructions, assuring his assistants: "Yes, that's fine. Be sure to check her blood. She may need a transfusion." Putting his hand on my arm affectionately, he softly added, "There we go now, girl. It's a good thing that's out." And with that he strode out of the operating room.

Henry was waiting as they wheeled me out. I gave him a wan smile and advised, "Wait around, Henry. They want to check if your blood matches mine. I may need a transfusion . . ." I didn't.

~ *Audition For Chorus* ~

What a surprise! During my brief sojourn at the Royal Victoria Hospital, my drawing board had been moved next to the Head of Department, denoting my status as a Senior Draftsman in the Nordyn Aircraft Drawing Office. I hadn't realized how much I had missed being there. Another happy reunion was meeting Shirley and June in the lunch break, especially to experience Shirley's bubbly, gushing enthusiasm for a local drama group who were doing a musical show.

"They're auditioning singers for the chorus," she announced. "It could be fun."

" I don't think I'd be any good in a musical show. I'd probably waste their time," I replied

"You won't. They can tell at the audition if you are suitable. Anyway, you don't sing by yourself. 'In the chorus' means you sing together with other people."

"I don't know. What do you say, June? Shall we give it a try?" I asked.

June was noncommittal, as usual. We dithered in making up our minds until Shirley pleaded, "I don't want to go alone. Please come with!"

We agreed to keep her company and later that week we were on our way to downtown Montreal.

The area looked familiar and as I looked across the park I realized that it was just up the road from where I used to live. I recognised the balcony where, as a child, I spent many hours. The imposing building spanned the width of the block and seemed to stretch as far in depth. Across the front, above the wide double doors were the letters YMHA (Young Men's Hebrew Association), carved into the stone lintel of the impressive doorway. It struck a chord; this was where my brother Henry sang years ago, with the Glee Club.

We entered, not knowing what to expect and found ourselves in a vibrant cultural centre. We were directed to the hall and were amazed to find ourselves in a fully fitted-out theatre. Someone standing by the door of the dimly lit auditorium put his finger to his lips, mouthing, "Shu . . .u . . ." implying silence and motioned us to join a long queue by the side wall. Obviously we weren't the only applicants.

Only part of the stage was lit. There was a pianist and someone with a notebook who announced the name and experience of each performer in turn. Seated in the theatre, about four rows from the front, a small group called out instructions. It was obvious right from the start that although this was rated in theory an amateur show, it was actually very professionally run. One by one, in turn, each person performed, singing something they knew. Every consideration allowed for nervousness as the pianist patiently sorted out the suitable key. The format was not unusual; you sang your piece and were told "Thank you very much, next" after which you waited around, listening and looking.

It was fascinating. When the auditions were over, we were each called in turn. Yes, for June. Yes, for me. Sorry for Shirley. She couldn't hold the tune. We were devastated; it had been her idea. She was great about it and laughingly said, "I didn't think it would notice in a crowd."

June and I signed on and rehearsals started the following week.

It transpired that the chorus formed the background for a traditional Minstrel Show, seated in three rows: black-faced men with fuzzy wigs, striped trousers and bow ties, behind two rows of brown-faced ladies in pretty colourful frocks. In the centre of the front row, the Interlocutor linked the dialogue between the soloists and chorus, as well as joining in the antics of the four comics, who were on stage throughout.

Rehearsals were carried out in sections, and until we reached the period of bringing everything together, it was impossible to know how it would all turn out. "Stars" did not rehearse with the chorus; at rehearsals someone else sang the part of the soloist. Sometimes I was chosen to fill in. As we progressed, occasionally the soloists would turn up and take their place in the arrangements. It was understandable then why they didn't have to practice. They were polished, superb artists. Each soloist had a unique personality and style and each one was perfection. The show began to pull together and it was interesting to see the story evolve. Individual acts, joined together by the Interlocutor and comics, resulted in a continuity of the plot. The show was a complete story in two acts.

Rehearsals went on right through the winter and by early spring we were nearly ready. Fittings for costumes and instructions on how to apply make-up were given: basically, dark-brown pancake for the girls, with black-faced men. The atmosphere at the dress rehearsal was electric, with the clowns in various ill-fitting jackets and outsized shoes. Everything was set for opening night.

The Minstrel Show was a major annual event for Montreal. It was the fund raiser for the Cultural Centre, but this year there was an added requirement. The troupe had received the status of an ENSA group, to entertain at military camps which had sprung up in the provinces of Quebec and Ontario. Much more money was needed to finance it. The show was scheduled to run for eight days instead of the usual three and every night was sold out.

The auditorium was full. Not an empty seat in the house. Everyone had taken their place on the stage; we all shared the buzz of excitement, but there was a flap: there was complete silence as the Producer and Musical Director strode onto the stage and beckoned everyone to gather round.

Peter, the Musical Director spoke, and announced: "Sadie (the star of the show) has lost her voice. There's no way she can go on." He looked on the verge of tears.

Everyone gasped. We all realized that Sadie held the key to the show. Without her, the show would not make sense.

He continued, "We've decided who must take her place."

There was a hush and everyone waited for him to continue. He walked along the line of the chorus and stopped.

I stared in disbelief as he reached out to me and said in a hushed voice, "Gwen, you know the words. You've sung them at rehearsals. We are all depending on you. Will you take her place?"

I was struck dumb, but when I came to, I realized that I had no choice. The producer locked himself in a back room to have a quiet nervous breakdown and I took my place in the wings.

The theatre lights dimmed, the leader raised his baton and the music filled the air. I watched as the curtains opened and the voices of the chorus filled the air. The audience was rapt with attention as the programme proceeded. Watching the clowns relaxed me a little and as, one by one, other soloists took their place and wished me luck, I seemed to gain in confidence. Then came the big number and I felt as if I was in a dream as the voices of the chorus rang out:

No gal made has got a shade on sweet Georgia Brown
It's been said..she knocks 'em dead when she lands in town.
Folks all sigh and want to die
for Sweet Georgia Brown . . .

I stood in the wings waiting for my cue as they sang about the merits of Georgia Brown, then strutted out when I heard:

Georgia claimed her
Georgia named her
Sweet Georgia Brown

Holding out my arms, I hollered out:

Just hold that kids and let it rest,
Cause you're looking at a baby who's termed the best!
Georgia may have been OK when rhythm was born
But she ain't the swinging kid she was! Today she's full of corn.

I strutted up and down the stage as the orchestra played the introductory notes of my song and went into the solo:

Who's got the guys all swingin'? Who's goin' right to town?
It goes without sayin' . . . Miss Hallelujah Brown.

I sang on:

Who's got a new sermon? She don't do no preachin' 'bout the Lord above
She confines her preachin' to that precious thing called love . .

At the end of the first chorus; the whole ensemble picked it up, clapping their hands with:

Hallelujah . . . Hallelujah . . . Miss Hallelujah Brown.

I strutted up and down as they continued singing:

Who's got the guys all swinging? Who's going right to town?

It goes without saying . . . Miss Hallelujah Brown.

As they reached the end of the song, I sang out, asking:

Don't blame the fellas, do you, the way they hang around?

And they replied with a crescendo:

Hats off and here's to you, Miss Hallelujah Brown!

And down came the curtain.

The applause was tumultuous. They had expected Sadie, but happily they accepted my performance and the show was a huge success.

My feet barely touched the ground as I made my way home and told Mama that a star was born. The next night I had to go on again, but this time they sent someone to bring Mama. It was rewarding to see her beaming smile as she watched from the front row. Sadie didn't recover her voice at all that week.

The reviews of the show were fantastic, beginning with:

"Her name is Gwendolyn Klein. Not long ago she was a kid in the chorus" and went on to explain how I replaced the star.

And so began an unexpected new phase in my life.

Following my debut at the Montreal show, when the ENSA show got on the road, the Musical Director worked on material for me. I was given my own solo as the "Forces' Sweetheart." My first song, 'I can't give you anything but love' alternated with 'Zing went the strings of my heart.' I was termed

WEDNESDAY, APRIL 7th, 1943

HER name is Gwendolyn Klein. Not so long ago she sat in the YMHA Minstrel Chorus — modest and unknown. A co-operative sort of kid, she obeyed immediately when Producer Sam Miller assigned her the thankless and usually wasted task of understudying Sadie Cohen. Sure enough, the one in a thousand chance materialized. On the Minstrels' Monday night, Sadie Cohen was ailing and young Gwen found herself sudenly catapulted into the public eye . . . .

WITHOUT a so much as "Gee, I feel nervous" the youngster stepped out of the chorus and sang two of Sadie's difficult numbers. Sang them beautifully who while everyone backstage chewed fingernails with anxiety and the chorus stood by ready to sing loud and furious. When the curtains closed on the first act finale, the cast swarmed around her and smothered her with affection and congratulations. Her face smudged with blackface kisses, the bewildered newly-hatched starlet ran happily upstairs to the dressing rooms. This hoary old lover of all things theatrical drank it all in from his vantage spot in the projection booth. Gave us a terrific lift to sense everyone pulling and praying for the green, unrehearsed youngster in her major stage debut....

A BOW in the direction of Sam Miller is definitely in order. The shrewd, far-seeing Minstrel producer handled the sudden emergency easily. Other Sadie Cohen solos were sung by Zelda Gordon, Sybil Rosen, Joe Spector and Bill Aaronson . . . So, as far as you civilians are concerned, the curtain has gone down on another successful Minstrel Show, perhaps the most successful in Y. M. H. A. history . . . Minstrel tickets were a priceless commodity. Sold like wildfire . . . The Minstrels really settle down to work now. Go on tour of the army camps immediately and will continue throughout the year. . . .

"the blues singer" and as songs became popular, they were put into the show.

The ENSA troupe numbered about fifty, which included the players, orchestra and wardrobe mistress. We entertained at military camps in the provinces of Quebec and Ontario, usually one evening a week, meeting at the bus at about six o'clock, travelling to camps within a reasonable distance. The format was basically the Minstrel Show but it varied, depending on whether soloists could make it. Sometimes, if there wasn't a booking at a camp, there would be a rehearsal; to keep everything fresh, new material was added and mediocre items replaced. The comedians kept the patter topical, which amused us as well as the audience.

The ENSA troupe was a serious commitment and ran for several years. When Winston Churchill and President Roosevelt had their meeting at Quebec, our troupe were asked to entertain at the Quebec Conference. After the show there was a special ceremony for eligible members of the troupe where we were each awarded a medallion commemorating one hundred performances to the troops.

Thanks to the Minstrels, I can now claim to be a "chanteuse".

~ VE-Day and Toronto ~

VE-Day at last! The war in Europe was over. The wonderful news brought in its wake thoughts that my days at the Nordyn Aircraft Plant would surely be numbered; war work would no longer be necessary. The war years had been challenging, interesting and exciting, but now it was time to move on.

I was in a quandary as to what to do. I was ready for a change, but I didn't know which way to turn. One idea from the world I had known in my childhood kept buzzing in my head and popped up again and again in my thoughts . . .

In frustration, I said to Mama, "If only life was as simple as when I was a child. I knew then what I wanted to do."

"What do you mean?" asked Mama.

"When I was little, all I ever wanted to do was to design clothes. It was a special treat when Papa took me to his factory. The war spoilt everything."

Mama seemed taken aback with my outburst and said, "You've never mentioned anything about wanting to do designing. You were always drawing or painting. That's why we arranged for you to go to Art College."

"I thought commercial art would be interesting, but I didn't find it so. Sketching samples for dress firms was not inspiring. The pittance they paid gave me the impression that they thought they were doing me a favour." I paused and continued, "If Papa was here, I'd know what to do."

"And what would that be?" asked Mama.

"He'd teach me to be a designer."

Mama was silent.

I felt that I had upset her and quickly added, "I'm sorry, Mama. I'm confused because I don't know what to do."

Mama smiled, saying, "I know, I was just thinking," adding, "Papa isn't here, but we have got his book. We can see if it really does explain everything. We can give it a try and I'll help you all I can."

I began helping Mama with her book, which she had started writing in Nottingham, taking dictation from Papa; she continued it with notes sent by Papa during the war. Dress designing seemed years away and yet so much I had seen as a child was stored deep in my memory. Papa explained each process in explicit detail; the book was like a catalyst stirring up the remnants of thought. I was returning to my first love: dress designing.

One thing I was adamant about was a refusal to look for work in Montreal where I could be patronised by former colleagues of Papa. I abhorred the thought of being taken on as a favour or duty; in that, I had Mama's agreement.

The clothing industry was like a large club. *The Draper's Record*, a prestigious trade journal, and *Women's Wear Daily*, a newspaper basically for the rag trade, carried information across the country of interest to the trade. Both catered to vacancies in different fields and I scanned the lists and selected one possible position, for a dress designer and pattern maker, in Toronto.

Plucking up all the courage I could muster, I went to Toronto for an interview. Two brothers, returned from the war, were just setting up in business with their demob. money. They had both worked in a dress factory before the war and understood the rag trade. They needed a designer and pattern-maker. I didn't have to tell them I was young and inexperienced; they could tell, because I hadn't worked anywhere, but they took me on.

"Mama, I got the job!" I excitedly told Mama on the phone. "I'm going to look for somewhere to live before coming back. I'll let you know how I get on. You can start packing."

I found two rooms sharing a widow's flat in a nice part of Toronto before going back to pack up and bring Mama to Toronto. We moved within a couple of weeks and settled in without any trouble. The bedroom with twin beds and the lounge with settee and easy chairs, were comfortable. The communal kitchen and bathroom were shared with the landlady, a lonely woman who poured out her heart if she managed to corner you. I felt very sorry for her and could understand her grief, knowing her daughter was living with a married man who would not leave his wife. She couldn't sleep and spent the nights rattling paper as she sorted out things in her room.

My two bosses, Moe and Sam, were in their mid- to late twenties and were fun to work for. We discussed the type of garments they wanted to make and I made sketches interpreting their ideas: modestly priced styles for a youthful clientèle. It brought to mind the Guinea Dresses Henry had made years before in London, which gave me a good insight into the type of garment required. The design sketches stretched my imagination to create interesting combinations taking into account the material and trimmings available. They gave their approval of the designs and I progressed to the next stage.

Moe and Sam watched as I began making my first pattern. I would soon know if I could manage to do it on my own. I worked directly according to Papa's radical methods in constructing the pattern, mindful of the need for everything to fit together, utilising the experience of accuracy gained in the Nordyn drawing office.

The brothers had never seen patterns made that way and Moe jokingly called me a witch, saying I was doing it with magic. It wasn't magic; it was Papa's practical brain which enabled one to position on the pattern exactly where it would be on a body, calculating and providing fullness and shape where necessary.

Moe and Sam were impressed by the speed with which the machinist matched up the coded seams, without measuring or adjusting, joining the garment together like clockwork. It quickly passed through to the finishing department, who added the trimmings. One final pressing and the dress was ready to be modelled by the pretty young girl standing by. Memories of my sketching days in Montreal flooded in.

The brothers were entranced with the sample dress. White pique collar and cuffs and narrow black patent leather belt highlighted a row of tiny black buttons dividing the centre panel of the black-and-white chequered fitted bodice with leg-of-mutton sleeves, the skirt divided into six panels. Simple and smart to relate with the obligatory hat and white gloves which were tantamount to standard dress. I must admit that I, too, was chuffed with the result of the sample. Compliments poured out. I had done it!

The designs I made were just what they were looking for. I sailed into producing work as if I had been doing it for years. As I finished a pattern, Moe, who was a cutter, would cut out the material and we'd watch the machinist sew it together.

Fashion in the 40s was detailed and complex. Formality was a priority, with an unspoken code of dress. The "cut" of the garment created the style. Clothes were shaped to the body and there were recognised modes of dress, used in varied combinations: a "Princess" dress was cut from shoulder to hem in panels which moulded the dress to the shape of the body; a "Shirtwaister" included a collar, with or without lapels; a "Coat Dress" was tailored and opened down the front; a "Gored Skirt" divided into panels and could be styled into a multitude of shapes, from a simple A-line to flaring out for a special effect. "Box Pleats" folded inward, either side of the "Box", while "Inverted Pleats" hid the folds of the pleat; "Straight Pleats" were in one direction. Pleats were usually stitched down to nine inches from the hem. Slits on straight skirts, at the side or back, modestly ensured that legs were always discreetly hidden by an overlap. "Dirndl" was a skirt gathered peasant-fashion into a waistband

The New York fashion shows are the highlight of the dress trade, very much like the Paris shows. They foretell the trend for the coming season and play an important part for manufacturers. The brothers suggested that it would be a good idea to go there to get fresh ideas. I well remember those few days. By sleeper to New York and three days of fashion shows and walking up Fifth Avenue, looking at glorious displays in windows, sketching everything in sight.

My two bosses were fantastic. I have a weakness for shoes, and as we passed a shop, a pair of black patent leather shoes with graceful high heels, caught my eye. They had flat bows across the square toes, which were shaped like ballet shoes.

I stopped in my tracks and said, "Oh! Aren't they fantastic?"

They couldn't stop laughing. I was embarrassed when they insisted that I must buy them. They propelled me into the shop and sat either side, grinning as the assistant shoe-horned them onto my tired feet. I was overwhelmed! They belonged on my feet and I couldn't resist wearing them as I walked out of the shop, much to the amusement of my two bosses. I loved and cherished those shoes for years. Though it was a business trip, it was better than a holiday.

On our return to Toronto, a wave of creativity followed, as I turned out casual wear and cocktail dresses for the new season, working from the sketches made in New York. It was exciting, adapting and sharing ideas with the two brothers. Wedding gowns and bridesmaid dresses were added to the range of young styles. Working for Moe and Sam was a wonderful experience.

Albert was stationed at Hamilton, just a short ride away. Being in a strange city with no friends did not present any problem. I introduced myself as an ENSA entertainer at the Servicemen's Club, which not only opened doors but also included the red carpet. Albert was beginning to accompany me on the piano and together we made a good team. Brother and sister going to a singles' club gave us an advantage to mingle without complications. It became a regular commitment and I became one of their regular entertainers.

A brief romance added to the excitement of Toronto. Ernie had served in the Mounties so he was special in many ways. The Royal Canadian Mounted Police are the highest branch of military in Canada and entrants have to be of the highest calibre to be accepted (or so it was then). Ernie was tall, good looking, rich and a really nice fellow. He courted me in the good, old-fashioned way. He would come right across Toronto in his open sports car every day to take me to lunch and return me to the factory at the end of my lunch hour. More often than not I would find him waiting as I left work. He called to take me to the Servicemen's Club and brought flowers and chocolates for Mama when calling for me on a date. He introduced me to his family and tried desperately to persuade me to let him take me up in his plane, but I refused. He was good company, the perfect escort and Mama thought he was marvellous. It was the first time that she tried to influence me. I knew that what she said was true and even my head told me he would make a good husband. My eyes told me he was handsome and my heart knew he was very much in love with me. But the magic was missing. The spark that makes the world light up when your hands touch. I liked and admired him and because of Mama I kept going out with him. She seemed to think that lightning would strike when I least expected it. Every time I came home after a date she'd be up: "Did you have a good time?" she'd ask.

And I'd answer, "Yes, it was very nice."

The trouble was I did always have a good time, but it wasn't "special".

I remembered Anne's warning: "Unless it feels right you're better off alone, getting on with what makes you happy."

Now I understood what she meant and my true feelings were unquestionable. Mama eventually agreed that I was making the right decision. It was hard finding the right words to end the relationship with Ernie. He was a great fellow, but not the one for me.

Mama was planning to return to England when news arrived that Eddie was back in Montreal and I realized with regret, that the period in Toronto was drawing to a close. It had been a memorable few months. Working with Moe and Sam had been a happy period of my life. I grew up in that year. I had a new career at my fingertips, proving to myself that I was a dress designer with confidence to cope with any conceivable obstacle.

~ Parting Of The Ways ~

A nightmare of emotional turmoil, triggered by the monotonous sound of wheels on the track, created an eerie illusion of a journey into the unknown. As the train sped along, the motion pitched me into a quandary, anticipating the reunion with Eddie with mixed feelings. Confused thoughts wavered back and forth with my moods changing from elation to despair. My feelings must have been obvious as I sat opposite Mama, my face drained of colour.

Mama reached out, asking, "What's troubling you, dear?"

"What's wrong with me, Mama? I should be deliriously happy, but I feel so wretched."

"It's natural for you to be worried and confused. You're not alone. Couples all over the world, in the same situation, are probably feeling the same as you. Everything will be all right. Just let things take their course."

"Thank you, Mama. You've made me feel better already," I replied, realizing that she had put my feelings into words.

There he was, his handsome face, deep blue eyes and saucy grin, standing out in the crowd. I waved from the train and he waved back, smiling, making his way through the crush of people. I gasped as I felt a surge of joy at that glimpse of him. All doubts disappeared with the pounding of my heart.

He helped us down from the train and gathered me up in his arms, making the years disappear. It was an era when porters vied for custom and rushed to assist with the luggage and while we waited, he looked me up and down.

His first comment took me by surprise. "You've changed!"

"For better or worse?" I enquired.

"I don't know. I'll have to think about it. You've grown up."

"Time didn't stand still, even for me," I admitted.

"Well, I suppose I'll get used to you," he kidded.

"Please list any faults and I'll see what can be done about it," I countered and we both laughed.

The tension had gone. It was wonderful having him home.

As we drove along I took a side glance to see if he'd changed. No, still the same thick hair curling slightly and clinging close to his head. The same straight nose and firm chin. A beautiful profile, an Adonis. He probably sensed my eyes on him and he looked round and smiled. He had the warmest smile of anyone I knew. His good nature shone through like a beacon.

"When did you get back?" I asked.

"Two days ago. I'm not demobbed yet, I'm just on leave."

"How long for?" I queried,

"Two weeks," he replied.

I nodded, thinking that we had so much to catch up.

We arrived at the block where we were staying with Henry and Eileen, with Peter, my nephew, running around wondering who we were.

After unloading the luggage and making all the right greetings, Eddie and I slipped out to be alone.

Not knowing the area, we wandered around until we found a small café and I laughed as Eddie ordered tea. We sat there solemnly holding hands across the table. I could see now that his face was thinner and that he was more serious than I remembered. I looked into his eyes; they looked sad. Suddenly I heard his voice and recalled how just listening to the sound always made me tingle.

"You've changed, you're not the girl I left behind."

I felt as if he'd thrown cold water over me. "Of course I've changed. I'm four years older. I had to grow up and take on responsibilities."

We were silent and I thought back to when we first met. I was a child then. I hadn't yet mixed in the world. He was right, he didn't know me, he only remembered the past.

"No doubt you've changed too," I suggested.

He looked surprised. The thought hadn't occurred to him. Suddenly, his face lit up as he relaxed and smiled. "You're right! I probably have and I remember the past too vividly."

"You, me and everyone else who's in the same boat," was my sombre reply, continuing with, "Look on the bright side. You're back in one piece and I'm still in one piece. Be thankful for small mercies."

He laughed again. He had a lovely laugh, rich and throaty; it was infectious and I found myself laughing too. He leaned across and kissed me. The magic was still there.

As the days sped by, we spoke of our thoughts and hopes. He'd gone away with the memory of a shy, insecure, love struck girl. I would even say child, because I was very immature. Four years later I had developed into a young woman. Had circumstances been different, I might have developed parallel to his thoughts of me. But I had gone into the business world and had been successful. And I loved it. And I had also been flung into the crazy theatrical world and I loved that too. We couldn't turn the clock back.

All his thoughts on returning had been focused on farming. Cultivating the land, living close to nature and becoming a farmer. Perhaps four years earlier I, too, could have contemplated that type of life. Certainly by the side of someone I loved, I could well have been persuaded and I may have even learnt to love it.

My thoughts turned to how I felt. I liked the hubbub of living in the city; I knew that I became alive when in contact with people. I needed people, I needed to be needed and most of all, I needed to be creative. The excitement of the commercial world was exhilarating. The country made me feel desolate and being alone in the country was purgatory. Much as I tried to dismiss the feeling, it seemed to get worse as I contemplated living in such circumstances. I knew I couldn't do it. I was demented with conflict; it just wouldn't work.

The thought that we were incompatible tormented me. If we both tried to adjust, in time we would both be unhappy. I couldn't face making the love of my life suffer and suffer he would, compelled to live in the city. As for me, it would kill me to live in isolation. If it didn't kill me, I would eventually kill myself. So strong were my beliefs. Too much time had passed and we had grown in opposite directions, through no fault of our own. It was the result of the war. The gap was too great and to mend it would end in failure.

I upset Eddie by telling him how I felt. He couldn't understand my feelings and as much as I tried, none of it made sense to him. I'm sure he regarded it as my rejection of him, but he couldn't have been more mistaken. Emotionally I was drawn to him, of that there was no doubt, but other factors stood in the way and that he could not understand. The memory I keep of him is full of tender love.

Three weeks later I boarded the *Queen Mary* and sailed to England.

The door closed on another chapter of my life. The dream I had harboured for four years was shattered.

I chanced to meet Eddie several years later on a visit to Canada when I stayed with my cousin, who was married to his uncle. When his uncle was taken ill, the first person she called for help was Eddie. I went with them to the hospital. We had to spend a long time together in the waiting room. He hadn't changed much, just a little older and more distinguished. He hadn't become a farmer after all. He was a schoolteacher. This time I did most of the talking about the years in between and about my children. He didn't speak of his life and I sensed that he had never forgiven me for leaving. The thought made me sad as I felt the strings of our first ties, but we didn't talk about old times.

PART TWO

~ Return To England ~

The ship was a shadow of its former self; the *Queen Mary* had lost her glamour. On one of Mama's earlier holidays to Canada, while seeing her off, we had toured the flagship of the Cunard Line, enthralled by the magnificence. Now she suffered the ravages of war, stripped of her embellishment and bearing signs of her service as a troopship.

Angry waves lashing the ship and spraying over the decks made it a very rough crossing. Walking was hazardous, with floors at a thirty-degree keel; it was imperative to hold the handrail, or any secured-down fitting, in case the angle shifted. It was unusual to feel lurching on the *Queen*, as it was amply fitted with stabilisers, but this trip was the exception, heaving with the swell of the sea. Dining tables had their edges raised and tablecloths were dampened to stop the dishes sliding about. Food slid back and forth on your plate even as you attempted to eat, if indeed you felt up to it.

There were still games like shuffleboard on deck, for those with hardy constitutions, but exercise mainly consisted of walking on deck and challenging the elements, to experience a breath of sea air, which was harsh and wild.

There were many young people aboard of a similar age to Albert and myself, and we swapped stories of our experiences in Canada. One such fellow, called Teddy, seemed to know, and have connections with, everybody in London. We promised to keep in touch when we got settled and he assured us that he would introduce us to loads of people our own age.

We sighted land, but freak gales added to the trauma of the rough crossing; the seas were so rough that the ship anchored outside Southampton for two days until the gales receded. We were able to see the harbour, while the wind and waves rocked the ship like a cradle.

At last we were able to land; our emotions were at bursting point. Papa was overjoyed and amazed to see how we had grown up. He still pictured us as schoolchildren. Mama, a shadow of herself, having endured the stormy crossing, was relieved that we were on dry land, as we made our way to London.

This was meant to be our "homecoming", but in reality we didn't know where it would be. Papa was now living in furnished rooms in London. We still owned the house in Nottingham and the furniture that had been in storage since we left for Canada. In fact, we were all looking forward to having a proper home and living in London.

Temporarily, we moved into rented accommodation in Maida Vale: bedsit land. Rows and rows of tall Victorian buildings, all the same, row after row, made it a challenge to find the right entrance. But they were lovely buildings, built to last, with interesting details. The rooms inside were spacious, with high ceilings alternating with odd-shaped box rooms. The kitchen gave the minimum convenience and ditto for the bathroom.

Priority to find a suitable home found Mama and me house-hunting, not an easy task in war-torn London. We concentrated on looking in the northwest area, which was convenient for Papa to travel to work in the West End. Also, Henry's in-laws lived there, and Mama assumed therefore, that it was a good district. Most of the houses we were shown were Victorian: large, rambling buildings, with basements and attic rooms, in a dilapidated state of disrepair.

46 Exeter Road, a detached Edwardian house in Brondesbury, was the answer to a prayer. Mama and I viewed the house with delight. The substantial panelled front door opened onto a tiled, square entrance hall. The door on the left revealed a long room, perfect for the William and Mary dining-room furniture in storage. To the right, a small study and straight ahead was the square lounge with French doors leading to the garden. The hall to the left of the lounge led to the breakfast room and scullery, very primitive, but with potential. Upstairs, the five well-proportioned bedrooms held a surprise. One bedroom had been delightfully "modernised" in the 30s; the black-and-chrome "Deco" room was stunning and perfect for Albert. The bathroom, too, was pure 30s Deco: walls lined with green vitrolite, a large, sculptured, green enamel bath and square pedestal basin. An inset mirror, lit by glass shaded wall lights, was fitted above the basin. The property, much nicer than anything else we had seen, was within our budget.

Mama had a talent for turning a sow's ear into a silk purse and in the minimum of time we had a lovely home. Luckily, Dad had not disposed of the car and we all welcomed the Ford Prefect which had been in mothballs for the duration of the war. Driving licences were issued without any problem and both Albert and I were allowed to use the car.

We took Teddy, the boy we met on the *Queen Mary*, at his word and contacted him. His boast actually turned out to be true and through him we were introduced to the Junior Three Cs Committee. They made us welcome, which gave us the opportunity of meeting people of our own age in northwest London. The Three Cs were an enthusiastic, hard-working group affiliated to the Senior Committee, who sponsored large fund-raising functions. We helped in carrying out nitty-gritty chores, doing the legwork of fetching and carrying gifts for tombolas. I remember selling brochures in the gods of the Palladium Theatre, wishing I had a parachute. It was an introduction and education into London life and we soon had a circle of good friends.

Albert and I went everywhere together as a couple. As brother and sister, we could circulate in a crowd, which made us very popular for invitations to parties and outings. Albert now accompanied me on the piano when I sang. As well as being two singles, we could also provide entertainment.

The 100 Club, at 100 Oxford Street, was the favourite haunt of all musicians and the centre for jazz. Anyone who was anyone met there. It was exhilarating and exciting and we were made welcome.

Many musicians were seeking to re-establish themselves after doing military service, for instance Stanley Black, who played piano, Jack Parnell on drums and Bob Farnham, who was in the process of forming his esteemed Robert Farnham Orchestra, to name but a few. Up and coming Ray Charles was a frequent performer, as yet relatively unknown. Victor Feldman was a child virtuoso who played drums; he was acknowledged as a genius and eventually played every instrument. Each of them was successful in reaching their goal. I too, became well known, and often joined in performing. Many musicians had taken on other careers, but returned for the sheer enjoyment of the music.

I was considering singing as a career when I was stopped by a head-hunter. In those days, we called it the grapevine, and word had got around that I was a dress designer. It culminated with meeting an entrepreneur, who had been informed that I had recently returned from Canada. He pointed out the difficulties and restrictions in England, explaining that rationing was not confined to food: clothing was on coupons. Materials for manufacturing were on allocated coupons and every commodity was on the shortlist. Men returning to civilian life were given priority to enable them to re-establish themselves in business and on demobilisation were granted an allocation of coupons. The proposition Mr Smith put before me was that his four partners had pooled their coupons to form a large firm and they needed a designer. The salary on offer was phenomenal. Once again I felt the bells ringing in my ears. Fate was handing me a golden opportunity and pointing the way.

Veering on the side of caution to be sure of the right decision, Mr Smith accepted my condition of a month's trial before agreement to our contract. The brief was to design moderately priced young fashion, at the newly set-up factory in Leyton. The month's trial went very well, even better than expected. Allocated material was assessed to make a certain number of garments. If a design was economical on fabric, the extra material was known as "cabbage". Cabbage was a desirable bonus and was my forte. Often a slight adaptation of a design resulted in less waste. The three year contract, at a fantastic salary, was negotiated. Also, on my recommendation, they agreed to engage Albert as factory manager. Despite the minimum amount of previous experience, designing came to me instinctively and the new range of designs produced for the season were greeted by the partners with rapture. Mr Smith purchased embroidery machines which afforded me even more scope to experiment. Indeed, I was in the fortunate position of getting paid for something I loved doing.

Albert and I were enjoying London. While I admitted to being a dress designer, I kept details of my position very private, as I found my salary an embarrassment. With young people trying to make up for the lost years in the forces, I found that if I chanced to mention my salary, they either considered me a liar and storyteller or else avoided me. Strangely enough, many of our friends did become millionaires.

For a brief period, every young man I went out with seemed to be a medical student. Philip was a prospective doctor who introduced me to the hectic world of hospital medics, not far removed from a *Carry On* film; I was full of admiration for their dedication and their ability to unwind. Philip was an intense person who took everything seriously, and eventually that included our relationship, as he went into great detail, explaining about the period of internship and of the hardship of managing on the meagre salary to follow. When I mentioned that it wasn't a consideration to worry about, he was completely put off at the mention of my salary. Instead of being an asset, it turned out to be a deterrent. It robbed him of his pride. After that episode, my salary was a moot point. I wasn't sure I'd make a good doctor's wife, anyway.

I was more impressed with that attitude than with another incident that made me suspicious as to why I was being dated, when the so-called suitor, a sales representative for a dress firm, calculated how many shops I could keep supplied with exclusive designs.

~ *Wedding Bells* ~

The Over Twenty-One Club created a certain curiosity. Drifts of snow settling on the roads, making them hazardous, didn't deter Clare from calling to take me to the opening night. We were a motley pair. Clare, a few years older than I, was small, fair-haired and sophisticated. In contrast, I looked even younger than my years, with hair hanging down to my shoulders, just a touch of lipstick, and my shy smile more in evidence than my conversation.

By the same token, Cecil called for Lally, who was having his customary sleep by the fire, loath to wander out on such a stormy night. However he was persuaded, despite the weather.

We were with a group of people making small talk when Cecil and Lally arrived at the club.

Looking around, Lally spotted us across the room and turning to his friend, said, "You see that girl in the red dress? I'm going to marry her."

"You must be mad!" laughed Cecil. "But I must say it's an original approach."

"You'll see," was Lally's serious reply.

Cecil found it difficult to contain his laughter as they made their way across the room and introduced themselves. By some strange coincidence, Cecil knew many of Clare's relations and they paired off.

Lally introduced himself to me. My first reaction was, why did he single me out? I'm not his type. But he had a wonderful sense of humour and liked to talk and I warmed to him.

The organizers were trying hard to interest the people there with quiz games, which didn't seem to interest Lally. He was more concerned for me to go out for coffee.

"I came here with Clare. I can't say I'm going home with someone else," I said.

"Why not?" he asked.

"Because it's rude," I replied.

"I'm sure she'd be more pleased to go with Cecil," was his comment.

Of course he was right! As soon as Clare heard, she quickly offered to take Cecil home, to leave me free to go with Lally.

Lally and I had coffee at the Cosmo in Swiss Cottage, and we arranged to meet two days later, in the West End.

That night, mulling things over, I came to the conclusion that Lally was really very nice, though not the type that I usually went out with. Lally had the confidence of a man who had achieved success; he was sure of himself and he knew where he was going and I liked it! Most of the boys I knew had spent the war years in the armed forces and were now in the throes of sorting out their lives and establishing themselves into civilian life. Lally, being a few years older, had the advantage of drawing on his pre-war experience.

We met in the West End two days later. He had theatre tickets for a play with Robert Morley and an added bonus of a box of handmade chocolates, a rare treat in food-restricted England. I later discovered that he'd made a special trip to his Uncle Newman's chocolate factory.

The following Sunday found us on a drive to the country, for tea. It was the first opportunity we had to sit and talk. Mind you, Lally did most of the talking, and I enjoyed listening to his perceptive and forthright outlook, which was interesting and amusing. He was rightly proud of the business he had built up, from a small workshop, to being one of the most reputable brush manufacturers in the country and revelled in recalling ventures, long past, that revealed his initiative.

To say he swept me off my feet was probably true. His co-ordinated, understated appearance and upright stature exuded confidence. His deep-brown eyes seemed to take in everything going on: dark pools in a strong, kind face with good features. I wondered why I hadn't noticed before how good-looking he was. It was probably the initial Marxist reaction to the Savile Row suits and the super Jaguar car.

Our third date began with a drive to a fashionable roadhouse for a romantic dinner. It was obviously planned and calculated to create the right atmosphere. The setting was intimate and beautiful: a small dance floor with an excellent band playing soft romantic music. He had a splendid style of dancing, his strong strident steps sweeping the floor in rhythm to the music was like poetry in motion. It was the first time we had talked much and it was exciting to discover that we had similar views to life as we chatted on and on between dancing.

The evening was drawing on when we took to the floor to the strains of 'Sonny Boy'' I was drifting in his arms when he softly whispered, "Will you marry me?"

I stopped in my tracks, doubting what I had heard.

"Goodness!" I said. "You've had much more to drink than I thought."

"I'm serious. I really mean it," he replied

"You're joking. You must be. Let's sit down."

I led the way to the table and listened to his unbelievable description of seeing me across the room and telling Cecil that I was the person he was going to marry. He added that now he was even more convinced. I listened, half believing, half doubting and completely confused.

Could one's whole life change in two weeks?

The following week Lally came to dinner to meet my family. This would be a telling test. The only one with any tact was Mama and I was anxious to hear her opinion. Lally created a good first impression when he arrived with flowers.

My family of academics were very forthright in stating their opinion about anything and everything. If he survived the scrutiny of Papa and my brothers, he was really serious. But I needn't have worried; Lally was a wonderful conversationalist and well able to stand up for himself. The first hurdle was crossed and he hadn't been put off.

Now I was invited to meet his folk. To say the least, his mother was very offhand and made it obvious that she didn't consider me a serious contender. I was downgraded a few notches when she discovered I had a career.

I can hear her warning words as she turned to Lally, saying, "She'll not make you a proper wife, my boy. You mark my words, when there's no dinner on the table when you get home from work."

Despite that, Lally continued with the courtship.

We had known each other just three weeks when I said: "Maybe, probably yes."

Lally requested a meeting with my father to formally ask for my hand in marriage. He was anxious to assure Papa that he was a responsible person. We waited in the lounge while the two of them went into the study. This meeting really amused Papa. He was a progressive and had, as a rebel, discarded convention. He listened patiently while Lally said his piece.

Papa smilingly replied, "Do you love each other? That is the most important issue. As far as supporting her, you have no need to worry about that. Gwen has a good job with a secure contract. She's one of the highest-paid designers in the country. You don't have to concern yourself about money."

Lally was stunned. We had never discussed the fact that I had a career, as such. He knew I had a job, but thought nothing of it. This was different.

He blurted, "I don't want my wife to have to work. I'm not interested in how much money she makes. I'm capable of supporting my wife."

Papa looked surprised and told him seriously, "There are not many women who can command such a large salary. She's a very clever girl. I can tell you it took me by surprise when she was offered this job. She even insisted on a month's trial before signing the contract. Anyway, if Gwen wants to marry you, my wife and I would welcome you as a son-in-law."

Papa got up from his chair. The meeting was over.

A few days later, my parents received an invitation to Lally's home. I had been to the house previously and was aware of the room kept for special occasions. Good, I thought, as we were led into a very pleasant panelled room. Lally's sister, Rose, was sitting by the fire, doing her nails. I had already met Rose and found her to be aloof, sensing that she didn't like me, but this took me unawares. She nodded her head in greeting and continued polishing her nails.

Lally's father stood up and greeted my parents. He was a fine man, tall and fair, with a jovial face. He looked the image of Maurice Chevalier and it wouldn't have surprised me if he had suddenly burst into song.

Lally's mother had an inbred contempt for everyone she came in contact with. Anyone close to her children was subject to the full force of her condemnation. After the preliminary introductions, she wasted no time in telling Mama, "I don't think it's a good match. With Lally's prospects, I think he could have done better, but there you are."

Mama was taken aback, but she rallied round, incensed by the effrontery, stating, "We're not here to defend our daughter. It was your son who proposed! Obviously he didn't ask your opinion, or we wouldn't be here. As far as my husband and I are concerned, if Gwen chooses to marry Lally, he will be the one benefiting the most." She stood up, saying, "I think we've said all we need to say."

The meeting came to an end.

Lally felt humiliated and livid. He had good reason to resent what his mother had done and was annoyed with himself for being caught off-guard. His mother was domineering and self-opinionated, but he hadn't expected her to disregard his feelings and to alienate the family of the girl he had chosen to marry.

After that there was a lot of soul-searching on both sides. Lally insisted that he wasn't concerned with his mother's opinion. She had tried to link him with many girls of her choice, but he was his own person. I was the one he wanted, nothing would change that.

It was my turn to rethink. I wasn't desperate to get married. I was still young, only twenty-two, with a brilliant career before me. I was very popular and never short of dates. I could follow my singing career in tandem with the designing. I had a great life.

But I was mesmerised by Lally. His determination fascinated me. He had taken me by surprise and for the first time, I felt that I had found the one I wanted to spend the rest of my life with. I felt his love enveloping me and I wanted to belong. He loved me for myself, not for what I could do or achieve. He just wanted me. He had woven a magic spell around me and nothing else mattered.

My parents questioned me, to be sure, but when we finally made up our minds, they gave us their support. Lally's father also added his support. His philosophy was that if I sang I must be a nice person. As my parents had bought me part of a set of luggage on our engagement, Lally's father offered to add the extra piece, which was a comforting gesture. However, instead of matching white hide, I was presented with what could only be described as a reject and in case the wedding didn't follow, he had it inscribed with Lally's initials.

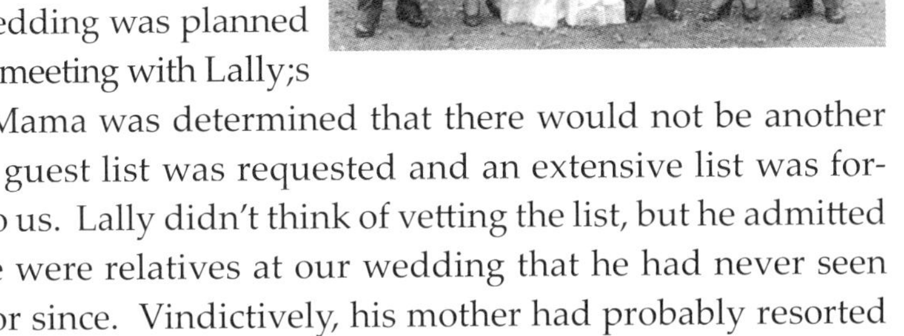

Lally surprised me by choosing my ring, a solitaire in an Edwardian setting, echoing his impeccable taste. It took time for me to get used to his extravagance, but it was exciting to be indulged.

The wedding was planned without a meeting with Lally;s parents. Mama was determined that there would not be another fiasco. A guest list was requested and an extensive list was forwarded to us. Lally didn't think of vetting the list, but he admitted that there were relatives at our wedding that he had never seen before, nor since. Vindictively, his mother had probably resorted to rent-a-mob.

The wedding reception was held in an exquisitely furnished house in Hampstead. My parents sold their house to pay for the wedding, but there was a bonus. The purchaser was the head pâtissie of the Lyons Corner House, who insisted on making our wedding cake and providing all the food, a fantastic gesture as it was a period of strict food rationing. True to her nature, my mother-in-law considered Hampstead a letdown and would have preferred a West End hotel; whatever or wherever it had been, she would have complained. But marrying Lally was no mistake. There have been hiccups and we've had our ups and downs, but our love remains something special.

~ *The Honeymoon and Our First Home* ~

This coastline had witnessed the Battle of Britain. It was over this terrain that the brave pilots of the Royal Air Force had manned their aircraft to keep the Luftwaffe of the German Air Force from destroying London and other vital cities of England. Bleak, silent fields keeping their secrets while groups of hop pickers gathered apples from laden branches of trees, added a note of hope to the desolate area. We were on our way to Dover, to catch the ferry which would take us across the Channel to Calais. The melody and words about bluebirds over the white cliffs of Dover echoed in my head and I anticipated their emergence when we saw the white cliffs as we approached the harbour. The whiteness of the cliffs were breathtaking and worthy of the song, but there weren't any bluebirds, only seagulls.

Crossing the Channel in those days was quite an experience. One did not drive onto the ferry; an overhead crane clamped the car by the wheels. The wire-spoked wheels of Lally's car were normally handled with kid gloves and lovingly burnished to a bright, glowing finish. The secured car was then swung up over the bow of the ship and supposedly deposited on the deck. Watching the car dangling mid-air over the harbour, made Lally gasp with horror, as the clamps released his precious Jaguar two feet from the ground, not a pleasant sight. Our destination was Zoute, a seaside resort by Knokke, in Belgium.

Thirty-five pounds each, the allowed currency, ruled out expensive seafront hotels. The Pavilion de Zoute, a hotel near to the Dutch border, suited our budget. Lally, having endured five years of rationing, was impressed with the food. I hadn't experienced his deprivation so it was touching to watch his eyes light up with each meal. At the amusement arcade opposite the hotel, Lally couldn't resist indulging in an additional daily waffle, smothered with cream.

Now, for the first time, we were on our own. To say the honeymoon was a disaster is partially true. It was a difficult period of learning and understanding. Hovering, was the special magic. The spark echoed in Lally's warm brown eyes and shy smile as his eyes met mine. It appeared to me as pride and pleasure, admiring the confidence with which he strode across a room and delight in the spontaneous original humour.

Sharing thoughts and opinions and doing things in unison was what I had anticipated, but Leader and Follower appeared to be the format. Lally's leadership was a quality I had admired, but now, it was fast becoming obvious to me that I was not happy with being ordered about and constantly being told what to do. The strong character, so admired during our courtship, was becoming too assertive. It was one thing to witness his authority, but quite another to be subjected to it.

"Hey!" I told myself, "This is supposed to be a partnership." Inner thoughts began to protest and I realized that it was a problem I couldn't run away from. Breaking point came suddenly, as I trailed behind in the Casino. Lally, oblivious of the fact that I was there, was deeply engrossed, as he flipped discs onto the roulette table.

Diverting his attention, I asked, "What are you doing?"

"Putting it on number nine," he replied.

"Shall I choose my number now?" I enquired.

"What do you mean?" he asked in surprise.

"If we're a pair, we choose a number together, or take turns."

"What are you talking about?" He stared at me as if I was demented, but I stood my ground and explained, "You're not an 'I' any more, no more 'I'. You are a 'we'. We do things together. You and me. WE."

And there in the casino was the first breakthrough. And we've been WE ever since.

Money raised its ugly head. It's not a commodity I covet as long as there's enough to get by. If the opposite were true, I would have married for money. The opportunity was there, but rejected. As far as earning money, I sacrificed a glowing career which had even made Papa sit up and take notice. And so it was a source of contention between Lally and me. He wasn't mean, just careful. Rightly so! He had worked hard to attain his wealth and therefore valued it. I respected him for his capabilities. The early days were hard, as I loathed asking for money. Hence, the first confrontation, when I was about to buy a scarf to go sailing. Lally protested, saying, "Use a towel from the hotel."

I laughed, but realising that he was serious, answered, "You must be joking!" I looked at him in disbelief, even more amused at the absurdity of the situation, as I stated, "It won't work. I don't anticipate having to ask your permission each time I need something."

The revolt shocked Lally, who was used to getting the better of an argument, but it helped him to understand my feelings.

Riding pillion on the hired motorbike was an exciting and economical way to get around Belgium, as we explored the countryside. Our money lasted two weeks on the Continent. On our return to England, we continued the honeymoon for two more weeks, touring the south coast through Devon as far as Land's End in Cornwall.

Slightly jaded, we arrived back from our honeymoon. Our problems had been sorted out to a point, but we still had to get used to our new status.

Mama, in her customary helpful way, had put a little milk, butter and sugar, part of her weekly rations, in our house for our breakfast. Obviously porridge was also there because that is what Lally requested. In my wifely role, I began cooking the porridge according to instructions.

"Put the milk in the porridge," ordered Lally.

"There's not much and we will need some for tea," I pointed out.

"Don't argue. We always cook it with the milk," Lally insisted.

I obeyed and the porridge turned to a rich, thick glue, which we attempted to eat, but gave up in fits of laughter. I couldn't resist saying, "I told you so," and we continued laughing.

The next morning Lally grandly handed me a five-pound note to buy supplies for supper as he set off to his business to earn more money to support the little woman left at home to dust and clean.

Making a note of the meagre supplies in the house, I ventured out to explore Edgware. The handful of shops, little more than a village, included an old-fashioned Sainsbury's, with tiled walls depicting rural scenes. Eager, clean-faced staff in stiffly starched white overalls stood behind immaculate marble counters, displaying their wares. Presenting my ration cards, I watched as the assistant deftly proceeded to chop a small lump of butter off the miniature butter mountain with a wooden palette, then pat it into shape with a palette in each hand, swivelling it round and round before wrapping it in greaseproof paper. He then cut off a miniature piece of cheese. A week's ration.

Smiling with pleasure at my first purchase, I took out my purse. The five-pound note wasn't in it. A search of my pockets revealed nothing. Confused, I had no alternative but to leave empty-handed, embarrassed by the crowd of waiting customers relegating me to "idiot" status.

I dreaded having to tell Lally: "Sorry! I lost the housekeeping money."

In fact, Lally found it hilarious; he couldn't stop laughing, remarking, "Don't tell my mother," and burst into another fit of laughter.

Then, sensing my distress, took me in his arms and holding me tight, softly whispered, "Just as long as I don't lose you."

The new experience of being the little housewife was actually enjoyable. Cookery became my main interest. The effort, however, was inadvertently laid to waste by Lally's mother. Lally and his two brothers travelled together to the factory in the city. Each day, they called in to visit their mother on the way home and she tempted them with special goodies, ready and waiting: bean and barley soup, chopped liver, gefilte fish. It seemed uncanny to my sisters-in-law and me that the brothers were never hungry. When the mystery was unearthed, Jill, Barbara and I went on strike, which put an end to the pre-dinner snack.

Attempts to make myself like the house always failed. Faults just stood out. The fact that the last owner had committed suicide within its walls formed the first strike against it. The vibes seemed to haunt me. The boiler in the kitchen kept going out and relighting it wasn't one of my best accomplishments. The kitchen sink under the large picture window overlooked the garden, but there wasn't a door from the kitchen to the garden. Access was through the side entrance in front of the locked garage doors, through the garage and the locked rear door. Eventually, with great difficulty, a door was fitted by cutting away the sink unit and picture window. Without central heating, the rooms, especially the bedrooms, were ice-cold and damp. Lally's mother knitted a balaclava, which somehow got lost, but remains our treasured memory of an odious passion-killer.

Lally embarked on a new idea, his imagination fired by exhibiting at the first Ideal Home Exhibition at Olympia. The company were expanding rapidly, making a wide range of brushes. He decided to use the opportunity to test the brushes by having the house painted. A team of men began removing picture rails and bedroom fireplaces to make clear, uncluttered rooms. Completing the theme, plywood panels concealed the balusters on the staircase. The house was beginning to look good when there was a knock on the door. It was the building inspector. Taken by surprise, I asked him in.

"I understand you're having some building work done," was his curt remark.

"Yes," I replied and smiled as it was so obvious.

"Are you aware that there's a five-pound limit without permission?"

"No," I said, shaking my head.

"You're not English, are you?"

"No, I'm Canadian," I replied.

"Oh, I see. Well I have to inform you about the limit."

"I'm sure we aren't going over it. Would you like to look around?" I enquired.

The house looked like a builder's yard as we walked upstairs, passing two workmen on our way. He made no remarks and when we'd gone over the whole house, he thanked me and left.

Shaking like a leaf, I phoned Lally, who was exhibiting at Olympia. My fetish about keeping within the law made me feel guilty.

Lally immediately left the exhibition and went to see his lawyer, explaining the situation and grim-faced, Laurie remarked to Lally, "It'll probably mean six months in prison."

For a couple of months we lived in terror of a knock on the door. After that we concluded that the Inspector took pity on my being Canadian and ignorant, or else he had dropped dead on the way home. Either way, we began to get back to normal. The house was painted cream throughout, a gift from one of the builder's merchants Lally supplied with brushes, and we settled down.

~ *Lally* ~

It came as a surprise to learn that Lally and his brothers not only looked like the Marx brothers, with the same characteristics and mannerisms, but were cousins once removed. The Marx brothers' father and Lally's grandfather were brothers. Lally had the bushy eyebrows and quick wit and humour of Groucho; Monty was gregarious, like the zany Chico and Harpo, chasing anything in a skirt; and Harold was introverted and always within reach of his moneybox and blood-pressure gauge. Living with duplicate Marx brothers was a daunting prospect, but it guaranteed that life would never be dull.

Lally was the third generation of his family dealing in brushes, following his grandfather, father and uncles. The war had interfered with his career. Now, with his discharge from the Air Force, he was seeking to re-establish himself.

Presenting himself to a small brush manufacturer with whom he had dealt prior to his military service, he was surprised by the offhand attitude as Charlie Page said, "I only supply regular customers."

"I can understand that," replied Lally. "Blame the war. I'm just starting up after my service in the Air Force," he explained.

"I said no and mean no," he growled. "I'm fed up with your type. You think the world owes you a living!" He disappeared into the workshop.

Lally was livid at the injustice. He wasn't asking for a handout. He recalled now how this maker had always been gruff and self-opinionated

He was still standing there when one of the workmen came out. Approaching him, he asked, "Are you a brush-maker?"

"Yes," was the reply.

"Would you like to earn some extra money?"

Dick Trew, one of the old school of brush-makers, proud of his craft, relished the opportunity of earning extra money for working on a Saturday, but he was a cautious man and warned, "It's not so easy, mate. Everything is on licence."

"Leave that to me," Lally replied. "Tell me what you need."

It wasn't difficult for Lally, as an ex-serviceman, to obtain necessary licences for the required items on Dick's list. One hundred pounds borrowed from his grandfather paid for the first week's bristle. Saturday morning found Dick Trew at Marlow Works, the small workshop in Shoreditch, fitted out with a workbench, boiler, oven, cones and combs with sundry additional items of glue and pins. Dick Trew converted handles and bristle into 6-inch wall brushes.

That was the start of Russell MacDonald, Brush Manufacturers. Week after week, Lally sold the brushes, ploughing all the profit back, doubling up on purchasing bristle and building up a substantial clientèle, concentrated on quality paint brushes for craftsmen. As soon as it was feasible, Dick Trew was employed fulltime, and Lally began looking for larger premises.

Great Sutton Street was a tumbledown building on three floors within reach of Marlow Works. As the company expanded, manufacturing was moved there, retaining the small workshop as a storeroom. The company was expanding and becoming recognised. Charlie Page, the manufacturer who had refused to supply

Lally, received word of his success and threatened to put him out of business. Lally laughed and a war began. The Bristle Merchants refused to be drawn into the argument and the threat that Charlie Page would not buy from them was ignored.

Lally's brothers were struggling to get established. Monty, now married to Barbara, was a puddings salesman without any prospects.

"Why don't you take Monty in with you?" asked Lally's mother. "I'm sure you could use another pair of hands."

True to his nature, good, kind and generous, Lally took him in and following on, took Harold into the business, making them partners. Each of the brothers performed their own function. Lally was responsible for the administration, Harold ran the factory and Monty managed the sales staff. The company grew and flourished, ranking as one of the major paint brush manufacturers in the country. The brushes were known as Armac.

That was the stage at which Lally and I met, when the ambition and determination shone through his unflappable exterior, someone sure of himself, resolute and reliable, masking a subtle, spontaneous humour.

Lally was quick to see the potential of paint rollers when he called at our home soon after we met, to find my brother Albert and me painting the kitchen. The commercial travellers considered them a joke and refused to show them, but the newspapers wrote a feature on them and paint rollers just took off. Wonderwork Paint Rollers, their trade name, became the foremost manufacturer in the country, used universally by Professionals and DIY.

At that time, they were having trouble in the old building with rats eating the bristle, which was causing havoc with their production. Rat-catchers came and put down poison, without success. The brothers managed to catch a rat and kept it in a cage for a week, feeding it with the rat-poison. It flourished, to the surprise of the rat-catchers.

The move to a modern factory in Pitfield Street gave them the added space they required, as new methods of manufacturing replaced outdated hand mixing of bristle. A large bristle-mixing machine, made in Canada, speeded up production, as well as creating uniformity. Brushes were still handmade, but methods to simplify the work were introduced.

The next big advance was their takeover of Christopher Leng, the oldest and most esteemed name in the trade, when they renamed their brushes Leng-Armac and Vulcaset.

Bristle, from the coat of wild boar, with a root and a flag end, is the most important component in brush-making. An inner tube, with its own strain of attached nodules not visible to the naked eye, holds and controls the flow of paint. China produces the best bristle for paint brushes, which vary in texture, depending on which Province they come from. To name a few, Chung King is stiff and the most expensive; Tiensen is medium to soft; Hankow and Tsinchow are firm; and Shanghai is very soft and the cheapest. They vary in length from two to seven inches.

The Bristle Auction, sponsored by China, was held once a year in London. Lots were viewed in advance, but bidding was limited to Bristle Importers. "Job lots" for each type of bristle and relative length were individually listed.

Harold was responsible for collating the complex order, based on the anticipated production for orders and the vast comprehensive selection of stock they carried of each range of paint brushes, from a half inch to four inches wide, each with their own blend of bristle and distinctive, dipped handles. Classic were the top of the range, all black with a gold band on the oval handle; Rembrandt, Adelphi and Gainsborough, with individual black markings on gold handles, were relatively downgrade; Warrior, Elite and Swift were economy brushes. Wall brushes ranged from four to seven inches wide; there were also Two-knots, Wash-downs, Fitches and

Paperhangers, as well as special specifications for the Government Ministry and British Standard. It would be impossible to list all the brushes; this is just an indication.

Harold usually placed the orders for bristle, but as he was under pressure in the factory, he gave the list to Monty, saying, "Here's the list, Monty. I've listed the first choice in each lot, with two alternatives. It has to be assigned to a Bristle Merchant to bid on our behalf at the Bristle Auction."

"OK Harold, leave it to me," Monty replied.

Inadvertently, Monty gave the same list to more than one merchant, all bidding against each other, running up the price on the first choice and then purchasing the alternatives. Monty had cornered the market, buying up all the bristle suitable for brush-making. Invoices, demanding payment forthwith for purchases made on their behalf, immediately followed the Bristle Auction. The office was in a turmoil, inundated with phone calls from the merchants self-satisfied with their successful bidding. Lally was devastated by all the incoming calls. They could lose everything.

Harold, on hearing the news, stormed into the office. "What have you done?" he shouted. "How could you be so stupid!"

Monty was taken unawares. Still not realising the situation, he began to laugh. Harold was about to strike Monty, but Lally grabbed his arm.

"Wipe the smile off your face. This isn't a joke, you bloody fool. This will finish us off. Everything we've built up will be down the drain."

The smile on Monty's face turned to fear. The gravity of his deed began to sink in.

"Get out. I don't want to see your face," Lally said, holding the door open.

The bank manager had watched Lally's steady progress in building up the company and was understanding, but he didn't have the thousands required. He had to get sanction from head office, who agreed to hold the bristle in bond. He told Lally:"They will back you on condition that Monty is given his marching orders."

In the end they were rescued. By some strange turn of fate, the world price of bristle escalated. Luckily, they were able to sell the bristle at a large profit.

Their mother intervened: "So Monty made a mistake!" and Monty was kept on.

One of the merchants involved claimed, " If Monty fell into a cesspool, he would come out smelling of roses."

Always on the lookout for a good opportunity, Lally's attention was drawn to the advantage of moving the business to Outer London. The discovery of a road-widening scheme in Pitfield Street made them eligible. Once more they were on the move, but this time to a one-floor factory in Borehamwood, built to their own specification, with an office block and canteen overlooking green fields.

A few years later, they built a second factory on their plot of land. Leng-Armac was now a leading contender for large contracts with the Ministry of Defence, which included the armed forces; with the Admiralty, British Rail and among others, the GLC, Greater London Council, and Borough Councils.

Wonderwork Paint Rollers were regarded as the best in the trade, with sheepskin supplied by Morlands. Many of the rollers on the market were invariably made by Leng Armac. With the influx of DIY, rollers were replacing the wall brushes favoured by craftsmen, but industrial rollers were even converting them.

Special pressure rollers were supplied for experiments carried out at the naval docks in Gibraltar, to paint the hull of ships underwater, thereby avoiding the cost of putting them into dry dock.

A useful innovation were Trim-it brushes, made with filaments within a tube. The worn end, when cut off, revealed a new section of brush. Trim-it, very aptly named, was featured on TV's Tomorrow's World. It replaced the old glue brush in industry and was used extensively by several trades.

A special pressure paint roller was made for British Airways for applying paint on Concord. Lally and I were invited to go over Concord when it was developed. Through an open doorway I saw workmen doing work outside, on the wing. They allowed me to step out and I had the amazing experience of walking on the wing of Concord. We were told that weight was of utmost concern; if the paint was too heavy, a seat would have to be removed.

For many years the annual Hardware Trade Fair included the decorating trade until Decorex, catering solely for builders' merchants, found favour with the wallpaper, paint and brush trade. I designed the exhibition stands for the trade shows. An early stand had a mixing machine and brush-maker making brushes, another had a full size stuffed wild boar, the firm's mascot, accompanied by turn-of-the century photographs of Chinese peasants gathering and sorting bristle into bundles. One year, each series of brushes were mounted in frames and displayed as an art collection. It was very effective and many merchants had them on loan for their company's promotion. The most unusual was a model brush, standing six feet high, decorated with a sequin ferrule and silver lettering. It created a sensation, with people asking if they could have the next dance. Occasionally, I was asked to do a promotional display for trade customers.

In 1983, the brothers decided that the time had come to retire. Reluctantly, the business was sold to a large public company.

The one hundred pounds borrowed to make the first batch of brushes at Marlow Works had come a long way.

~ *The Riviera: 1948* ~

"How about a drive down to the South of France?"

The question took me by surprise. I looked at Lally to see if he was *compos mentis*. He looked normal enough, grinning in his mysterious way, and I wondered what was coming next.

"What better way to run in a new engine?" he asked.

Of course! He was referring to the new 3.8 litre Jaguar based on the pre-war design, its leaping jaguar poised above the long bonnet, with distinctive radiator and large, round, shining head-lamps: the epitome of elegance.

I smiled, catching his excitement. "It sounds wonderful! However, you've forgotten one little detail. Holidays cost money. The restricted currency we can take out of the country won't go far on the Riviera."

The mysterious smile broadened. "I've just met a friend of a friend who owns a share of an hotel at Juan les Pains. He lives in England and he'd like to be paid here."

I stared in surprise. "Where's Juan les Pains?"

Laughingly, he explained, "It's on the coast between Cannes and Nice. The hotel is on the seafront and he can guarantee a first-floor room overlooking the sea."

"Sounds too good to be true," was my sceptical reply.

But it was true and a few days later we were on our way.

Collecting the Continental Kit at Dover seemed an unnecessary precaution with a brand-new car, but the AA man practically insisted. It was a gesture of goodwill for members, and there was no charge if it was unused.

The sea crossing from Dover to Calais was as smooth as a lake, with perfect weather as we headed for Paris. The detour to Paris was a special treat for me and I anticipated its magic. Lally, though unpredictable, was a romantic, and I looked forward to any surprise he chose to spring on me.

Barely perceptible at first, the gentle purring of the engine began to give an occasional splutter. As it increased, Lally remarked that it sounded like the petrol pump and he'd attend to it when we arrived at the hotel. The hustle and bustle of traffic was the first indication that we were in Paris, with traffic at crossroads controlled by a gendarme standing on a small platform in the middle of the intersection, giving directions. As we approached, the gendarme waved his arm, indicating to us to stop. As the car stopped, so did the engine. Lally jumped out, ran around the car, lifted the bonnet and jiggled the petrol pump up and down, which started the engine; he closed the bonnet and ran back to the driving seat. The gendarme quickly reversed the traffic and waved us on. Unfortunately he was unable to pass the message to the next gendarme, whose raised arm again implied, "Arrêtez-vous" and so the whole episode had to be repeated. In fact, it had to be repeated six or seven times until we finally reached the hotel.

The sun had long gone down by the time we arrived at the hotel, but Lally was still wearing sunglasses. His sight glasses could not be found. It was dark by this time and it was impossible to see anything in the car. He had difficulty seeing anything in the dimly lit hotel. We were both frayed at the edges from our day's travel, and the thought hung over the evening that unless we found Lally's spectacles, we'd have to cancel our holiday; happily, we found them the next day under one of the seats.

The Continental kit didn't contain anything to replace the fault of the petrol pump, but Lally's tinkering around managed to make it work reasonably well. This was the era when cars were not just vehicles of transportation; cars were a hobby and a way of life. Lally was a car buff and well-versed with Jaguars.

We bade farewell to Paris and began our journey south. The sun shining on the clear wide French motorway with pasture fields either side and the humming motor in tune, was exciting as we approached Fontainebleau. Suddenly, the car lurched as the rear wheel emitted a loud noise. We had a blowout.

While I panicked, Lally calmly said, "It's not too serious. I'll put on the spare."

I was quite impressed as I watched him take it in his stride. Out came the jack and in no time at all, it was placed in position to raise the offending wheel off the ground. Off came the wheel cover and I gazed with admiration as he systematically removed bolts, lifted off the heavy wheel and put on the spare.

Every village, at that time, had water troughs for the animals and I was surprised when Lally stopped at the next one to repair the flat tyre. It wasn't difficult as Lally knew exactly what to do. The inner tube was pumped with air like a balloon, then moved about in the water till bubbles were located. Patches and adhesive from the Continental kit sealed the leaks. The repaired tube was replaced in the tyre and pumped to the correct pressure. We smiled at each other with satisfaction. It was a new world for me and an appreciation for Lally's capabilities and most of all it was fun doing it together.

It was very hot, much too hot to eat, but the open roof and windows were refreshing. Suddenly, to our surprise, there was another blowout. We set about it the same way and wasted no time before repairing the second tube. After the third blowout we began to get worried. Veering on the side of caution, we bought two buckets. At each water trough we splashed water onto the wheels to cool them.

When we approached Avignon, the back wheel went; simultaneously, the front wheel burst, which sent us careering off the road into a large tree. The extent of damage was not good. The inner tubes were ripped to pieces and we only had one spare. We were in the middle of France with only three usable tyres.

There was a farmhouse nearby. The farmer and his wife came out to see what the trouble was. They both stood there shaking their heads from side to side. "Ah! Très mal!"

We were grateful when the farmer offered to take a wheel into Avignon in the sidecar of his motorbike. He was gone for hours. All we could do was wait in our propped-up car, exhausted, hot, tired and hungry. A long time elapsed before the farmer's wife asked if we would like something to drink. We were shocked, but still grateful, when she charged a ransom for it. We declined later when she offered something to eat. She'd already had what we had budgeted for the whole day's food.

At last the farmer returned. He had brought the wheel back with a tyre fitted on. It looked like a tractor tyre, much fatter and heavier. Would it fit on the car? It did, in a way. We put it at the back, which made it higher than the three other wheels, causing the car to tip diagonally. But at least we were mobile.

Limping into Avignon, we discovered that all the hotels were fully booked. Hotel after hotel could not offer any accommodation. At last, we gratefully took a single attic room in a grubby pension. Lally, completely exhausted, fell asleep the minute his head hit the pillow. The room was stifling. I opened the window overlooking a flat roof, horrified to see dozens of large rats running about. Shuddering, I quickly closed the window and sat there till morning, petrified in the suffocating heat.

The next morning Lally looked refreshed and ready to take on the world. He smiled as we helped ourselves to breakfast. "Well," he said, "what's it to be? We can have the car transported home, or we can chance it and go on."

It took me by surprise. The thought of giving up hadn't occurred to me, but he was giving me a choice. We optimistically concluded that the holiday could only get better and decided to go on

From Avignon there are two alternative routes to the south. One is through the French Alps and Grenoble; the other is the coastal road, the Corniche. Pandering to my fear of heights, we decided on the coastal road, even though it was longer. I was horrified to discover that the lower Corniche Road is suspended halfway down a sheer cliff. As we drove on to it, I was panic-stricken; the pounding in my chest was so intense, I thought it would explode. I couldn't look up. I couldn't look down and I dared not close my eyes. The fear within me was indescribable. Phobia experts believe that if one is placed in a position which causes panic, it cures you of your fear. It isn't so. I've never been so terrified. Here we were in mid-air, in a lopsided car, with faulty tyres liable to burst and swerve any minute. All I wanted at that point was to arrive at Juan les Pains safely.

Juan les Pains was welcoming as the gates of Heaven. The hotel was on the seafront and we were shown to our first-floor corner room with double aspect. Two windows overlooked the sea and a side window gave a wide view of the coastline.

Juan was everything it promised. A small haven with just a few houses forming a small village, stretches of golden sand and little more than a café, our hotel and a larger, walled-off hotel, with its privately walled-off section of beach nearby. Delighted with everything, we quickly changed to stroll along the golden, peaceful sandy beach.

"POW! BAM . . .BAM . . .BAM!" The first thought, when the room started to vibrate, was that it was an earth tremor, but the impact of accompanying music seemed odd. Chattering and shouting was coming from just below our room. Putting my head out of the side window, I could see people milling about as passengers alighted from cars lining the road, slamming doors shut, oblivious of the fact that it was eleven o'clock at night. We had not been told that our room was immediately above a night club turning out ear-shattering music till four in the morning.

A request to change our room was greeted with contempt by the maître d'hôtel, who remarked, "People don't come to Juan to sleep. They come here to enjoy themselves. This is the room you paid for." He was adamant. "Take it or leave it."

Though I proceeded with caution, sun umbrella, large hat, the brief exposure to sun while swimming in the sea was too much. That first evening found me suffering with sunstroke. I had no idea of how serious it could be. The kindly, grey-haired doctor tut-tutted, and gave the hotel staff instructions, while I became disoriented and wanted to die. They enclosed me in mosquito netting and plied me with drinks, which proved to be hazardous; ants swarmed and wriggled all over bottles and glasses. When I emerged from the mosquito net, the corner room proved to be a boon. I watched and waved to Lally from the window, as he enjoyed the beach, until I was well enough to enjoy the holiday.

And we did enjoy the holiday! The beach had to be avoided, but we discovered the Casino and Sporting Club at Monte Carlo. The sheltered pool at Eden Roc became a haven, where we were witness to the traumatic real-life drama of Elizabeth Taylor and Nick Hilton. The scenario of their turbulent honeymoon surpassed any script; the animosity was there for all to see, with no restraint on strong language and fiery action, until he hurled her into the pool and strode off as she shouted abuse. A saga not unlike her later role as the wife in Who's Afraid of Virginia Woolf?, for which she won an award.

Petrified as I was of the sea, I succumbed to Lally's enthusiasm in hiring a sailing boat to view American Navy ships anchored along the coast. The distance was much greater than he realized and we were a barely noticeable speck on the vast Mediterranean when the wind dropped and we were becalmed. It was as if time stood still. Not a movement, not a puff of wind, but utter, complete calm. An eerie feeling crept over me, which turned to panic as a spike cut through the surface of the water, heading in our direction.

With fright I shouted, "Look, a shark! It's coming straight for us!"

Lally helplessly raised his arms up in the air. "There's nothing I can do. We haven't even got a paddle!"

We watched, sharing the same thought of being overturned and swallowed up. I'm not religious, but I confess to a silent prayer: "Dear God, if you are up there, please help us."

The spike was about ten feet from us as it rose in the air; the sea all around began to bubble and foam and broke to reveal a submarine surfacing. The sailors emerged laughing. They had witnessed our torment and found it very funny. I felt I had died a thousand deaths.

As suddenly as it had dropped, the wind returned, and Lally resumed tacking to take us safely back to shore.

Lally's brothers had contacted Dunlop regarding the faulty tyres, and replacements, together with a petrol pump, arrived and were refitted.

Strangely enough, I didn't mind the return journey through the French Alps. Perhaps facing a hazard does cure a phobia after all.

~ We Are A Family ~

"Rest and eat enough for two."

Such was the advice given in the 40s. No, I wasn't ill, I was going to have a baby. Mystery and ignorance abounded: no clinics, no prenatal talks, just a monthly visit to the gynaecologist, whose comment, "Good, make an appointment for next month," had to suffice.

The doctor made up for the lack of information by keeping the mother in hospital for two weeks after the baby's arrival. Combined with that, if finance allowed, a maternity nurse cared for mother and child for the first month at home.

We began preparing the cream-painted nursery by painting and cutting out figures of Bambi and mounting the plywood animals onto the doors of two cream-painted utility cupboards. We bought a comfortable wicker nursing chair, a cot, a glass-shelved hospital trolley and a metal-framed portable fabric bath, the top cover of which was used as a changing table. Linoleum, with a white, grey and red square pattern, covered the floor.

My Canadian passport enabled me to purchase the larger export Silver Cross pram, silver in colour with a large and small white wheel each side. An extension flap by the handle provided additional length and an umbrella holder and sunshade were useful extras.

In my search for a nurse, I discovered that Mothercraft ran a Training Society, with a centre in Highgate where they cared for waifs and strays. In addition to nurse's training, expectant mothers were allowed to help with bathing and feeding the babies, to learn how to hold a baby correctly. I was grateful for that little bit of experience and knowledge.

The layette was standard. Two dozen Harrington muslin nappies, two dozen terry-towelling nappies, four Viyella nightgowns, four flannelette sheets, two cellular blankets and two shawls, were basic items. Additionally, one needed bonnets, booties, mittens, matinée coats and dresses or rompers which had elastic around the legs and buttons under the crotch. Knitting was a useful occupation, as bootees, mittens and cardigans shrank with constant washing and needed to be replaced. More ambitious knitters made gossamer shawls, which were a useful luxury.

Barry arrived at two o' clock in the morning, 6th February 1949. Lally and I agreed that, with his wizened face with wisps of black hair, he was the most beautiful baby in the world.

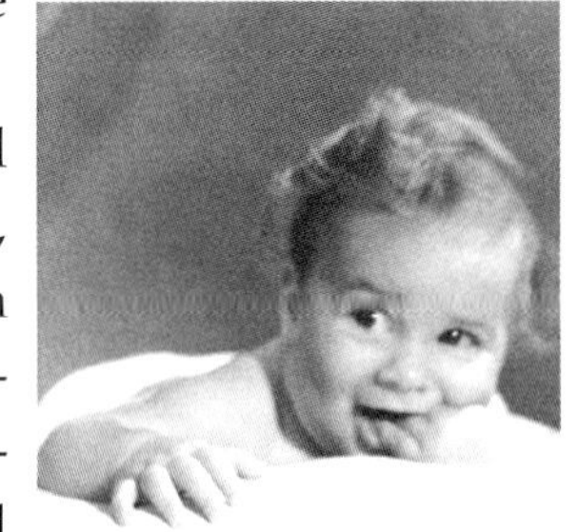

White-haired Nanny Smith, a typical grandmother, was our maternity nurse, exuding confidence and sound advice on how to cope with the strict, rigorous routine based on feeding at four-hourly intervals to allow time for necessary tasks and which started with the first feed at six o'clock in the morning.

Washing was done by hand on a scrubbing board and nappies were boiled in a copper; the wet clothes were then wrung on a mangle. Lally had presented the copper and mangle to me shortly after we moved into the house and I admit that they were not appreciated at the time. Now I was grateful for them as we had to cope with a constant line of washing hanging in the garden or on a rack in the kitchen, operated by a pulley.

Ten a.m. was bath time. Nanny Smith demonstrated its simplicity; the top lid slipped down the back of the bath, which she filled with a bucket of water. Testing the temperature with her elbow, she explained: "It's the most sensitive area of the arm. Hands are hardened and it's very easy to scald a baby."

Following the feed, Barry was put to sleep in the pram, in the fresh air, sheltered by the hood and the cat net. Time now allowed for cleaning the nursery, having lunch and doing odds and ends.

Two o'clock: another feed, followed by a walk in the pram. Nanny preferred the park, but I liked to walk to the High Street. Late afternoon was playtime until the six o'clock feed. A change into night clothes and tucked down until the ten o'clock feed and then, hopefully, down for the night. If he woke in the night, a little cuddle, a little water and down again to sleep. It sounds a doddle, but keeping the baby clean and dry, supplied with clean clothes and nappies – all of which were ironed to take away the roughness – was a time-consuming task. I was breastfeeding, so there was some respite, but there were still bottles of water to be sterilised, bouts of colic and sleepless nights.

Nanny Smith's departure heralded the daily trauma of coping with the washing of countless nappies, made easy by the purchase of a Bendix washing machine, so powerful that it had to be bolted to the floor. I continued with the routine Nanny Smith had started, keeping everything spotlessly hygienic. The nursery, as sterile as an operating room, was washed daily with disinfectant, making it germ-free. Without a chance to grow any antibodies, Barry caught every illness going. Anything that struck had a field day; a lesson in how one can be killed with kindness.

Papa, in his wisdom remarked, "Bringing up children is a job for professionals, but it's put into the hands of amateurs."

The arrival of Barry brought out the inner Lally and exposed the love he had hidden away. Barry was a lovely baby, everything one could wish for and Lally doted on him. Everybody's baby is special to the parents and we were no exceptions. Barry was a tough boy, and as he began to toddle around, Lally took to building a coal-shed in the garden. Each weekend would find him knee deep in bricks and cement, with Barry, barely walking, helping with his bucket and spade, pottering together side-by-side. Barry was a fine boy, sturdy, good-looking and strong willed, with an inquisitive mind. Everything in the environment interested him more than toys. His favourites were a pile of interlocking electrical plugs that Mama kept for him to play with when we visited.

I certainly didn't miss my career; I had one now that was much more rewarding and it was expanding even further.

Small workshops were springing up in the city, close to Lally's factory and regulations were being lifted; I was delighted when Lally arrived home with a round, polished-mahogany coffee table and demonstrated how four small quarter tables slipped underneath.

"That's clever," I said, as I watched him slide the fourth table underneath.

"We did a good deal on the price when I said we would take three," Lally proudly stated.

"Why would you want three?" I asked.

"Monty and Harold each had one, as well as one for us," Lally replied.

"Are you saying that your brothers bought identical tables?" I asked.

"Yes, and Mum wants one, too." Lally replied.

I stood there, stunned by the thought of all of us living in duplicate.

"Well she can have this one!" I said.

"What do you mean?" Lally asked. "You said you liked it."

"I did, when I thought it was something special. But with all the family having the same thing, it has lost its appeal. It will be yet another addition to the hodgepodge of furniture I loathe."

It was the first time I'd expressed such emotion and Lally was taken aback, as I confessed, "This isn't my home. I don't like the house, I never have and I don't like anything in it. You've never given me a chance to choose, unless it's a choice between two things you've already selected. I have no intention of continuing in this way. I have an opinion and you must recognise that."

Lally was mortified to think he had caused so much antagonism. But I was to blame as much, or even more than, him. For years I had kept my innermost thoughts to myself. Now I had to learn to express my opinion openly, which at first I found difficult.

Things changed after that, in fact to the opposite extreme. "You choose what you want," Lally insisted.

"No, if we choose things together then we will both like what we have," I maintained.

Not long after, Lally arranged for a builder and decorator to call, with this message: "Tell him to do anything you want in the house that will make you happy."

The most dramatic and effective alteration was to break through and remove the wall between the two box-like reception rooms; it changed the atmosphere of the house. The gloom disappeared as the graceful sweep of the arch, linking the two areas, allowed light and sunshine to flow in from each end. The house began to feel like home. But, more important, it was a turning-point; it proved to Lally that I had flair and gave credence to my opinion. From then on, our relationship never faltered.

The Ideal Home Exhibition, 1950, was a revelation with the re-emergence of the furniture trade. Large manufacturers, whose factories had been converted during the war to support the war effort, were now exhibiting displays of new products. Restrictions and regulations were obsolete and firms were anxiously attempting to re-establish themselves. The accent was on quality, displayed by old established firms exhibiting for the first time, showing a range of furniture which would be filtered onto the market.

The Regency mahogany table and lyre-back chairs, together with the breakfront sideboard, with four drawers in the centre and a cupboard with a small drawer above on each side, had a simplicity and elegance.

"This is the type of furniture I like," I said, turning to Lally.

"Do you think it will fit in the house?" Lally asked.

"Oh, yes, perfectly," I replied.

The representative for Tibbenhams told Lally: "It's not in production yet. We're showing it to see what response we get."

"Can I buy the display?" Lally asked.

"Yes, but you'll have to wait for delivery until we finish showing it to the trade," the salesman replied.

"Fine! We'll have the display, as it is here. The table, six chairs, two carvers and the sideboard."

I was in a trance as we walked away.

"Happy?" Lally asked.

"In seventh heaven," I replied.

"We're going away for a few days," Lally stated, adding, before I could respond, "It's all arranged. Your Mum is coming to keep an eye on Barry and Sheila says she can manage."

I was surprised, but not unduly. Lally had a way of springing surprises.

"Where are we going?" I asked, accepting the inevitable.

"Paris," was the simple reply.

I smiled, realizing that it included the 16th of February, the date we met and always celebrated. Paris was a touch extravagant, but the holiday would have to suffice for some time, as I was expecting another baby.

Wandering around the streets of Paris, absorbing its culture, was exhilarating. Paris had not suffered the ravages of war torn London and shops displayed their wares with panache. I had to be careful with items I admired as Lally was in one of his indulgent moods, ready to buy anything and everything I liked, often given later as a surprise.

The recently ordered Regency dining suite needed chair covering. What better place than Paris to look for tapestries of the period? We made an appointment to visit the Beauvais showroom, where a tall, distinguished, white-haired man with a small, elegant white beard, descended the magnificent, curved balustraded staircase and approached us.

Extending his hand in greeting, he asked how he could help. I explained about the chair covering and he graciously led us into another room and proceeded to show us appropriate designs. We were overawed, but not as much as when we were told the cost of each one. Lally was speechless as I apologised and told this wonderful man that we had made a terrible mistake. They were obviously way out of our bracket. He was one of the principals and amused with our reaction, but obvious admiration. He declared that it would give him great pleasure to show us some of the original tapestries and drawings. It was a most memorable day. His Gallic charm and specific descriptions of the historical battles, given with such pride, was an exclusive experience and one we both treasure.

Four months later and three weeks overdue, Marcia was born on the 30th June, 1951, at the Westminster Hospital. We wanted a girl and Marcia was a dream come true. Her beautiful, angelic face, with blue eyes and a halo of fair hair, was in contrast to Barry's dark features.

I had arranged for Barry to stay with Monty and Barbara, Lally's brother and sister-in-law, whose daughter, Amanda, was the same age as Barry and a constant companion, happy with the thought that he was with his cousin in familiar surroundings.

It was fortunate that Barbara reacted without delay to summon their doctor when Barry suddenly became ill. The doctor immediately rushed Barry into Great Ormond Street, the hospital for sick children, where they diagnosed that he was suffering from a blood breakdown. Completely unaware that anything was amiss and not at all suspicious that anything was other than perfect, I was surprised when Lally told me that children under five could not visit,

Lally would spend time with Barry at the hospital in Great Ormond Street and then come to visit me. Westminster Hospital was run on very strict lines, with specified visiting hours which catered to the routine of feeding the babies. I complained when Lally was always late, unaware of the cause, but Lally smiled and made up some story about Barry, never mentioning any problem. Mama, too, did the same, saying how nice everything was.

Babies were kept together in the nursery and I was at the stage of collecting Marcia, taking her to my room to have her feed and returning her to the nursery, changed and ready to be put down to sleep. My confinement was nearly at an end and I was looking forward to going home.

The next thing I knew was that I was found on the corridor floor. A group of doctors were assessing the problem of why I had collapsed after taking Marcia back to the nursery.

The doctor was waiting for Lally when he arrived at the hospital, greeting him with, "Mr Leigh, I have bad news for you. Your wife is seriously ill. She has phlebitis, a blood condition. Blood clots have blocked the circulation of both legs."

Lally had to break the news to me. He explained about my legs and told me I would have to stay in hospital until the danger was over. Looking down I could see that my legs looked like tree trunks. I had been aware of the heaviness, but I put it down to excess weight after having a baby and a good reason to watch my diet. The pain had worried me. Now I knew why.

Not a lot was known by way of treatment in those days, just bed rest, with crepe bandage to keep the swelling down. My legs were bound from toe to thigh, the end of the bed was raised higher than my head, and a large cage kept the pressure of blankets off my legs. Daily exercise was done lying on the floor with my legs supported by the wall, as well as alternately stepping in hot and cold water, to promote circulation to my toes. Walking was kept to a minimum.

Blood samples taken daily – which made me feel like a pin cushion – eventually caused problems for nurses unable to find suitable veins, and the doctor had to be called.

In all this time not a murmur of the trouble with Barry had been mentioned. Barry's blood had righted itself and he was able to go home, though still not very well. Lally suggested that he was going to take Barry away to Brighton for a few days, to make a fuss of him. I agreed that it was a good idea. We still had no idea of how much longer I would have to remain in hospital.

Mama moved in to our home and she and Sheila looked after Barry to ease Lally's burden. Lally spoke about Mama being at home with Barry, but I assumed that Barbara had just had enough.

After six long weeks, I left the hospital and went home, still confined to bed, but out of danger. Barry stood in the doorway, just looking, and slowly walked to the side of my bed. His deep-brown eyes looked twice as large as he came closer to make sure it was me, and I gathered him up in my arms.

Lally had been anxiously waiting for this reunion, to tell me, "Barry has been very ill! We nearly lost him, but for quick action by Barbara." He continued, saying, "You can see that he is fine now and it's better that you know what happened."

Barry was a shadow of the bumptious boy I had left behind, but he looked well and happy, thanks to Lally, whose love and strength had no limit.

The tiny house was bulging; in addition to Lally and me, there was a maternity nurse to care for Marcia, Sheila looking after Barry, Mama cooking, and Bridie, Sheila's aunt, coming in daily to clean.

I was devastated when the invitation arrived for Rose and Jack's wedding at the Metropole Hotel in Brighton. How could I refuse to go to the wedding of Lally's sister? And yet the problem of attending seemed insurmountable.

"I have nothing to wear except my maternity dress," was my lament. Jill, my sister-in-law, came to the rescue by taking me shopping. I managed to find a ballerina gown of black and blue shot silk taffeta, with a small gold thread motif. Shoes were a major problem, but flat navy suède loafers fitted over the bandages, giving me the elegance of a penguin. Shopping for a hat was too much, but with time on my hands and a crochet needle, I made a juliet cap in gold thread, mounted on a padded band with thick strands of gold thread wound round. The little hat was the perfect complement and the nicest part of the outfit.

The exodus for the wedding was traumatic. A roof rack fitted on the car took the luggage. A vague recollection of the journey exists, but the lines of wet, hanging nappies across each of the two bedrooms of the Metropole Hotel are still a vivid memory.

My foolish mind does recall a simple episode during our stay at the Metropole. At the hotel was Lally's former fiancée. I had been told about Myah's beauty many times by members of the family: "A Hartnell model, with poise and glamour." When Lally introduced me, her eyes took in my dumpiness, making me feel like an elephant in drag.

I doubted Lally's, "You're much lovelier and prettier than her." But realising that I was the one he married and his eyesight is obviously faulty, I'm confident that he does love me.

By Christmas I was able to leave off the bandages. Marcia was weaned and I was able to resume normal living.

It had been a trying period.

~ *Moving House* ~

"Building plots around here are impossible to find, so don't waste your time," was the advice given by my brother's wife, Helen.

The "impossible" turned out to be a building plot on the best side of Winnington Road, with part of Kenwood included in the three hundred feet of garden. House hunting had been a weekly chore, which did much to clarify features of houses that appealed to both of us. The purchase of land in Winnington Road put us in the enviable position of including all the details we wanted into the specification drawn up by the architect, Alexander Flinder.

The plans were approaching completion when Lally's brother, Monty, told us about a derelict house in Canons Drive, which had been requisitioned in the war. "It's in a state, but it's worth having a look," was Monty's understatement, but he aroused our curiosity and we followed it up.

There was something magical on entering the drive to Canons, once the home of the Earl of Chandos. At once, the avenue of trees conveyed a bygone grandeur and tranquillity. A short way on, gently merging into the setting, swans and ducks nestled beneath the branches of a tall willow tree, its branches touching the still water of the pond.

Houses almost hidden behind the trees added their charm. A short distance further on, majestically side by side, five superior houses stood out, dignified by their classical stature. "Dalla" was semi-obscured by overgrowth, but the roofline proclaimed its existence. The house had been requisitioned during the war by the Admiralty and after the war, inhabited by squatters.

Making our way past the bushes, we entered the sheltered front door. No amount of warning could have prepared us for the squalid devastation; we found ourselves in a ruin. The enormous lounge hall had a splendour which shone through the chaos of decay. Tall windows with low sills either side of the entrance door were elegant. On the right, a large fireplace; the remnants of a fire in the hearth gave the impression of burnt wood, with broken pieces of wood splayed over the grimy floor. To the left, double-glazed doors revealed a large reception room. A third reception room, larger and more grand, had French doors and windows opening onto the garden. The staircase was set in a well and the kitchen area was to the right. Missing floorboards taken up and used for firewood endangered walking, in case one fell through a hole. Five bedrooms and a bathroom on the upper floor left much to the imagination.

The state of the house was atrocious, to the extent that it needed fumigating. There was wet rot, dry rot and rising damp. The entire terrace surrounding the house was above damp course and needed to be dug up and lowered. The garden, which had a tennis court, was completely overgrown. A mound of asphalt, obviously delivered pre-war, overgrown with weeds, added to the desolation. The house was nothing but a shell. It had been on the market for years, but nobody would touch it.

Lally and I viewed the house in silence, each of us absorbing the beauty and the horror. Plans for Winnington Road were now complete. Due to building regulations for new houses, there was a restriction on the size one could build. This house was considerably larger than planning permission for a new house would permit. It would have to be gutted and presented much more of a challenge. Another consideration was the fact that Lally had recently built a new factory in Borehamwood, which was quite nearby. We left the house unsure of what to do.

As we drove down Canons Drive I asked, "What did you think about the house?"

"It will be a mammoth task to put it right," was his practical reply.

I nodded in agreement. "You're right. It will take courage. But if we don't, I think it will be an opportunity missed."

"Think about it. It's a big decision," Lally advised, but after a short time, added, "I'll call the estate agent tomorrow."

The following morning, I put in my vote for Canons Drive, saying, "I can't get the house out of my mind. Let's go for it."

Lally had come to the same decision and we were back to the drawing board. Work started almost at once. I undertook the planning and supervision, calling on the architect for advice when necessary. My days were now filled with seeking out the best available in an exciting period of innovation in British industry. We planned the work giving priority to basics: new electrical installation, plumbing and heating, kitchen, bathroom and children's rooms. Lally's connection in the building trade was a boon, giving us access to trade suppliers and superior craftsmen.

After years of deprivation, firms now introducing new products vied for recognition. Leisure Kitchens competed with Elizabeth Rose. Leisure, less luxurious and simpler, was my choice. The white wall cabinets and lower cupboards with red Formica counter tops, which included swivelling corner shelves, were revolutionary. A counter unit, with curved open shelves at one end, divided the working space from the bench seats and oblong table.

A streamlined Cannon cooker with eye-level grill, ventaxia, venetian blinds and Swan Maid dishwasher, were all new and desirable. The laundry room included the Bendix Washing Machine and clothes-airer above the Trianco Boiler, which never went out.

We had one of the first Marley vinyl floors to be introduced onto the market; it featured a border, outlining a white and red diagonal design. A photograph of the kitchen was featured in *Modern Woma*n magazine, October 1958, as an example of kitchen planning.

Overgrown trees had obscured part of the house and their removal revealed a feature window and roofline above the triple arches of the front of the house. The unusual room in the centre of the house became the bathroom, a superior example of its day, installed by Boldings of Davies Street, the doyen of bathroom installations. Grey tiles formed the walk-in shower in the corner and continued down the wall with a mural of birds in flight above the large, low, pink bath flanked by grey tiled piers each end. The opposite wall included a large square pedestal basin and inset mirror below a thirties-style diffused light fitting. The low ceiling, caused by the roofline, created a problem which was overcome by inserting four fittings into the void: a forerunner, now known as “downlighters”.

Barry’s large room with yellow walls, yellow cord carpet and Venetian blind, made an excellent playroom, with white shelves displaying toys and books between two deep cupboards. A made-to-measure blackboard filled the right wall. On the left, set back in an alcove, was a ship’s cabin, constructed in a combination of light and dark timber, with brass portholes either side of the open doorway, with a ship’s lantern and a red and white life-belt above the bunk bed. A haven, to retreat into and set sail for dreamland.

Jim Baldwin’s firm of decorators was the best, normally working for large contractors and regularly decorating Sanderson’s showrooms. He found my requests amusing, especially when I told him that I wanted the ceiling of Marcia's room wallpapered the same as the walls.

Jim laughed and said, "OK, if that's what you want."

White-dotted pink wallpaper covered the sloping ceiling and walls of Marcia's room, except for the "Milkmaid Panels" which were inset on every flat wall. Dolls and teddies abounded on a padded window-seat, below the wide dormer window, with more toys hidden by a curtain, in the same material as the bedcover.

The lounge hall was the hub of the house, a beautiful large room, a forerunner to open planning. The original parquet floor, when restored, had a patina new floors attempt to copy and although the floor we had laid in the lounge was the same in detail, it didn't have the charm of age. The walls, which included the staircase and upper hall, were in traditional grey and white hand-blocked wallpaper by Coles of Mortimer Street. Red silk brocade curtains with stiff pelmets, trimmed with gold tassel braid, were made for the windows, entrance doorway and half landing; burgundy carpet was fitted on the stairs and the upper hall. The room was empty of furniture, but a fire in the hearth gave it a welcoming warmth.

The next room we concentrated on was the drawing room: wide French windows into the garden, flanked on each side by tall, low windows. Brass curtain rails were not obtainable; instead, poles were covered with gold satin, with brass handles forming the end knobs. Swags and tails of apricot silk were draped over and under to give the effect of being wound around the pole, which formed the pelmet for the wall of curtains. In a sale, we were fortunate to find an Aubusson floral design carpet, which fitted the room. Four wall lights, shaped as branches, replaced the centre fitting. The piano I had grown up with in Canada had pride of place and the pale-blue and cream upholstery, made for us when we married, made up the one semi-complete room of the house.

The front room with double doors became the dining room. I found a niche in an auction. The fireplace was removed and the niche was built into the chimney breast. The Regency table was placed across the room beneath a chandelier, with the sideboard on the right. Turquoise walls and soft concealed lighting was delightful, viewed from the hall through the double-glazed doors. Burgundy carpet was salvaged from Broadfields Avenue, with sufficient for this room and the main bedroom. Burgundy velvet curtains with swags and tails, were temporarily put on hold.

Mrs Lerner, a widow, bubbling over with energy, belying her short and dumpy stature, dealt in fabrics and carpets, with a vast trade connection to supply whatever anyone needed. She seemed surprised when I questioned the quotation for the four dining room curtains, which was much more than our budget allowed.

"How I can I cut down the cost?" I asked.

Mrs Lerner explained, "Prices depend on the quality of the material, the lining, interlining and what's included in the standard of workmanship," and smiled as she added, "You get what you pay for."

"What does that mean?" I asked.

"Some makers skimp on interlining, sometimes without adequate stitching to give stability in wear, others use machines which tend to pull the material." A thoughtful look came over her face as she asked, "Have you ever seen curtains made?"

"No," was my frank reply.

"I'll take you to a good outworker and you can see what's involved."

The following week found us in a large workshop. Flat tables, long rods with a variety of hanging curtains stretched out, women concentrating on sewing across flat expanses of folds of lining, others making pleats and stitching braid.

Mrs Lerner confided, "This is one of the best workrooms. If a large firm needs a special, this firm does it."

She introduced me to Doris, explaining why I was there.

"'Ello love. Want to learn the trade, eh?" Doris laughed.

Doris was about forty, tall, well built, her fair hair held close to her head with slides. I followed her around while she explained why certain methods were followed.

When we finished she added, “If you ever need any help give us a call on the blower and if you’re really good, we’ll give you a job, eh, Mrs Lerner?” she added jokingly.

The prospect of making curtains was daunting, but I was loath to accept inferior work, because I knew that in the end, I would regret it.

Lally was adamant. “Here’s what you can spend. It’s up to you to do what you want.”

The next day I set up the largest table I could fit into the spare room. I enjoyed the challenge of hand-making floor-length curtains for the four dining room windows: burgundy velvet, interlined, each with three swags and pleated tails, all trimmed with gold bobble braid.

Mrs Lerner not only helped me with advice, but allowed me to draw on her knowledge and years of experience by opening doors and showing me the way. I’m grateful for her guidance.

There was still a lot to do. We were now keeping to a budget and looking for unusual furnishings. I began hunting for them in auctions. Every day would find me looking in London and at weekends, Lally and I would go to country sales.

Auctions are exciting and a challenge. You have to be decisive: “YES” or “NO”. Tomorrow it will be gone. The real value of an item doesn’t really count. What matters is how much you’re prepared to pay. Sometimes you find you have a real bargain, others may be a disappointment and occasionally there’s an added bonus when an unexpected extra item is included in the job lot. Many's the time an additional item turned out to be more valuable than the one bid for.

I viewed four auction rooms in London regularly each week: Phillips, Son and Neale; Bonham’s; Coe; and Harrods. I’d make my assessment and leave my bid with a porter. I rarely went to the actual sale, but if I did, I would still have the porter bidding. Dealers could and would run the price up if they spotted a stranger bidding. They would form a ring, which was illegal. On one occasion they ran the price up for me, but the auctioneer spotted it and knocked the price right down to rock bottom.

Country sales were more fun and better value. The most exciting were auctions at large mansions and stately homes. A stroke of genius was when Lally arrived home with a drop-head Ford Zephyr, operated by the simple touch of a button. It became a hobby, to go to sales and auctions and arrive home with the back of the car laden with bargains, much to the amusement of friends.

"Lally, look at this mirror." I pointed to a large frame carved in dark wood that attracted my attention.

"You wouldn't want to hang a mirror like that in our house!" was his surprised reply.

"Of course not! But it would make a fabulous headboard."

The anticipated price was not reached and it was knocked down to us for forty-seven pounds and loaded on to the Zephyr.

"I could think of better things to waste my money on," was the comment of a friend, when asked to help carry the large frame into the house.

The padded and buttoned headboard, converted from the antique Italian mirror now coloured soft white and delicately picked out in gold leaf by a very able gilder, is a rare and beautiful piece.

But that wasn't necessarily our best buy. So many items were "going for a song". It was the post-war period with a general attitude of "out with the old and in with the new". Things were being discarded as if they were rubbish. The dilapidated Victorian sofa from the gardener's cottage of a Rothschild estate was neglected, but the shape and frame with the added feature of a drop-end, were good. In fact it was a gem. Re-upholstered, it has pride of place in our home.

The His and Her boudoir chairs also turned out to be a snip. Exquisitely buttoned, with carved mahogany frames, they linked perfectly with the sofa. Together with a washed Chinese carpet, they formed the basic furniture of the lounge hall.

The main bedroom developed in stages. Green silk wallpaper contrasted with ivory built-in wardrobes. Over the bed, an antique ormolu coronet was hung with drapery. The French boulle marble-topped dressing table of inlaid tortoiseshell and brass, was a special piece. On top, an oval ormolu mirror was surrounded by a bevy of silver-framed photographs.

I decided to make the bedroom curtains and bedcover myself. The small embroidered flowers of the ivory silk brocade were enhanced by the addition of green satin. It was an ambitious and successful effort that included floor-length, interlined curtains with triple swags and tails for the two windows.

By now the house was more or less furnished, but it was only the start of our quest to fill our home with beautiful things. Sale rooms, auctions and markets became our pastime. The hunt was on, not for specific articles, but for items that we found desirable; we became avid collectors.

~ *Barry And Marcia* ~

The continuous ringing brought us rushing to the door to find a small child, her flashing black eyes and tousled long hair echoing her panic.

"Stop the fight!" she shouted. "It's a mistake. Lawrence could never do what Barry says he did."

That was our first glimpse of Amanda Kayne. Lally intervened in the skirmish and made the boys shake hands. Sheepishly, they smiled at each other and apologized.

"You probably dropped your pen. I'll help you find it," Lawrence offered.

That was the start of a wonderful friendship; even more than that, it formed an inseparable bond which lasted until adulthood. The Kaynes lived six houses up the road; Barry and Lawrence were eight years old and their sisters, Amanda and Marcia, were six. The four children became close friends and lived parallel lives throughout their childhood.

Little did we realize how much this estate had to offer when we chose it in lieu of building the house in Winnington Road. The relative privacy made the roads comparatively safe as there was no throughway for traffic or pedestrians; it meant that the children could safely play out of doors. Barry and Lawrence took full advantage of this freedom. Roller skates led to constructing a vehicle using the skates. They improvised and experimented with planks of wood, and by using scrap materials, adding brakes and steering, they culminated with a viable go-cart. It took them a long time, but they never tired of the challenge and one could sense their joy as they took turns sitting in the cart, with the other one running behind, pushing it down the slight slope of the pavement.

They kept in constant touch with each other by connecting their houses with some form of communication. The neighbours didn't object when the children ran wires along the dividing fences. The boys were able to alert each other and speak through their self-made Walky-Talky.

For a brief spell they joined the Boy Scouts to go camping. The "back to nature" phase continued when they returned home; throughout the summer months, they slept out of doors in their tent which was pitched in the middle of our garden. They cooked their meals on an open fire, which played havoc with the lawn, but they so enjoyed it that we couldn't object.

As they grew sufficiently responsible, they were allowed access to the seven-acre lake. The seven-acre lake, tended and maintained by the residents, was another bonus of the Canons Estate. It was well stocked with fish and regularly checked for swimming. Changing huts, a raft and diving board, provided the youngsters with the advantages of a nature reserve. Lally kept his boat, *Little Armac,* moored at the side, and when they were old enough, they had use of it.

Barry had to make an early start to get the Green Line bus to Shirley House, his prep school in Watford. It was clear from the start that Barry was clever. A stubborn streak was not apparent until he attended school, when we received a notice that he was uncontrollable.

We sought out the highest authority at Great Ormond Street Hospital, Dr Newns, who commented, "There's nothing to worry about. Barry is highly intelligent. It is the teachers who are at fault. The boy is obviously bored."

His school reports confirmed the problem. Term-time assessment placed him bottom of the class, but he attained excellent exam results. The teacher's comment corroborated Barry's stance: "Barry sleeps through the term but manages to get good exam results. If he paid more attention in class he would do very well indeed."

"Don't deliberately provoke the teachers," fell on deaf ears.

I have no doubt that Barry was Papa's favourite gradchild. When Barry was quite young, it was Papa's pleasure to plan a day's outing and to take Barry with him. Papa recognized his keen mind and determination. They had a bond, and though it wasn't obvious to me at the time, I can now see their similarities: their love of books and inquiring minds; their regard for tradition and heritage; their interest in the future; and their amazing reservoir of useless, but interesting, information. Idealists, sensitive to the faults of this world.

We should have paid more attention to Papa's observation when he said, "Bringing up children is very complex, but it's put into the hands of amateurs."

How true that was! He probably could have told us much more about Barry's thoughts and aspirations, but we didn't ask and he didn't say. We treated it as a huge joke.

We wanted the best for Barry, but in retrospect, we made mistakes. The prep school – Shirley House, in Watford – which Barry attended, was highly regarded. Mr Walters, the Headmaster, had recognized Barry's lack of interest during lessons with repetition of a subject. To accommodate his brilliant mind, he initiated alternative interests. Barry was happy; there was no doubt that he would do well in attaining a place at a public school.

It was some time before we realized that Mr Mold, the new Headmaster, held a different view. Mr Mold favoured using the cane, which escalated as Barry showed his contempt by deliberately provoking him. In later life, Barry remarked that Mr Mold was an idiot, and I quote: "Mr Mold didn't question the problem, he just wielded the stick," adding the sad recollection, "How can an 'r' written back to front merit six of the best?"

Barry didn't complain and it took too long for us to realize the true situation. But Barry's progress through life is a story in itself.

Marcia was something special. Beautiful from the day she was born, with the face of a cherub beneath a crown of golden curls, Marcia was charm personified, with an inner glow that shone through. She excelled in all the social graces: elocution and drama, swimming and diving, as well as superb horsemanship. Show-jumping and dressage were her forte. Everyone adored Marcia.

I indulged myself by making her clothes which made her even more noticeable. Not until she grew up did she confess that she longed to have something that was bought in a shop. However, her friends appreciated them and were constantly going through her cupboard to see what they could borrow.

Gwendolyn, a large rag doll, came on the scene shortly after Mama died, to keep Marcia company, as she was not happy to be left alone. I kept secret the fact that I was making the doll until she was ready. Gwendolyn was life-size, the same size as Marcia. She had a shaped head and body; sturdy arms, long enough to give her a cuddle, were secured to her body with strong twine, which gave them the flexibility of normal arm movement. Long legs were joined to her body in the same way. A pretty face with blue, felt eyes, black eyelashes and a red mouth, was surrounded by strands of flaxen hair made of wool hanging down to her shoulders. I made special felt shoes for her feet with elastic to hold them firmly in place over Marcia's shoes.

"That's so you can dance together, with her feet over yours," I explained.

Gwendolyn was her constant companion and a huge success.

Marcia and Amanda were joined by two more friends, Jane and Stephanie, in the school run to St Hilda's, in Bushey. The mothers took it in turns and through the daily contact, Pamela, Gina, Barbara and I, also became friends. We were a motley collection, but great together. Stephanie was a leader, self-assured and full of fun. So, indeed, was her mother, Barbara, who, it transpired, was one of Lally's former girlfriends. Barbara and I became firm friends.

Marcia's fear of dogs was a problem, especially as nearly every house in Canons Drive had one. Marcia wouldn't walk up the road in fear of meeting one. The one exception was the long-haired dachshund belonging to Barbara.

"You can't be frightened of Snuffy," was the amazed remark of Barbara. "Come, give her a little stroke and watch her wag her tail," she commanded.

Marcia did as she was told, but she wasn't convinced. A few days later, Barbara suggested that she would like to take Marcia to see something and could I collect her later.

I rang the doorbell. Marcia came running to the door, so excited that the words were tumbling out. "Mummy, you must ask Auntie Barbara to show you what we saw today."

I laughed and turning to Barbara remarked, "You always sort out interesting things, but this sounds like something special."

"It is and I will take you. Keep your coat on. We're going out," she replied.

A short walk brought us to the door with a grey-haired lady saying, "Hello Barbara. You back again?"

"I've brought Marcia's mother," Barbara explained.

She ushered us in, led the way through the kitchen and pointed in the direction of the floor.

"I should have guessed that it would involve a dog," I commented.

Barbara knew all about every dog in the neighbourhood.

This was something special! A beautiful long-haired dachshund surrounded by her litter, puppies so small that they didn't look real.

"You're not frightened of these dogs, are you?" I asked Marcia.

"No, they're wonderful," she whispered.

"Could we have one of the puppies?" I inquired.

"They're all spoken for except this little male dog," she replied, pointing to the smallest one, obviously the runt of the litter, struggling to find a space.

"I like that one best of all," Marcia stated.

The deal was done. It was decided that the puppy would remain with the mother for at least eight to ten weeks. Marcia counted the days and at last we went to collect him. He had grown into a sturdy, lively puppy.

Marcia took one look and rejected him, saying, "That's not the one I chose. Where's the little one?"

It took a lot to convince her that he had grown so much and that he would continue to grow until he was full size.

The first walk in Canons Drive was hilarious. As another dog appeared Marcia shouted, "Pick him up. That dog will eat him." Eventually, she realized that the dogs were only playful and her fear vanished.

The breeders had called him Slipper and we continued to do so. Slipper was beautiful and had we been so inclined, could easily have entered him for Cruft's. The little runt grew into a tough "boss" dog who made even the largest dog cringe.

Marcia yearned to have her own pony, but it wasn't practical. Together with Jane and Amanda, riding was their all-absorbing interest. Weekends were spent at the local riding school, doing all the tasks required. The girls more or less adopted resident ponies which became their regular rides. They were all good riders with Marcia excelling in show jumping and dressage. Their interests revolved around the Pony Club. Several of their summers were enhanced when they were boarders at Benenden and gained superb experience with show-jumping and dressage. Marcia's love of horses has never waned.

In school sports, Marcia's forte was swimming. She had beautiful style and grace which I didn't often get the opportunity to witness, due to Marcia's request: "Don't come to Sports Day, Mummy. You'll make me nervous."

On the one occasion that I did go, in her final year, when I decided it was now or never, I saw her deliberately slow down to let her friend win. When I questioned her about it, she laughingly replied, "It upsets her if she is not first."

Drama was an additional bonus. No one who watched her performance of Pooh Bear will forget her struggle to get through the hole; she was so convincing, that everyone really believed that she was stuck.

Marcia was truly "sugar and spice and everything nice".

The years flew by. Nowhere seemed more appropriate to have Barry's bar mitzvah than at home. I started making plans to cater for the evening, mulling over details with the super daily woman working for me at the time, when Mrs Smith said, "You needn't bother yourself with that, Mrs Leigh. I'll get a few of my friends to help."

We had two celebrations, one a formal one for the adults, which included family and friends. But the highlight of Barry's bar mitzvah was the teenage party, the first of many teenage parties which were to follow. With the rooms stripped of furniture, loudspeakers blasted out pop music; there was buffet-style food, large tubs of ice cream with do-it-yourself-toppings, and a birthday cake with dancing swinging figures atop. It was a huge success

It was the formation of one of the best caterers in northwest London. Mrs Smith went from strength to strength to build up a very successful business.

Mrs Smith never forgot her beginnings. Thereafter, we had access to her catering equipment. Every Christmas, Barry and Marcia had an enormous party.

~ *Mama and Rabbi Leigh's Book* ~

"We should consider the future," said Mama, "and our financial position when you are no longer able to work." Mama's initiative throughout their married life had created a sense of security, but Papa's response made her furious.

"Why?" he questioned. "I have always worked and provided. I shall continue to do so."

"There may come a time when you will find it too much. It's only sensible to plan for the future," Mama stated.

Papa was adamant and stubbornly said, "I don't need much and our three children won't let us starve."

"That's selfish and unfair," was Mama's reply and she frowned as Papa said, "I'd be quite content to go to an old people's home and be with old dodderers my own age. My needs are very modest."

"You're an old fool. I can just imagine you being regimented by some young matron insisting you eat the food whether you like it or not and being told what to do and when to get up or go to bed." She laughed and continued, "Well, that wouldn't include me because I don't intend to be a burden to my children."

She sat pensively thinking about the situation, then suddenly said, "I've seen an investment property in Cricklewood Lane. I'm going to view it today and I wondered if you would like to come with."

Papa was taken aback. He paused in thought and then said, "No, I'll leave it to you. I'm a stubborn old fool and I would only be in the way. You've made up your mind what you want to do and as usual, you're always right."

Cricklewood Lane was Mama's first investment. It brought her endless pleasure and though she could have had a managing agent, it was her delight personally to collect the rent. She liked me to accompany her so I could share her pleasure, but it didn't have the same meaning for me. The greengrocer greeted Mama in his shop on the ground floor as if she was a celebrity. His wife and daughter, in the middle floor, made us welcome, as did the two gravediggers on the top floor. Other properties were acquired, but none had the magic of Cricklewood Lane. Mama had business acumen and quietly and efficiently built up a considerable portfolio of properties, shares and investments which assured that she and Papa would be independent and secure in their old age and not a burden to their children. Sadly, she didn't have a chance to experience the benefits.

Mama's joie de vivre was deceptive. It didn't occur to us that lurking behind the facade was a very ill person. We regarded her admission to the National Heart Hospital as a routine check-up. But days turned into weeks and weeks became months. The only treatment in those days was rest and care. Heart surgery was unheard-of and preventive drugs undiscovered. Two visitors were allowed between five and six p.m. each day. Papa and I worked out a rota to visit on alternating days. It worked well, with the advantage of allowing friends to visit and time to talk.

Mama doted on the antics of Barry and Marcia and begged for details, devouring every word.

Three months elapsed. It wasn't my day to visit Mama, but I felt a compulsion to go to the hospital. For some unknown reason I bought a bed-jacket and a large bunch of roses. With the pretence that Mama needed the bed-jacket, I called at reception. Sister would not let me up to the ward to see Mama, explaining that everyone would demand the same privilege. She acted as messenger to get Mama's approval of the jacket and came down to tell me that Mama loved it, adding, "I wish you could see your mother. She's holding the lovely red roses in her arms and smiling. She looks radiant. You've made her very happy."

"Tell her that I love her," were my parting words as I left to meet my friend Jean in the West End.

I was surprised to see Papa at the house when I arrived home.

"Papa, why aren't you at the hospital?" I asked. "Isn't it your turn?"

Papa seemed lost for words. It was then that I noticed Lally was there too.

At last, Papa said in a hoarse whisper, "Mama's gone!"

"What do you mean, she's gone? Gone where? Matron didn't say anything about her going anywhere when I called in."

Papa took a deep breath and said in a hollow voice: "Mama died this afternoon, holding your flowers," and he added, "Matron said it was as if she waited to say goodbye."

I was dumbfounded! A sense of looming disaster had hung over me all day. The realisation that I had lost Mama, my rock, my friend and confidante, was devastating.

Mama died on 23rd July, 1957. The Shiva was my first experience of death. Mama and Papa both regarded death as a taboo subject, but to me, the Shiva ritual period of mourning, was a comfort and solace. Having Papa and my two brothers, Henry and Albert, there for seven days, eased the pain. But losing Mama was something I could never come to terms with. I was riddled with guilt and filled with remorse. Why hadn't I spent more time with her? My conscience kept reminding me how undemanding and understanding she was. To this day, forty-odd years on, I still miss her.

Mama had provided Papa with the security he had craved and he was humble in his appreciation of a comfortable home, a companion, housekeeper, winters in Israel and his independence.

Thoughts of Mama, who had taught us our traditional heritage, struck a chord when I was asked to illustrate a book written by Rabbi Leigh: *Jewish Observance in the Home* was something I believed in. I was, however, concerned that my minimum knowledge of religion would be a problem.

Lally and I joined the United Synagogue, in Mowbray Road, Edgware, when we got married. My first encounter of going to shul for a religious service was disconcerting. Anxious to participate in the prayers, I found myself on the upper floor surrounded by chattering women, discussing the latest styles, trouble with hired help, recipes, everything but the prayers! No one appeared to open a prayer book. It was impossible to follow the service and I admit to feeling I was in an alien world. Perhaps Papa was right about religion. The women around me had no respect.

"Come to the Reform Synagogue." Lally's brother, Monty, an active member of the Synagogue, aroused our curiosity. The first encounter was a revelation. The barn-like building reflected the period of post-war Britain, but despite the stark simplicity, the atmosphere conveyed a dignified serenity. The revised approach to religion was in keeping with the period in which we were living. Men and women were not segregated and all the family sat together. The Hebrew service, interspersed with a large proportion in English, made it understandable and gave it meaning, allowing those not versed with the knowledge of Hebrew to experience the reverence and worship. The solemn ritual of the Scrolls, carried out with the decorum of generations past, symbolised the significance of Judaism. There was complete participation, with respect and contemplation of the Minister's sermon. No chatter or diversions but undivided commitment to the solemn spiritual environment. Laws regarding activities such as driving cars on the Sabbath, were considered inappropriate to the period in which we were living, and women were encouraged actively to partake in the service. We became members.

Rabbi Michael Leigh was the Minister of the Reform Synagogue in Edgware. Monty became Chairman of the Edgware Reform Committee and it was he who put my name forward to illustrate the book Rabbi Leigh was writing.

Rabbi Leigh's unpretentious approach to religion stresses the importance of fundamentally creating a basis of tradition in the home. It begins with how and where to fix a mezuzah on the front door, including the dedication ceremony, to which family and friends are invited.

Every chapter relates to family life, with the addition of suggested prayers and books of learning. Treasured symbolic items of a committed Jewish home include candlesticks for the Sabbath, a kiddush cup, Bible and prayer books. Additional items refer to a Chanukah Menorah and a set of Haggadot for Passover. Comprehensive and informative dietary laws are also dealt with.

The importance of communication between parents and children is emphasized, especially to observe the Sabbath in an atmosphere of peace and enjoy the company of each other. The Sabbath, with the lighting of candles and prayers, is sensitively described.

The book continues to when life is sad, with prayers to help in times of anxiety. The illustrations amusingly reflect my own family in each interesting and relevant chapter.

In retrospect, I can relate to Rabbi Leigh's appraisal of Jewish life. Mama and Papa, echoed their commitment; a home filled with love, friendship and debate, although our books were based on knowledge, not prayer

Despite his religious beliefs, Papa took an interest when I was illustrating the book and came to synagogue every Friday night to discuss details with Rabbi Leigh. I drew on his knowledge, which, later, inspired me to do a series of religious paintings.

For many years, the Rabbi of the Reform Synagogue gave the book to the bride and groom at weddings and to boys and girls at their bar and bat mitzvahs.

I really enjoyed doing the illustrations and am proud to have had the opportunity of participating in it.

~ The In-between Years ~

"It will soon be Passover and this year I would like to make a proper family Seder."

Lally looked surprised and asked, "What's special about this year?"

"I want to include all the family," I replied.

"Such as?" he asked.

"Don't be funny. Family! Your parents, Papa, your brothers, their children, my brothers and their children."

"Where would you be able to seat so many?" he asked.

"There's no problem. We'll put the settee and other furniture in the garage and borrow trestle tables from your canteen. There's plenty of room," I replied.

"Well, it's all right with me. I hope the others are as keen as you are in celebrating Pesach," was his dry comment.

After countless telephone calls, I was happily rewarded by the response. They were all keen, even eager, to participate, with one exception: my brother Albert and his wife Helen, together with their daughters Cheryl and Gillian, would be going to her parents.

Lally was forthcoming with the trestle tables, which we formed into a long line running the length of the room. My first symbolic gesture was to unpack the yellow-bordered white Passover dishes that Mama used to use. This was for Mama!

It's amazing how much detail remained in my memory as I recalled Mama roasting a bone on an open flame until it was charred black, and doing the same with an egg; hard-boiled eggs in a bowl sprinkled with chopped spring onions were waiting for the jug of salted water to be poured over. Mama grated enough apples mixed with nuts and kosher wine to have some left over for breakfast. I smiled to myself as I remembered that Papa always did the horseradish because it made Mama's eyes tear. There were little sprigs of parsley and, of course, lots of matzos.

My Florence Greenberg cookery book explained everything in detail, including recipes for cakes, macaroons and coconut pyramids. Papa advised me on the procedures and setting of the Seder table and provided Haggadahs, (Passover-Service books), for everyone to read.

We decided to seat everyone in order of seniority. Papa sat at the head of the table. To his right were Lally's parents, Grandma and Grandpa Leigh and to his left, Rosa, Lally's sister and her husband Jack. My brother Henry, his wife Eileen and their children, Peter and Angela, sat next to them. Lally, Barry, Marcia and I sat opposite. Next to me, at the end of the table, were Lally's brother Monty, his wife Barbara and their daughters, Amanda and Nicola; opposite them were Lally's brother Harold and his wife Jill, with their children, Andrew and Lorraine.

Papa took the service and I listened with pride as he related the meaning of various passages. How Mama would have loved it! He gained the interest of the children when he broke the middle matzo in half and made a big show of hiding it. The promise of a present to the lucky one who found it went down well. He patiently pointed to or held up each dish in turn and explained the symbolic meaning throughout the service. He encouraged us to take turns in reading so that everyone felt they were participating. It was a wonderful evening.

How well I remember that first Passover in our home in Canons Drive. It brought to fruition my dream of having a family celebration. It epitomized everything I held dear, setting a precedent for love and tradition with all the family.

Jazz evenings began informally around the piano; a few enthusiasts getting together just for the fun if it. Peter Natley and friends were on drums and double bass; John Goldcrown's fantastic harmonica could vie with Larry Adler. Many others joined the group: Monty Raymond on trumpet, Harold with his guitar and top-raters like Lenny Felix occasionally put in an appearance, while Moss Kaye couldn't resist sitting-in with tenor saxophone. Friends came to listen.

Additionally, poetry and jazz evenings were held at other venues to raise funds for charities. They were great fun and I enjoyed joining-in with the occasional solo.

Europe appeared to be on the holiday agenda for Canadian and American relatives and friends and we were inundated with visitors. We appeared to be number one on the contact list and we made the most of it by entertaining and showing off the treasures of Great Britain.

Invitations from them to reciprocate did not appeal to Lally. "Don't let it stop you from going. I'll stay here and look after the children," he suggested.

The best laid plans can go awry and this was no exception. I discovered that many things were missing and became suspicious of the new daily woman I had engaged. When she disappeared without trace, I called the police, only to discover that she was a recognized thief and they were looking for her.

"You go and enjoy yourself. We'll manage," Lally insisted.

The three of them took me to the airport to see me off. Flying was still primitive and London Airport was just one building with a lookout on the roof to watch the planes take off. I waved to them as I boarded the plane.

Little did I realize as I careered towards another continent what chaos lay in my wake, as Lally took charge, saying,

"We'll all have to join in to keep everything in order while Mummy's away. Barry, you will help with washing up and polishing the floors. Marcia, you'll do the front doorstep. You're used to polishing brass." He considered that he was letting her off easily, as she polished brass at the stables every weekend.

Marcia came downstairs with her suitcase and he saw her making her way across the road. He knew where she was heading, as he phoned: "Gina, Marcia is on her way over to you and I believe she's leaving home. Don't say anything to her and I'll be over to collect her for supper."

No further mention was made of the front step.

I remember the flight so well, seated next to an American who must have been amused at my excitement. He chatted a lot about America and plied me with champagne, saying, "It's the best way to travel." He was an executive at Fort Knox, very charming and amusing. He gave me his card saying, "If you have any problems anywhere while you're in the States, call me."

Touchdown in Montreal! Of all my cousins, Queenie was my favourite, and there she was at the airport to meet me. I had admired her since childhood and if I had to choose a role model, it would be her. It's strange, I'd never noticed it before, but she was just like Mama.

It was great to see relatives and friends and a thrill to recognize places. How Montreal had grown! But the holiday did not start off well. The flight affected my legs but the local doctor refused to prescribe treatment. I phoned Lally and pills were flown out to me. The first thing I did was to buy a box of Laura Secord chocolates, which were in turn posted home.

During my stay, Queenie's husband Henry was taken ill. She phoned her nephew, Eddie, for help and I went with them to the hospital. It was a strange reunion with Eddie. We had planned to marry when he returned from the war, but I changed my mind and went back to England. We didn't talk much. In fact, I think that I did all the talking. I felt that he had never forgiven me, which made me sad.

From Montreal I made a short stop at Toronto, where I was met by another cousin Queenie, and her daughter, Natalie. Queenie had been a frequent visitor to our home when we lived in Montreal. She was always in trouble, coming to Mama for help. I was a very young observer, just listening, aware of the goings-on. She made me laugh when she remarked, "I didn't think you could speak!"

I think I made up for it during that short stay.

Landing in Chicago, I expected Al Capone's henchmen to be lurking in the background. Instead, I discovered that Chicago is really a lovely city. I stayed with Hilda and Ed in their bungalow near to the lake which confirmed why it's called the "windy city". Hilda was Papa's cousin and she introduced me to members of the family I didn't even know existed. She was a well-known artist and we spent a week painting in her studio and going to exhibitions. She taught me a lot. It was a most enjoyable stay.

Two memorable days in Pittsburgh was really not enough, but it renewed the friendship with Reah and Irving and had me wishing for more. Reah, my cousin from Chattanooga and Irving, a professor who regularly lectured in London and Europe, were frequent visitors to London. We shared a lifetime of close friendship, despite the distance. Their three sons were about the same age as Barry; I enjoyed meeting them and the many friends invited to meet me. I still occasionally make my version of the instant chicken salad she made, which brings back fond memories.

The last lap of my holiday took me to New York, where I had reserved accommodation in a small hotel overlooking Central Park. The friendly taxi driver, as he drove me to Manhattan, pointed out historical sights, accompanied by tittle-tattle about local gossip and restaurants. The hotel had been recommended and was first-rate, close to the shops and theatres. I found it exciting to wander out and absorb the atmosphere, choosing to have breakfast at small local cafés. One of my first forays was to the Automat, the memory of which remained vivid, as I recalled when my brother Albert upset the cutlery table which crashed onto the marble floor and brought the entire restaurant to a standstill.

The reunion with Reah's brother Erwin had spanned possibly thirty years, with the recollection of him as a child playing tennis with my brother Henry, during our visit to Chattanooga. He and his wife Jo had moved to New York from there and were enamoured with the city. No sightseer could have been shown the sights with more enthusiasm. We took the ferry to Staten Island and sailed by the Statue of Liberty with reference throughout to historical data, including Rockefeller Center, Times Square and Broadway. I managed to get theatre seats, allegedly impossible, for the musical show *Mame* to reciprocate their generosity.

The stay in New York was divided between fraternizing with them and my pal Audrey, who was bridesmaid at our wedding; she was now married to David, an American. We kept in touch on her frequent visits to her parents in London. I was impressed with their family and lovely home in Far Rockaway, and delightful garden featuring a bridge over a stream. She took me shopping for presents and souvenirs, guiding me to all the stores in Fifth Avenue. Memorable days!

Three weeks seemed to pass in a flash and I was on my way home. It had been a great holiday. Just as moving was the enormous WELCOME HOME above the front door. It was good to be home.

"I've got something for you."

I never ceased to be surprised by some unexpected item Lally brought home.

"Another piece of jewellery?" I asked.

"No, not this time," Lally laughed, holding out a large parcel.

"Where did you find time to go shopping in Borehamwood?" I asked.

"The clue is inside," he replied.

I stripped off the wrapping to reveal a large, metal attaché case.

"What is it for?" I asked, as I unclicked two clasps on the front and raised the lid, part of which folded back, revealing a flat, white board.

"Put your thumb in the hole and slide that out sideways," he suggested.

The interior was divided into little compartments. The centre displayed two rows of coloured tubes. Square bottles at each side had small metal containers above. A long section at the bottom held brushes.

"It's a paint box!" I gasped, with surprise.

"Do you like it?" Lally's voice brought me back to earth.

"It's fantastic!" I replied and laughingly added, "It's a far cry from the small box Henry gave me when I was seven."

"It's Windsor and Newton's best, made for export and not generally available in this country." Lally announced proudly. "I told them that you were an artist and they sent it especially for you."

I can't recall how I came to the Arthur Segal school of painting, in a large Victorian house in England's Lane, but I'm pleased that I did. The school, started by Arthur Segal, an eminent German painter, was carried on by his wife and daughter after his death. They were both fine artists and brilliant teachers.

One day a week I made the journey to Hampstead. I progressed from still-life painting, to painting flowers and followed onto experimenting with different methods of paint application, including life paintings and portraiture, which I found fascinating. The vast number of self-portraits displayed in my home may appear to be vanity. Not so! It avoided offending "sitters" who appeared dismayed by my interpretation. It took a lot of effort before I became confident. I'm particularly proud of my portrait of Papa.

~ *Pamela and the Dolls* ~

Extravagant, unrestrained, captivating: all describe Pamela Kayne. Everyone and everything appeared mediocre in comparison. Black hair melted into the black, flowing cape she usually wore, flashing black eyes, white face, a slash of red, revealing gleaming white teeth, she'd sweep in like a beautiful witch and suddenly the room was full.

"Could you design some furry animals like that large doll you made for Marcia?" she asked.

The question took me by surprise, but then, Pamela always took me by surprise.

"What do you want them for?" I asked.

"They could make good pyjama bags," she declared. "Edna has a workshop of outworkers and she could make them up."

"It sounds interesting. Have you anything specific in mind?" I asked.

"Yes, I have, but I suggest that we have a look around and I can point them out to you. It's easier than trying to explain."

The following week found us in Fortnum and Mason looking at stuffed animals in the toy department. Within a short time, the orderly displays were devastated, as Pamela pulled out one after another of the animals and dolls on display. The assistants looked on helplessly as she dismissed their offer to help.

I was mortified by the havoc she created. "You don't need to pull everything down!" I said. "We're only looking for ideas. I'm not going to copy them."

To which she haughtily replied, "They'll soon put everything back. That's their job."

The fabric department didn't suffer as much as Pamela rummaged through and pulled out rolls of material, depositing them nearby to open them out. Eventually, we selected a few sample lengths of fur fabrics in various colours. We ravaged Harrods next, followed by John Lewis, where we purchased more sample lengths, check cottons, satins, suedette and felt.

The doll that had fired Pamela's imagination was Gwendolyn, the life-size rag doll, with long arms and legs and hair hanging down to her shoulders, above, her smiling face. She shared Marcia's clothes and was usually found sitting on the window-seat, or a chair. Pamela's interest dated back to when she mistook Gwendolyn for one of Marcia's friends; to our amusement, she asked her if she went to the same school.

Working from rough sketches, a format began to evolve with elongated arms and legs which could be posed in different positions, equivalent in height to a child of six or seven. An opening at the back of the body accommodated pyjamas.

A pink, furry pussycat in a pink-and-white gingham dress became the first sample and prototype. Following on, a donkey scarecrow with ears peeping out of his hat, with rolled-up trouser legs, revealing striped socks; next was a furry, blue dog pop star in satin, as Elvis.

Pamela was delighted, but I wasn't so sure. "I think making characters of personalities will be more interesting," I told Pamela.

"Fine, I leave it to you," Pamela replied.

I toyed with different ideas and eventually came up with Grandma, wearing gold-rimmed spectacles and a lace-edged mob cap over her grey hair; an apron protected her lace-trimmed print dress from her knitting. Beside her, moustached Grandpa was in shirt-sleeves and tie, red braces holding up his tweed trousers, reading the newspaper. There was Pierrot, barely concealing a tear, his half-mask, white conical hat and ruffle collar above a silvery blue-and-white diamond patterned costume; and his Columbine, a classical graceful ballerina, her long, white satin legs with ballet shoes tied with ribbon, peeped out from the layered tutu. Three clowns with funny faces followed: the first one, with black pom-poms down the front of a yellow tunic and pom-poms on a yellow pointed hat; half-red, half-blue with contrasting spots, was basically number two; the third was black and white stripes and squares. The best of the range were sophisticated fashion dolls: suède faces and large eyes with long lashes in glamorous dresses bedecked with jewellery: Penny in black velvet bedecked with gold chains; Hilary's white tucked bib, lace-trimmed petticoat peeping out below the rose-pink moiré flared skirt; Sandy's large glittering earrings and bracelets complemented her blue satin gown with white feather boa, in contrast to Melanie's ribbon-trimmed pale lemon silk, with layers of tulle petticoats.

Pamela was pleased with the progress, but it was my turn to be surprised when she said, "I've booked a stand at the Gift Fair in Blackpool."

"You what?" I said flabbergasted. "All you have are the samples. You haven't made any in the workroom and you can have no idea of cost," I said in disbelief.

"It's the best way to see if they're saleable," she replied in a matter-of-fact voice.

"You are asking for trouble," was all I could say.

Ignoring my reply, she continued, "It will be fun and you can treat it as a holiday."

"When is it?" I asked, accepting the inevitable.

"Next month. By the way, it is the Buy British Festival. Special attention will be given to everything made in Britain."

The stimulus of exhibiting at the Gift Fair put a new slant on the project. I was inspired into making something typically British, which resulted in the Grenadier Guard: black fur Busby, red jacket with gold-trimmed epaulettes and red-trimmed navy trousers. In view of the impending exhibition, I made three more Guards. Additionally, I set the proud head of the British Lion on a lion-shaped fur mat as a nursery rug.

That last week in January, Pamela, her sister and I set off in two cars with several boxes and suitcases laden with the dolls for the five days of the Gift Fair. Additionally, we had with us rolls of white muslin, rope, tape, tools and other miscellaneous items.

Although quite excited at the prospect of seeing Blackpool, a highly regarded Victorian seaside resort, I discovered that it was not at its best on this cold, winter day. However, the vast number of stately hotels, each more grand than the next, which stretched for miles along the seafront, had me in awe, even more so when I discovered that all the hotels were participating in the Festival of Britain; for the five days of the Gift Fair, they were providing accommodation for five thousand exhibitors.

Setting up the stand was exciting, exhilarating, exasperating, exhausting and a miracle. Basically, all we had were the two rolls of muslin. We tied rope at the top of the corner poles, cut muslin double the length to the floor, hanging it over the rope on three sides of the stand. The boxes were arranged in one corner, like a pyramid, coming down in varied steps and draped in muslin to form the background; finally, the dolls were added, in animated groups, down to the lion rug on the floor at the front of the stand. Two Grenadier Guards stood at the front corners of the stand; the other two mingled with the animals. The display was magnificent. There was really no place to sit, but we took turns in one small space at the corner of the display.

Interest in the dolls was gratifying and Pamela secured an excellent outlet for them in the Etcetera chain of gift shops.

It was far from a holiday, much more like hard work. We didn't even get to see any of the stands at the other hotels, but it made me realize how much I had enjoyed the commercial world and how much I missed it.

Oh yes! A television crew came to report about new products at the fair. They photographed the Grenadier Guards and then came back to photograph the Lion Rug. They were both included in the ten-minute BBC TV *News* of the Gift Fair at Blackpool.

~ *Disaster Of 1963* ~

I must have been blind not to see danger looming into my life. I did, however, have a strange premonition as 1963 turned into a nightmare,

"Is something the matter?" I asked Lally as he walked into the kitchen.

"Yes and no," he replied.

"Which is it?" I queried.

He hesitated before saying, "I've arranged to have a small operation to cure me of my insomnia."

I stared at him in disbelief. "I don't think I understood what you said. Is this some special sort of treatment?"

"Yes! A simple incision and I'll be back to normal," he replied.

"But why do you need an operation?"

"To help me sleep," he said.

"Sleeping pills do that," I countered.

"You know how I feel about taking sleeping pills. According to Dr Rose, this will cure me of any anxiety," was his confident reply.

"Any operation sounds drastic to me. Have you had a second opinion?" I asked.

"I phoned Alfred [our doctor]. He hasn't heard about it, but he believes that Dr Rose has a good reputation."

"What do your brothers think about it?" I persisted.

"I haven't told them," he replied. "They'll know about it when it's all over."

"When is this going to happen?" I asked.

"Today! It's scheduled at the Royal Northern Hospital in Holloway Road."

"What about the children?" I asked.

"There's no need to trouble them. Just say I'll be away for a few days," he replied. "I'll be home soon."

This was his way of telling me that he didn't want anyone to know. In this era one didn't talk about anxiety or depression; reference to a problem that had mental connotations bore the stigma of insanity. I respected his wish for secrecy.

I packed Lally's personal things into a bag and we drove to the Royal Northern Hospital in Holloway Road. The grey stone building, dating back to Dickens's period, was eerie and unwelcoming. We entered into a maze of corridors; cold, dank, cream-painted walls exuded an odour of foul disinfectant. We were directed to a sparsely furnished room on the first floor.

There was no pre-preparation, and without any preamble, Lally was taken away. I was directed to a bench seat, situated in an alcove near to the room, to sit and wait. Eventually, he was wheeled back, his head swathed in bandages, and heavily sedated. The nurse at his bedside told me he was sleeping.

After what seemed like an eternity, the Matron smiled as she approached, saying, "He's awake now. You can come in."

He looked awful! The bandages partially hid his drawn face and he seemed confused.

I took his hand, saying, "Hello, remember me?"

He stared at me and gave the flicker of a smile.

"That's not much of a greeting," I admonished, but Matron cautioned me, "It's early days yet, my dear. It will take him time."

"What do you mean?" I asked.

"He's been through an ordeal with this operation," she explained.

"But I was under the impression that it was only something minor!" I responded.

She looked surprised and replied, "I'm only concerned with the aftermath," adding, "You'd best go home now. He'll sleep through the night. There's no point in your staying around. We'll keep a watchful eye on him."

It was good advice. The children would be waiting. I told them that Daddy was in hospital, but didn't consider it necessary to worry them about the operation and just generalized about Lally's health. The restrictive visiting hours, which were in keeping with the Victorian era of the hospital, made it easier to limit visits by Barry and Marcia.

The next morning, by chance, I saw Dr Rose leaving as I arrived at the hospital. Hurriedly catching up to him, I breathlessly asked, "Did everything go according to plan with the operation?"

"We have to wait and see. It is a delicate operation," he replied

"But you said it was quite minor," I stated.

"I just generalized" he said. "We didn't go into detail."

"Do you mean that you didn't tell him what was involved?" I asked.

"My dear child, one always takes a risk with surgery."

"He was under the impression that he would be home the following day."

"Maybe I was a little too optimistic. I don't wish to discuss the matter any further." With that curt remark, he got into his car and drove off.

I learnt from probing questions that the leucotomy operation was not the anticipated simple snip, but a last resort if all else had failed. I realized that Lally had agreed to the operation to cure his insomnia, oblivious of the fact that the risks were critical and of the possibility, if things went wrong, that he could suffer brain damage.

Recovery was slow, as day after day I watched, listened to delirious ramblings and waited to learn the results. Being unsure of the facts created genuine fear.

I should have been warned when the bandages were removed. A horrifying, abhorrent sight of mutilation; the two holes drilled through his skull were badly repositioned, leaving unsightly indentations.

"Matron wants to see you," said the nurse, which softened the shock.

Matron took me to one side, saying, "I'm pleased you're here. We need your help."

"What do you want me to do?" I asked.

"We have to get your husband to talk. We need to get him to hold a conversation. Talk about anything that will stimulate his memory."

"Why? Is there a problem?" I asked.

"We don't know. We're never sure with this operation. The familiarity of your voice will help." Her warm smile gave me courage.

She left the room and I turned my attention to Lally. And I started to talk. I'm not normally chatty, but somehow words came from nowhere. I droned on and on about events long past; gossip about neighbours; places I would like us to go to and things I would like to do or buy. Matron came in to give moral support and ended up chatting too. Some utterances were so absurd that we started to laugh. Suddenly, the whole atmosphere changed; the gloom that had hung over like a cloud seemed to disperse. I looked at Lally.

He was smiling, almost laughing, as his weak voice rang out: "That was funny," he said.

Matron looked from him to me; her smile was reassuring as she said, "He's alright! There's no need to worry."

The need for the operation was misjudged. It did not cure the insomnia and yielded no obvious benefit. Fortunately, no harm was done, but there remained in my mind the fact that insufficient opinions had been sought. Several years later we learnt that the leucotomy was no longer viable.

Strangely, I suffered the strain of the operation much more than Lally, who merely considered it a useless incident, with the witty comment,

"I needed it like I need a hole in my head."

But Lally was not ready to give up. After a short recuperation, he was back again with Dr Rose. This time he reverted to pills and shock treatment.

"I've had enough!" I still bear the vivid memory of storming out of the house, getting in the car and driving off. I had no idea why, or where, I was going. I just drove and drove. I finally pulled up in a lay-by. I just sat there not knowing what to do, numbed with the realization that I had no one to turn to. I sat there for some time and eventually I went home.

Lally and Marcia were in a panic. They had been calling everyone to find me and I felt guilty for causing them such distress, but it made me realize that I needed help.

A few days in hospital under observation convinced the staff that I did not have a mental problem. Dr Rose took charge, assuring me that I would benefit with some sedation and the addition of shock treatment.

He didn't encourage me to speak of my problems, but assured me that I suffered from depression. He failed to differentiate between that and the stress I was under. He did, however, talk about himself: his beautiful wife; his beautiful flat in High Point; his beautiful Rolls Royce and his son at Harrow.

I didn't have many close friends. My confidante was Barbara, the only person to whom I revealed that I was suffering from depression and that the doctor had given me tablets.

Her response struck me to the core: "I don't like being with people with mental problems," she said. "It's better that we don't see each other till you're better."

Now I knew why Lally had sworn me to secrecy for his operation.

Lally's determination to seek further for a remedy for his sleeplessness led him to Dr William Sargent, who was highly regarded for the work he was doing in treating patients with phobias.

"I've made an appointment to see Dr Sargent. Do you want to come with?" Lally asked.

Dr Sargent was a stern man; he peered across his desk, his gaunt face bereft of emotion as he listened to Lally's problem.

I must admit that he was convincing in his claim that he would be successful. A flicker of a smile crossed his face as Lally accepted the treatment; he was prescribed Valium, the miracle drug.

His first reaction seemed good, but that was short-lived. The Valium was not having the anticipated effect and alternative Valium injections and shock treatment were prescribed. And so began Lally's journey down the "slippery slope". Hindsight revealed that side effects of agoraphobia eventually took hold, causing more anxiety than his original problem.

Dr Sargent was considered the doyen of the day for the treatment of depression, but with hindsight, he was not good for me. He was a pill-pusher; his theory was: "Never mind the problem, have a pill." Additionally, he prescribed shock treatment. I welcomed the relief of escaping into oblivion, but it didn't do much good otherwise. I wonder what harm it did to my brain as in error, they gave me double the maximum dosage.

I didn't benefit from the progression of pills which put me into more confusion, ending up in the perilous situation of being out of control. I didn't trust myself to walk into a shop in case I inadvertently absconded with an article I hadn't purchased. I was unsteady on my feet and it occurred to me that just walking across a road was hazardous, should I lose my balance and fall in front of a moving vehicle.

"I can't live like this, Dr Sargent," I complained.

"You'll get used to it," was his indifferent reply.

"There must be some other way," I insisted.

He laughed, saying," You'll be back."

"Over my dead body," were my parting words.

I flushed all my pills down the toilet and I did suffer from withdrawal, but I never went back.

"What's the matter with Gwen?" queried Pamela Barnet, a good friend who spent much of her life travelling around the world.

"I wish I knew," Lally replied.

"It sounds like she needs help like I did a few years ago. I'll have a word with her."

I was fascinated and interested and I had nothing to lose when she explained, "This doctor uses hypnosis."

Hypnosis delved into the depths of my despair and brought out the hidden me, riddled with frustration and self-doubt. I was also tarred with the mentality of a slave: "Tell me what you want and I will do your bidding."

The hypnosis did cure me. More than that, it confirmed that the depression was caused by stress and frustration. I had to be taught to accept my self-worth and give some priority to things I wanted to do and achieve, but it's something I've never fully mastered.

~ Troubled Schooldays ~

I thought everything was going well until we were alerted to the fact that Barry had defied the Headmaster and had walked out of school. He eventually returned home, surprised to find us in a panic.

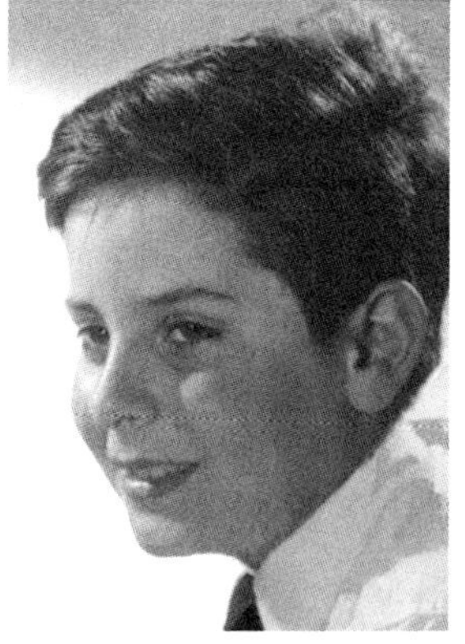

"Why did you walk out of school and become a truant?" I asked.

A surprised look crossed his face as he replied, "I've just had enough of Mr Mold's bullying. He didn't even query the problem; he just wielded the stick," and he continued, "He doesn't like me. He's critical of everything I do, though I've really tried to do what he wants."

Mr Mold had recently taken over the post of headmaster at Shirley House School from Mr Walters and as yet we had not had the opportunity of meeting him. We were, however, aware of Barry's dislike of the man.

Our investigation revealed that Mr Mold demanded strict obedience regardless of reason. It transpired that Barry had been subjected to maltreatment, the only apparent cause being that he was free-thinking, with an enquiring mind. The fact that he was slightly dyslexic seemed to spur Mr Mold's anger. Such a tyrant was not fit to be a headmaster.

It was a crucial time for Barry. Having achieved the required exam results, he was in the throes of interviews for a place at one of the public schools. This episode made him sufficiently aware of his problem to stipulate: "I'm not going to another school with strict discipline and I won't go to boarding school. If you insist on sending me to one [which was on the cards], I shall run away."

We took him away from Shirley House and sent him to Davis's, a reputable crammer school, until we could sort out the problem.

The offer of two boarding public schools were rejected outright. There was no point pursuing the matter: he had suffered enough as a victim subjected to abuse without cause. We decided that he needed time without strict discipline to allow his potential to develop.

The "swinging sixties" heralded a new era, and Barry was a true product of the age, growing up under the spell of the "flower people", rebelling at everything conventional. He even played truant at the crammer, but we never discovered what he did or where he got to.

Eventually he opted to join Lally and go into the brush trade. He began by working in the factory and found it very interesting. However, Lally's brother, Harold, resented the interference when Barry began making suggestions to improve production; Monty also gave him a hard time with his surveillance, both of which put an end to that avenue.

His enrolment to take his A-Levels at the Barnet College of Further Education took us by surprise. He sat the English and Physics exams., but refused to take his A-Level Maths, saying, "It's just a piece of paper."

"He's my best pupil," was the lament of the teacher, who phoned to persuade me to try to change his mind, to no avail.

Nevertheless, on the teacher's recommendation, he was articled to a prestigious London firm of accountants, who gave favourable reports of his progress. He had been there about a year when I received a surprising phone call from Mr Citroen, one of the principals of Citroen Wells, the Accountancy firm, as he announced: "Barry has given notice!" He continued, "Don't let him do this, Mrs Leigh. He's doing so well. He's a credit to the firm."

"I'll do my best, but once he makes up his mind there's not much chance of changing it," I replied.

Barry's new aspiration was to do Economics.

"You need three A-Levels to go to University and you refused to take the Maths," I reminded him.

"So I'll take the exam," he replied.

He attained his A-Level without any problem and was offered a place at Swansea University. He no sooner got to Swansea, when he switched courses to do Psychology. We were surprised and disappointed, but we really didn't mind.

Meanwhile, Barry had settled in at the University of Swansea; Lally and I duly made the journey to visit him and were pleasantly surprised.

I had built up in my mind a picture of the Welsh countryside as a black landscape, with weary people rather down-at-heel, carrying bags of coal on their shoulders. How wrong I was. Wales is beautiful!

Barry was sharing an imposing house with three other students, in a tree-lined road close to the village shops, just a stone's throw from the seafront. He had gone to a lot of trouble to prepare tea, which was beautifully set out, and we were joined by two of his fellow students, both of them doing engineering, one of whom was sponsored by Rolls Royce for their design department.

After tea, Barry took us on a tour of the University and then for a drive, to show us the countryside. Mumbles and the surrounding panorama could compete with any place on the Riviera, and Barry was appreciative of being associated with it.

Barry was showing us his true colours and we were so proud of him. My heart warms to the recollection and I'll never forget that wonderful day.

In the meantime, all was not well with Marcia, which began out of the blue, with her wan, "I don't feel well, Mummy."

I took one look, put her to bed and called the doctor. As luck would have it, Alfred, who was a close friend as well as our doctor, was on holiday.

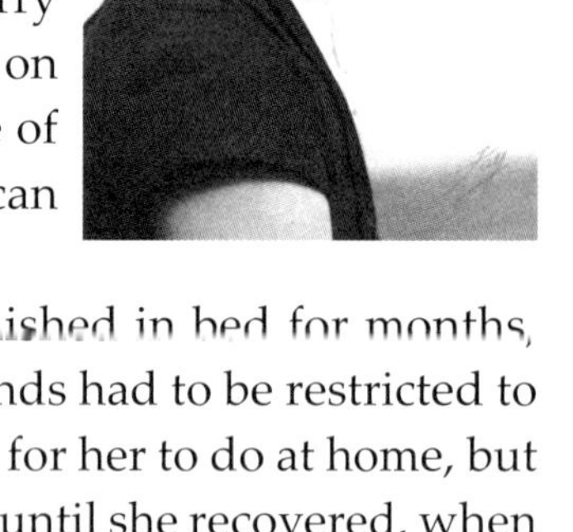

Dr Hanks' wife was curt as she replied, "Bring her to the surgery."

"No way," I replied. "She's much too ill."

"Nonsense," she retorted. "You Jewish mothers make too much fuss. You are so inconsiderate."

Dr Hanks, however, did call. "I'm sorry about my wife. You were right to insist on a house visit. Marcia has a serious case of glandular fever. There's not much we can do. Just rest and she'll get over it."

But it was not so simple. She languished in bed for months, too fatigued to go to school and her friends had to be restricted to short visits. At first St Hilda's sent work for her to do at home, but eventually we had her privately tutored until she recovered, when arrangements were made for her to take her O-Level exams.

That summer I arranged for Marcia to go to Canada. Susan, my cousin Penny's daughter, was fifteen, the same age as Marcia, and the two of them became counsellors at the B'nai B'rith holiday camp for deprived children. Further education depended on her exam results and during the three months she was away, Lally and I visited various possible colleges and picked out those we considered suitable. When Marcia was offered a place at Queen's

College, in Harley Street, I phoned her with the good news to get her approval to register her for the place in September.

"Thank you, Mummy. That's wonderful! It's a relief to know what I am going to do," she replied.

However, we hadn't reckoned on Susan's "How come you let your mother make decisions for you?"

At the end of summer, Marcia returned and I was taken aback when she suddenly came out with, "Don't you think you should have asked me if I wanted to go to Queen's College?"

"Don't you want to go?" I asked.

"Yes, but I should have made the decision," she replied.

"You did! I phoned you and you said 'yes'."

I was dumbfounded. An angel had gone to Canada, but a monster had come back. Try as I might, she remained a rebel without a cause.

Repercussions followed her return. She had extended an invitation to come and stay to one and all at the camp; a progression of teenagers regularly appeared on the doorstep,

"Marcia invited me," no longer took me by surprise. One or two at a time were easy to cope with, but things became a little hectic when Susan arrived with a retinue of friends. Sleeping bags used up all the floor space in Marcia's room, Barry's room, the dining room and studio. Breakfasts taken in shifts were a nightmare as I tried to keep everything under control and remember each one's name.

"Ziggy wants to know what he should do," I asked as the boy waited around downstairs.

"Tell him to drop dead," answered Susan.

Barry, too, contributed to the hospitality. "Barry said I could stay a few nights," was no longer a surprise.

During the Vietnam War, I was aware that some of the boys were draft-dodgers. I didn't blame them for not wanting to fight someone else's war, but I discouraged long-term stays. The visiting eventually died down and the household returned to a normal pattern.

Queen's College was the perfect choice for Marcia. As well as knowledge, it was a school for "young ladies", where they developed decorum and sophistication. Marcia settled in like a fish to water and the two years there were well-spent. New friends opened up a wider spectrum of life; among them were Margot and Vanessa, who held similar interests, and they developed a close relationship both in and out of school.

We thought it interesting when they asked if they could spend a short break in Israel, working on a kibbutz, all the more interesting as the two girls were not Jewish. The kibbutz near Akka welcomed them with open arms for the fruit-picking season. Free time was spent at the Youth Hostel on the edge of the Sea of Galilee, in Tiberius, where Marcia had worked on a previous visit.

The best laid plans go awry and so it was when I received an unexpected phone call:

"Mrs Leigh, I'm calling from the telephone exchange in Israel."

"What for?" I asked.

"Your daughter, Marcia, has been in an accident. The doctor at the kibbutz does not speak English and I am calling on his behalf. She is in good hands and will receive the finest treatment. I have been advised to give you the option, should you so wish, that we will fly her home by ambulance. Personally, I have to say she'd be better off staying here." She continued, "I will keep you informed of her condition and in the meantime, all the lines here are open to your calls and will immediately be put through to me, should you have any query."

The next communication confirmed that the condition was not as serious as they had anticipated and that Marcia was adamant that she would not go home on a stretcher.

Word got back to the Youth Hostel in Tiberius; David, who was in charge, phoned the kibbutz offering to care for her at the hostel, which she happily accepted and after a few weeks, she returned home. All I can add is, all's well that ends well.

Postscript: The following year, some of my paintings were due to be exhibited at a gallery in Caesarea, which gave Lally and me a good reason to holiday in Israel. Unfortunately, we arrived there to find that excavation for the site had revealed an important archaeological find and they could not proceed with building the gallery.

However, the visit to Israel was not wasted as it gave us the opportunity to visit the Youth Hostel at Tiberius and to meet and thank David for his kindness to Marcia.

I loved Israel! I was impressed by the enthusiasm and warmth of the Israelis and had I been younger, could have enjoyed helping in the growth of the country.

~ *Shattered Glass* ~

A shattered windscreen triggered a turning point in my life. The glass, in a heap on the floor of the car, seemed too precious to discard.

"Don't throw it away," I called out as Lally began sweeping it into a dustpan.

"What else should I do with it ? " he asked in surprise.

"I don't know, but it's so beautiful. I'll do something with it. Put it in a box," I suggested.

Lally frowned. "Another hoard of rubbish," he grumbled as he went to find a suitable box. He was getting used to my eccentricity.

This was the anticlimax of a carefully planned seventeenth birthday for our son Barry. A suppressed air of excitement and secrecy prevailed until the black-roofed, white Mini, complete with L- plates, pulled into the driveway. The new car on the doorstep took Barry completely by surprise. He had learnt to drive long before, taught by friends on private roads and had prepared for this day by applying in advance for his provisional licence. He was car mad, studying engines and doing body work, while working in a local repair shop in his holidays. The cold, damp day in early February was no deterrent to taking a drive out to the country to quiet roads where Barry could take the wheel. I was a back-seat driver while Lally supervised Barry.

We had been out a couple of hours and we were returning home when the windscreen was suddenly shattered by a pebble. Barry coped extremely well by knocking out a section of the crazed glass to see enough to pull into the kurb. We had to remove most of the remaining windscreen to have sufficient visibility. Barry had to take a back seat while I took the wheel for a nightmare journey; twilight, light rain and freezing temperature are no fun without a shielding windscreen, but we made it home safely. A sad ending for a day that started out with such joy.

Still, I had a box full of beautiful broken glass.

Fascinated by the glistening mass which sparkled like jewels in the light, I pondered on how I could harness the small glass facets. I decided to try the same painting method I had used with eggshells. Eggshell inlay had proved to be an excellent medium which I had used successfully for much of the painting done in my religious period, culminating with a painting of 'Footsteps on the Moon'. Eggshells produced a muted, inlaid effect, totally opposite to the vitality anticipated from glass. Textures, too, would have to balance with a hard, glittering surface. Canvas was insufficiently rigid to support the weight of the glass and caused the surface to sag.

Using a narrow plywood board horizontally, I captured the magic while experimenting with the combination of paint and glass and 'An Elephant's Necklace' was the result. As a painting, it could not be deemed "a work of art" but it was a vehicle which opened a potential panorama in its wake. Paintings evolved from this first effort, encompassing a variety of subjects, using differing methods of application.

'Friday Night' – burning candles in a pair of silver candlesticks, the flames glinting from reflected light – was a successful traditional painting that followed.

'Twelve Tribes' had a large Star of David divided into twelve, each glass section denoting the colour and emblem of the twelve Tribes of Israel. The surrounding border is symbolic of the Exodus. Narrow lines bearing the colours of all the tribes are textured to show vitality and imply kinship with individuality. The painting, set off the wall, is unframed, to signify the tribes going out into the world.

'Blessing': the words of blessing at the close of a synagogue service by Rabbi Maybaum was very moving, which prompted the painting of a Rabbi with his arms held out. Superimposed in fragmented glass, were the words: "The Lord bless you and keep you and give you peace". I gave the painting to my brother.

'Conversation Piece' contained three silhouetted standing figures in a shaded purple background; 'Jazz' depicted shadowy musicians in blue and black backing the main guitarist in the foreground, glistening as he gets caught by the light; 'Chessmen' were three pieces on a chessboard.

'Vortex', a swirl of abstract black glass with a tiny touch of red, on a textured white background, led to a range of textured abstract paintings which were to form the nucleus of a large proportion of work which was to follow. The glass became more subtle, blending into the texture and colours of paint. 'Sea Urchin', 'Autumn', 'Wild Snowdrops' and 'Blue Orchid' followed.

By now, glass paintings were predominant on the walls of our home in Canons Drive. They were exciting to live with, as the unexpected reflected light added an air of mystery. Friends were intrigued by them, none more so than Pamela Barnet, when she and her husband Laurie came to visit.

Pamela was strangely quiet that evening and I was taken unawares when she suddenly asked, "How many painting have you done?"

"I'm not sure," I replied. "Why do you ask?"

"I know a gallery who I feel sure will mount an exhibition of your work. Would you be interested to make enough to make a good showing?"

I looked to see if she was leading me on, but she was really serious.

"How many would they need?" I asked.

"About thirty, I would think," she replied.

"Just give me the word and consider it done," I said confidently.

"Good. I'll ring you tomorrow."

The next day Pamela phoned. "The gallery are interested. They want to see a sample of your work."

I let Pamela have a few paintings to show the gallery and after that it was up to me.

Until then I had relied on the odd broken windscreen salvaged from the roadside and brought in by friends, mainly as a joke. Now I was forced to find a proper source, looking for rejects in scrap yards, of old wrecks precariously balanced on other wrecks. Barry was helpful in sorting through the rubble, but when the windows were cleaned, many were found to be scratched and stained. Others were difficult to remove from the vehicles. We discovered, too, that patterns of shattered glass differed according to the make of car.

Eventually I found a source who could provide Jaguar windscreens. They looked perfect, except for a small chip or mark – which was not acceptable on a new vehicle – and had to be scrapped and replaced. They were also the best in providing variations of glass with sections of large clear pieces from vision areas in an otherwise blanket screen. The firm had any amount and they were there for the taking.

"How many would you like?" was a welcome response to my enquiry.

Derek was the manager of Lally's factory; he cut the large sheets of plywood into specified sizes. There was never any waste as one foot squares and narrow panels were cut from odd sizes. On one visit to the factory, my eyes alighted on the shiny gold contents of a large box under a workbench. On inspection I found it full of small brass discs.

"What are these for?" I asked.

"The scrap yard," was the blunt reply.

This was confirmed by Lally, who laughed as he said, "They're stamped out to make insets for the ferrules of the brushes. If you want to add them to your pile of rubbish, take all you want." And I did!

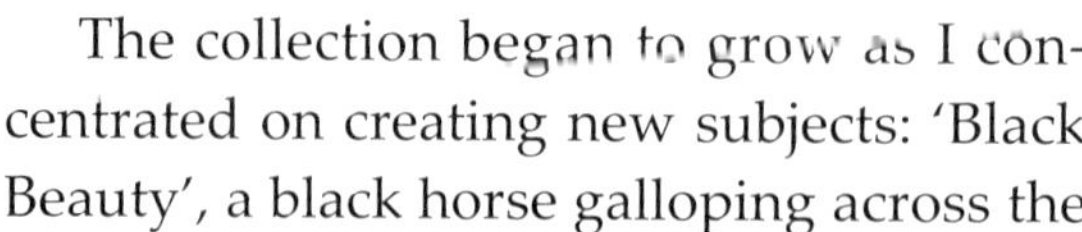

The collection began to grow as I concentrated on creating new subjects: 'Black Beauty', a black horse galloping across the horizon of a red sunset; 'Wheatsheaf', husks of wheat and a mill wheel; 'Deal', a seaside village of terraced cottages; 'Cornucopia', long red and orange shapes erupting onto a brown textured background from a black centre, studded with brass.

An unexpected visit from my friend Barbara took me by surprise as she tossed five playing cards on the table. "Here's your first commission. I want a painting of them for Leslie." 'Royal Flush' was the special request for her poker playing husband.

Jewel-coloured shapes in small square frames became a speciality, among them 'Jewels', 'Aquamarine', 'Ruby', 'Topaz', 'Fire Opal', 'Emerald', 'Citroen', 'Peridot', 'Garnet', 'Amethyst', 'Amber', 'Coral' and 'Sapphire'.

Among my favourites were additional paintings such as 'Wild Thistle', 'Blue Daisies', 'Early Autumn' and 'Shades of Autumn', together with 'The Kiss' and 'Mother and Child', which were the most powerful subjects.

The Comedy Gallery, in the Haymarket, opened to a private view on Wednesday, 15th October,1969,

The exhibition was successful. Many commissions followed with special requests for specific rooms of homes. One client bought a small collection to show at a gallery in Israel; another had a painting of her racehorse. The Londoner Hotel took a selection of 'Jewels' which they displayed for sale in the foyer.

Following the exhibition, my friend, Gina, took sample paintings to Liberty's in Regent Street. They took everything I could supply as well as taking orders for copies, following feature window displays.

It was a satisfying and rewarding period which came to a close when I was snared into another project . . . but that's another story.

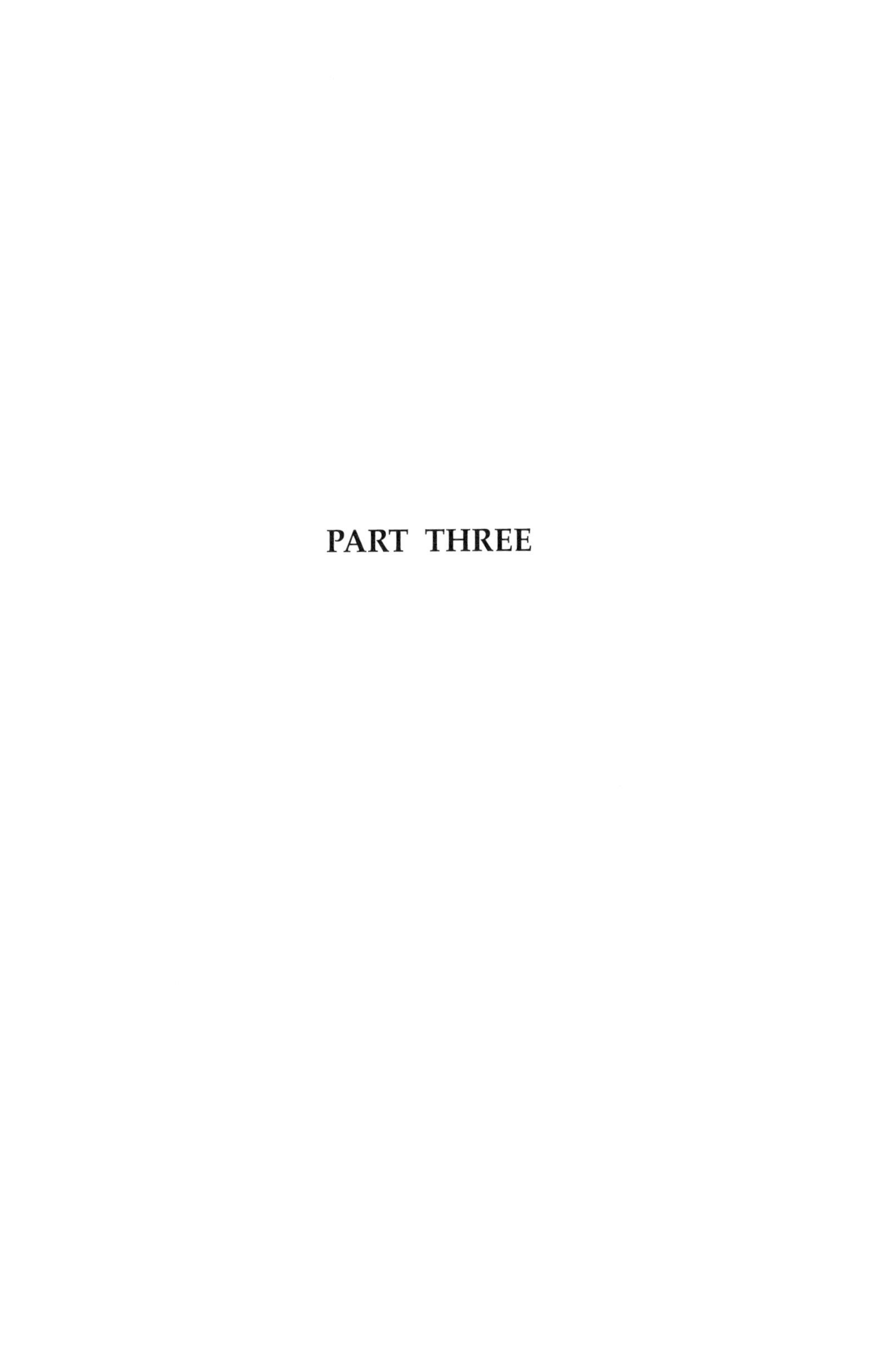

PART THREE

~ Caledonian Suite ~

"Telephone for Mrs Gwen Leigh!" The voice rang out on the tannoy loudspeaker, disturbing the peace of the Green Park Hotel garden overlooking the swimming pool, in Bournemouth. Everything became hushed for a moment and then everyone reverted to what they were doing. Everyone, that is, except me. I was on my way to Reception.

"You have a call for me," I said breathlessly.

"Oh yes, Mrs Leigh. You can take it in booth one."

I picked up the phone, prepared for whatever tragedy was in store, saying, "Hello."

"Gwen, how's the holiday?" My pulse stopped racing; as I recognised Cecil's voice, the panic subsided.

"Cecil, what a surprise! Are you coming down?" I asked.

"We don't all have time to laze about," he replied with his customary humour.

I laughed, answering, "Tough, just a minute while I dry my tears," and added on a more serious note, "Sorry, Cecil, what did you call about?"

"I have a bit of a problem and I wondered if you can help." His voice was serious now and he continued, "I've had three artists' impressions for a brochure I have to produce, but the client says none of them are right. I'm stuck. Could you do a brochure?"

"I'll have a try. I don't guarantee the result, but I'll do my best," was my prompt reply, continuing with, " We're coming back tomorrow. I'll call you as soon as we get back and you can put me in the picture."

"Thanks, Gwen. I'll wait for your call," and he rang off.

As promised, I called Cecil on our return to London and he came round to brief me on the project in preparation for a meeting with the client next day. It was simply 'A Scottish evening in London'.

"Is that it?" I asked.

"Does it conjure up any startling ideas in your head, because it didn't inspire any of the others," he said in a matter-of-fact voice.

"I don't know, but I'll have a go," I replied shrugging my shoulders. "Let's see what happens tomorrow."

It was obvious that Joe Lewis, Cecil's client, didn't think much of my potential. He was a young entrepreneur surrounded by bright young assistants buzzing around offering advice. As he politely explained what he wanted, it was clear that he didn't really have anything specific in mind. "Look," he said, "I want this Scottish Evening to look so exciting that it's at the top of the tourist list. I'm off to Paris today, but I'll be back Thursday. Will you have something ready then?"

I nodded and asked, "Can I see the premises?"

"Sure. One of the girls will take you over."

Northumberland Avenue, off Trafalgar Square and south of the Strand, seemed a little off the beaten track. A dilapidated canopy over the pavement emphasized the wide pedestrian way to the entrance, which was set back to accommodate a doorway to a club in the basement.

One stepped straight into the foyer, a bleak room with a lot of doors; double doors lay directly ahead, double doors to the left led to the cloakrooms and double doors in the middle of the left-hand wall opened to reveal a room of magnificent, elegant proportions, abysmally neglected. Large marble columns supported a lofty, original decorative ceiling and there were panelled walls. At the far end, a throughway led to another large room, not of the same calibre, but well proportioned. Kitchens were situated to the back of these two rooms. We made our way through the second room and found ourselves back in the foyer. I made a few sketches to give myself inspiration, thanked the young assistant and made my way home, to get started.

Thursday afternoon, Cecil and I went to meet Joe. Cecil had no interest in looking at my work in advance because, as he said, it didn't matter what he thought: Joe had to like it. The atmosphere was electric as I passed the work to Joe.

"Hey! This is terrific! It's exactly what I wanted. You know, I must confess, I didn't think you could do it." He laughed at his confession; he rarely admitted that he was wrong.

"Can you do another one for the middle page?" he asked.

"Yes, of course," I replied, giving Cecil a big grin.

Cecil was now ready to take over. "Tell me Joe, who's going to supervise the decorating?"

"I hadn't thought about it. I suppose one of the girls," he replied offhandedly.

"Give the job to Gwen. She's got an eye for that sort of thing."

"Yes? Would you like to do it, Gwen?" he asked.

"Very much so," I replied.

"Fine. The job is yours."

I was stunned. This was a new challenge and I welcomed it.

Joe liked the centrefold artist's impression as much, or even more than, the cover. "Great, isn't it? Look, she's made it look just like the room," he said, showing it to his young assistant, Jane, which made me smile. It was such an obvious thing to do.

Norman was employed by Hanover Grand to do the maintenance on all their premises, which included building work and decorating. It was a surprise for him to learn that the design work for the Caledonian Suite was to be done by me. For years he had made his own decisions and was of the ilk who considered that building was a man's trade and he had contempt for interfering women. He grudgingly helped, but I had the feeling that he would be happy to prove me wrong. With the passing of time, when he realized that I wasn't trying to usurp his position, he became more amenable. The place had to be stripped. Layer upon layer of paint had to be burnt off, cracks filled, wiring and sanitary fittings checked and floors made good. Norman was left to carry on with the groundwork, while I began researching Scottish history.

Tartan, denoting a clan, conveyed the most meaningful Scottish characteristic. Through a connection in the carpet industry, I had a carpet sample made in the guise of a tartan, in the colours of the brochure, using purple, shocking pink and olive green. It was sensational, creating an exciting identification for the Caledonian Suite. The carpet would run throughout, linking all the rooms. Another friend put me in touch with an obliging mill to weave matching fabric; the ensuing tartan provided staff uniforms, as well as kilts and scarves for sale to tourists.

I had difficulty finding a decorative finish for the walls that related to the tartan; wallpapers were too textured, or too fancy, and paint seemed too bland.

A chance remark by one of the workmen aroused my curiosity: "You should see what they're doing in a flat in St John's Wood."

It was by luck that I was told to go and look at that flat in St John's Wood. The walls were beautiful, smart and sophisticated. It was flocking, not the garish patterned flock, but smooth as velvet, elegant and sumptuous. I watched as the magnetically controlled fibres were sprayed onto a prepared wall, each fibre standing on end, resulting in a smooth velvet-pile finish. It was amazing!

"We can do it in any colour and spray it onto any surface," I was told by Ron Goff, as he continued, "It's hard-wearing and washable."

Samples of the three colours – purple, shocking pink and olive green – were submitted, put through rigorous tests and approved. The basic idea was to create a sequence of colour: olive green in the foyer, shocking pink in the reception, moving through to the subdued purple banqueting room, all linked with the carpet underfoot.

A concept began to emerge by updating the drab canopy at the entrance. Gold fibreglass rope edges, looped with tassels, accentuated the gold Caledonian Suite mounted on the complementary purple background. Small inset light bulbs, like small stars, replaced florescent tubes. Life sized figures of Highlanders on the right wall gave an illusion of their presence, until one realized it was a photograph of Highlanders in battle.

This was where the 'Scottish Evening in London' began. As one entered the foyer, the tartan carpet on the wall behind the reception desk, flanked by carpet-clad pilasters, emphasized the sombre, olive-green flocking on the walls and doors. Guests were greeted and given their allocated table number. Gold handles opened double doors into the Reception room as the tartan carpet led the way.

This room now displayed its elegance. Vibrant, shocking-pink velvet flocking revealed the well-proportioned panelled room. Two imposing marble columns, veined with yellow ochre, supported beams in the high ceiling, dividing it into three sections, each with a large crystal chandelier hanging from the ornate centre and heavily patterned cornice surround, picked out in colours complementary to the columns.

The personnel at the National Portrait Gallery were helpful with my research of Scottish history. I recognised their giggles and undisguised amusement as I approached: "Here she comes again!" became an ongoing joke.

"Sorry! Yes, it's me again!" and we all laughed.

I plied them with questions and delved through the archives; this brought me to the decision to have a large portrait of Mary, Queen of Scots, on the central wall. They recommended me to their photographer, who advised me about it and produced the facsimile portrait paintings. Slightly smaller paintings on either side were Robert Burns and Bonnie Prince Charlie, even though I was made aware that the feud still remains and resentment shown by some, at the inclusion of a Campbell.

Tommy Wayne ran shops for Hanover Grand. He explained that a suitable place to sell souvenirs had to be included in the Caledonian Suite. The boutique, in the u-shaped carved wood counter and display, was positioned under the portrait of the Queen.

Guests were made welcome by the "Laird" who greeted them as host of the evening and were offered Scottish hospitality of scotch or other drinks, by staff dressed in the tartan kilts with a scarf over one shoulder. They consisted of out-of-work actors, mainly entertainers, who were "resting" in between engagements; they waited on tables and took part in the floorshow. They mingled with the guests, who browsed over items in the boutique, until all the guests on the list arrived. Highlanders with bagpipes led them into the Banqueting Suite.

Despite its size, the dimly lit Banqueting Room had an intimate, romantic atmosphere. The left, semi-circular window wall was curtained from ceiling to floor in purple dupion, to match the flocked walls. Gold chairs around candlelit tables, with a scroll of the set menu at each place, were positioned around the dance floor, which, when raised, doubled as a stage for the cabaret, and for the ceremonial Cutting the Haggis, brought in by Highlanders playing bagpipes.

To add a note of authenticity, I sought to introduce traditional tartans into the décor, drawing from the limited selection available at The Scotch House. Each tartan had its own Coat of Arms.

Those of Royal descent could display the crown above the coat-of-arms. I was advised to consult the Scottish Office, as an ancestral authority, to corroborate facts of lineage and verify that the tartan and coat-of-arms were correctly correlated. The Scottish representative spoke passionately about his heritage, outraged with indignation at seeing people with no affinity to the clan, wearing tartan. He vented his anger at tartan displayed in shop windows being sold to the general public.

"I'm pleased to say that we won't be party to offending anyone with the colours we are using in our tartan," I explained.

I felt the venom in his rebuke: "Madam, that is not a tartan. You have made a check material."

I enquired as to which clan he belonged and carefully noted, "Do not use."

Eight tartan panels were inset in the flocked purple walls, two each side of the stage and four on the opposite wall, each displaying the Crown and authentic coat-of-arms. I toyed with several ideas of finish and decided to make them myself, in the special glass painting medium I had pursued in the past, with crowns of brass, another medium I had previously used. For this I secured the assistance of my very talented Japanese au pair. The shields were magnificent: vibrant colours with an incandescent glow beneath opulent gold crowns made of brass. It added an air of mystery and excitement.

This pilot scheme was a resounding success. Before long, the seven evenings a week bookings were increased to two settings, seven evenings a week. Joe Lewis congratulated me on the ambience of the project on the opening night, followed up by a touching letter of appreciation, which I have since lost.

The Caledonian Suite project carved out a new and exciting career for me as the designated designer for Hanover Grand.

~ *Hanover Grand and Verry's* ~

I could now think the unthinkable. My world had turned full circle and I was on the brink of a compelling career, joyful at the realisation that Lally had discarded his Victorian attitude to working wives. My two children, both happily at university, no longer in need of parental supervision, left me free. I hadn't contemplated employment, but the elation experienced in the transformation of the Caledonian Suite made me realize that interior design gave me ultimate satisfaction. Being presented with an open-ended offer by Joe Lewis to update all the premises of Hanover Grand, was a dream come true.

My first assignment was a small suite on the left as one entered Hanover Grand. A window at the front overlooked Hanover Street, and at the far end, an internal staircase led to the lower floor. A bandstand was built into the recess by the side of the stairs, with a small dance floor in front, which gave it the atmosphere of a club. It needed little more than refurbishing: wallpaper, improved lighting, drapes, carpets and pictures. Furniture was not included, which made it adaptable for any occasion and perfect for small functions.

Tommy Wayne, who ran the Hanover Boutique next door, kept a watchful eye on what I was doing. He was determined that his shop would have priority as my next project.

As soon as the reception room neared completion, he was there, saying, "Come and see what you can suggest."

My first impression was that the place needed a facelift, as I asked, "How much are they prepared to have done?"

"Whatever needs doing," said Tommy, adding as an afterthought, "And a new shop front."

This was new territory for me, but unabashed, I approached it as a project, beginning with the exterior. I knew that as the building was in a Conservation area, it would require Town and Country planning permission; I determined to obtain that before wasting time on taboo schemes.

I took measurements and made drawings of the shop frontage. The existing entrance door to the shop was set back, level with the entrance door to the upper floors. By creating a wall between the doors, the entrance to the shop was brought forward, in line with the requested bow-window, making the entrance more prominent. The man at the planning office was very helpful, suggesting that I invest in a book about Victorian and Edwardian shop fronts. It was back to the drawing board, this time to include the facade of the whole beautiful building in which an affinity and balance of the shop front was created. The plans were approved and I could concentrate on details of finish for the polished wood structure, signs and door furniture.

The interior of the shop was inadequate, but the articles for sale were name products, in fact, the best of British.

"It's a very old-fashioned shop, Tommy. Tell me, do you attract customers who think they're getting something old and original?" I asked.

Tommy took me aside and explained, "The major proportion of customers are tourists, mainly Japanese, but others too, of course, who come in coach loads to buy traditional British classics such as Burberry and Dunhill. Stock has to be readily at hand to serve them quickly because they are only here for a restricted time."

"What happens then? Does the coach just wait for them?" I asked.

"Oh, no," replied Tommy. "First they are dropped off next door to have lunch or tea in the place you just decorated. They come here to shop and the coach picks them up and takes them back to their hotel."

"I'm pleased you told me, Tommy. It makes everything clearer and certainly will influence my concept of the shop."

Work for the shop followed and proved to be practical, especially the window display which attracted additional customers. The interior display consisted of cubby-holes for pullovers and shirts lining the walls. Glass-topped counters in front, either side of the shop, displayed small items such as cuff links, lighters and pipes, scarves, gloves and Celtic jewellery. Additional stock was stored below on sliding trays. The lower floor, approached by a sturdy staircase, had large items: Burberry coats and jackets, Church shoes and Golf clubs, as well as an additional stockroom.

Tommy was a charming man, offering advice, always framed as a question: "Do you think?" Full of enthusiasm, he hung around like a mother hen when the work was being done. His office, at the rear of the shop, served for both administration and meetings. Another small room next to it accommodated staff.

All the woodwork was finished in polished mahogany with gold signs. The shop front and interior units were executed by a reputable firm of shop fitters, who also supplied directional downlighters and brown carpet.

Verry's Restaurant, in Regent Street, was my next assignment. The actual size of the premises took me by surprise and yet, it had an intimate ambience. The establishment had the well-deserved status of being a good eating house, catering to a business clientèle and frequented by celebrities and dignitaries. They specialized in English fare: large joints of beef and lamb on silver-domed heated trolleys and other specialities, carved, prepared and served at individual tables.

I was shown to a small, rundown area catering for approximately fifty people, situated off the main restaurant. The partitioning had been done without due consideration, resulting in a boxed-in atmosphere. It needed change, which I put as suggestions to Joe Lewis, but he wasn't interested in discussing details:

"Just get on with what needs to be done," was his reply. "Norman will get you anything you want."

It was a comparatively small job and Norman felt that he could cope with doing the building work himself. It presented a good opportunity to work with him. The whole area was gutted and rewired. The hanging light-fittings were replaced by indirect lighting concealed in cornice set lower down on the walls to reduce the height of the ceiling. Upholstered seating was fitted below a dado rail. Panelling on the walls above the dado added interest and warmth, enhanced with a series of framed, colourful prints, each softly lit by a small brass picture-light, giving the room a soft glow. Shaded paint on the woodwork blended with apricot wallpaper. The patterned carpet to match the main restaurant, remained.

As soon as I completed the small dining room, Joe presented me with another challenge:

"See what you can make of this," he said, handing me a grubby parcel wrapped in brown paper.

I began opening it, but he interrupted, "Take it home and go through it there."

I couldn't wait to get home to see what was hidden away in the mysterious package. It was treasured, interesting memorabilia.

The history of Verry's dated back to 1821, when Emile Verry, a Swiss confectioner, opened the restaurant. It was the custom of his beautiful daughter, Fanny, to help in the shop, preparing cakes and ices in view of the window.

The fame of her beauty spread far and wide and the bucks of the late Georgian era came to drink coffee at the shrine. The business grew and it became the rendezvous of Upper Bohemia.

Crowds would gather around the window to watch Fanny and one day, the crowd was so large that it overflowed into the road. The police ordered her arrest for causing an obstruction of the King's Highway while King George IV's carriage was passing up Regent Street. The magistrate advised M. Verry to send his daughter out of town until the public curiosity had subsided and she was kept out of public view in the rear of the premises. Sadly, the episode caused a decline in her health and she died of melancholy.

The entire story of Verry's is told in newspaper clippings, a poem by Lord Petersham to Miss Verry, letters to the editor from "A Gentleman", dated 1828 and 1837, photographs of the restaurant in 1905 and a 1913 and 1936 menu.

I had them all framed and put on view in the foyer.

"Do you think the menu merits a new image?" I was asked by Cecil, who was concerned with the printing.

"Of course," I replied, " and the history should be printed at the back."

Joe was in full agreement and approved of the new format on the front and the history.

A brief resume of additional work carried out at Verry's began with refurbishing the front and entrance to bring back some of the grandeur of a bygone age. Acid-treated glass in the internal doors was reinstated as close as possible to the original, with the ambience of Victoriana, when elegant design was a requisite.

Plasterwork on the staircase walls leading to the main restaurant was repaired, revealing an interesting coat-of-arms which was picked out in colour.

Christopher Wray's Lighting Emporium was new to the London scene and was the source of new lighting, together with old prints above re-upholstered seating in the Bar. The grandeur of the original long bar was brought back to its old glory.

A restored fireplace, one of the original features, added character to the lower floor Main Restaurant and the formal Blue Room to the side of the Main Restaurant – required relief from the overpowering colour.

The Powder Room was given a complete facelift, but as hard as I tried, I couldn't get Joe to agree to hot-air hand driers.

An occasional treat while working at Verry's was lunch in the Main Restaurant: definitely first rate.

The London Room in Drury Lane was a new acquisition, in pristine condition, sophisticated and smart, but it lacked warmth. I suggested and bought, long Victorian Laura Ashley dresses, stiff white aprons and mob caps for the staff, a boost for Laura Ashley, who had just opened their first Fulham Road shop, and it added an unusual informality.

Joe Lewis was a practical joker and I was a little wary of him. Was he serious or was it frivolity when he asked, "When can you come to Blackpool? Your next job is the Cliffs Hotel."

~ Cliffs Hotel, Blackpool ~

I had no idea of what I was letting myself in for, but felt the excitement in anticipation of a new adventure as we sped north to Blackpool, with Joe at the wheel and Jane, who accompanied him everywhere, at his side. The coastline, when at last we reached it, took me by surprise; I hadn't expected Blackpool to be so beautiful.

Joe drove along the sea front pointing out landmarks and then stopped opposite an enormous dilapidated Victorian Hotel.

"That's it," he said, waving his arm in the direction of the building.

Indeed, I could now see the large letters CLIFFS HOTEL across the front.

Caught off guard, I heard myself say, "I didn't think it would be so big."

Jane laughed, saying, "You should know by now that Joe does things in a big way," and we all laughed.

Once inside, I had the eerie feeling of being in a time warp. The Victorian elegance had been untouched and the spacious reception, with marble floor, featured a wide staircase; the ornate balustrading formed a well which reached up to the top of the building.

"Come look at the rooms," said Joe excitedly, propelling me into the dining room. "Nothing's been done here since before the war."

"And I should think not for a long time before that," I remarked, looking around at the decorative cornice on high ceilings supported by columns and pilasters on panelled walls. It was a large room, the tables, with stiff white tablecloths, beautifully set; a glass-fronted area overlooked the sea front. Despite the antiquarian character, the hotel was well maintained.

"It's a good dining room. All it needs is the Palm Court orchestra."

Joe nodded his head. "That's why you are here. I want it brought up-to-date and made into a three-star family hotel."

The ballroom was much larger than the dining room, with a large stage, square columns up to the decorative ceiling and a row of high, arched windows along the length of one wall. This room belonged in grottsville.

Joe obviously sensed my revulsion, saying, "Think about drinking and dancing. Blackpool has a reputation for people having fun. A live band plays every night and it's usually filled to capacity."

That evening I had a chance to see how true that was. Drinks were served in the ballroom, the band played non-stop and the leader's rapport was good, creating a feeling of camaraderie. The bar next door was practically empty.

The several lounges don't merit mention, but the worst area was the enormous basement, referred to as the Lower Ground Floor, which was a disaster. Its only redeeming feature was an excellent billiard table.

The next day was spent measuring and making notes of the ballroom and dining room. A plan of the maze in the basement revealed one room originally built for a masonic lodge, fairly large, with an interesting sunken floor. I took measurements and made notes of all the rooms. In my mind, the whole area of the lower ground floor was destined to be a leisure centre, but it would need careful planning.

Joe introduced me to all the staff, explaining what I would be doing, and instructing them to give me every assistance.

In the evening, Joe and Jane took me on a tour of Blackpool, pointing out the highlights. We returned to London next day and I began making drawings, plans, mainly for myself, followed by artist's impressions.

I began by spending three days a week in Blackpool, catching an early train on Monday and returning home late on Thursday. I looked forward to having a leisurely relaxed breakfast in the Pullman train and arriving at Blackpool ready for work. The introduction of separate carriages had a harrowing effect on me; I was alone when a man suddenly opened the door and jumped in as the train pulled out at one of the final stations near Blackpool. We sat in opposite corners; something in his appearance made me feel uncomfortable. I watched as he reached into his bag and took out a pair of gloves, pulling each one on slowly. My thoughts raced ahead: "He could strangle me without leaving fingerprints." I was petrified as he stared in my direction; and reached in his bag again. I consoled myself thinking, "Being stabbed is better than being strangled." I practically collapsed with relief as he took out a newspaper and began reading. However, from then on, I drove up. The Jaguar made light work of the journey and I became quite used to travelling alone.

The first area to receive redecoration was the main dining room. Drastic treatment was not required; the room was beautifully proportioned, with all the original features, which I had picked out in pastel colours. Adjoining the dining room was a bleak, cold glazed area, with a wonderful view overlooking the sea front, frequented by the occasional guest who would sit there enjoying the view. By painting the walls green, putting white arched trellis over the green background and adding garden furniture, it was converted into a garden room with flora and greenery; the regular florist of the hotel was very helpful in selecting suitable plants. I named it The Terrace; the snack café was a good addition and proved to be popular with the guests for breakfast as well as lunches and tea. It gave the hotel the required sense of informality and complemented the charm of the dining room.

Despite the distance, Ron Goff, who had flocked the walls of the Caledonian Suite and Royston Locke, who had made the curtains, came to estimate for doing work in Blackpool. Without delay, the artist's impression became a reality. Honey-coloured flocking for the ballroom was luxurious and uncluttered; as it was sprayed on it brought out details of the beautifully panelled walls. The honey colour echoed in the bank of silk-curtained windows, each with a red silk border on the leading edge, below a draped swag and tails, also red-bordered. Tasselled gold rope tie-backs matched the rope piping between the honey and red silk border. Matching honey and red blinds were drawn over the windows at night. Curtains for the stage on the opposite wall echoed the colouring, reversing to red as the backdrop. Crystal wall-lights, within panels on the walls and large crystal chandeliers, centralised either side of the revolving mirror ball in the centre of the dance floor, provided sparkle to the basic lighting. Specialized stage lighting was included. Carpet and similarly patterned upholstered chairs were arranged in clusters around small marble tables on the perimeter of the large dance floor. An antiqued mirror was fitted to add interest on the square columns.

The lower-ground floor demanded the most attention to turn this into a family hotel. With plans in hand which entailed a lot of work and expense I sought Joe's approval before proceeding. We descended to the large open room on the lower floor; set back at one side was the cloakroom for coats and straight ahead, double doors led to the ladies' and gents'.

We stood in the empty space as I explained: "This will be a games room for youngsters, with table tennis and other games, which have to be sorted out. It needs better overhead lighting and a vinyl floor. It could also interest guests who come to the cloakrooms."

Joe seemed to think it over and asked, "What other games do you have in mind?"

"Pinball machines. They keep kids engrossed for hours," I replied.

Joe laughed. "You're right. And not just kids. All ages including my son. Are we finished?"

"No, not yet," I said as I led the way through a small passage to the billiard room. "This room just needs refurbishing, re-upholstered seats, carpet and curtains. The billiard table is in very good condition. The last owners must have been keen players." I spoke generally as I made my way to a small room leading off. "This needs more attention," I said, opening the door to the Masonic Room.

Joe was really surprised. "I don't remember this room. What do you have in mind?" he asked.

"I'd like to make it into a disco," I replied.

"But we already have a ballroom upstairs," he said.

"That's for older people. You want to give the younger set something they'll stay in for. Parents will be pleased to know where their kids are," I suggested, adding, "You do want to make it a family hotel."

"You've been right with everything you've done so far so I'll give you the benefit of the doubt," he said with enthusiasm. He turned to leave as I stopped him in the ante room, opening another door.

"Just one more room," I said stepping inside.

"What now?" he asked in surprise.

"A babies' playroom for under-fives."

He looked at me in amazement, with the query, "Do you honestly think it's necessary?"

"It's such a little room. How can we go wrong?"

"All right, do what you like," he said, exasperated.

As he started to leave, I asked, "Do you want to look at the Ladies and Gents, or will you leave it to me?"

"You're the expert. Just get on with it."

The meeting was over.

Back in London next day, I sought information on pinball machines and was put in touch with Associated Leisure. They were helpful in advising me about regulations, followed with confusion in making a selection: pinballs, football, hockey – the variety was enormous. I chose six. No gambling machines were allowed.

The next selection was for the playroom and included a made-to-measure blackboard, miniature table and chairs, a slide, dolls, a cradle, pram, cooker, large bricks, a train set, cars, paint, paper and storybooks.

By way of creating a fun area, I decorated the small passage with figures from the *Magic Roundabout* (the popular children's TV programme), much to Joe's amusement.

I struck lucky with the disco. I didn't know the man, but I knew a man who did and so I obtained the services of the technician who set up *Top of the Pops*. He came up to Blackpool and set up the sound system.

Decorating the disco was a doddle. Everything was painted black except for eight white circles, measuring four feet in diameter, which I positioned on the walls. Pulsating kinetic lights linked to the music, threw out exciting colours in rhythm, changing the white circles into animated colour. Brightly coloured bean bags were strewn about the surrounding raised, black-carpeted floor, above the sunken white-tiled dance floor with an inset black, key-design border. Habitués of Blackpool, the City of Lights, proclaimed this a winner.

The Ladies and Gents throughout the hotel were thoroughly renovated, with up-to-date cubicles, plumbing and décor. Lounges were also updated and upholstered furniture either re-covered or replaced.

Barry came to Blackpool to assist me with the mammoth task of reviewing the bedrooms to upgrade the hotel by providing en suite facilities. While this is very simple in a modern establishment, the era in which this hotel was built did not adhere to identical rooms; each room was individual. The principle followed that three rooms provide two rooms en suite. A tedious study followed, measuring each room and assessing the best way to divide the middle room. We jointly drew up a comprehensive plan, following consultation with local commercial furnishers of measurements for suitable available fitments. These plans were submitted to Joe to be put in the hands of a local overseer.

By then I had had enough commuting to Blackpool, but I loved every minute of this enormous challenge.

~ Time For Change ~

The university years had flown by as we watched, with pride, Barry, in cap and gown, receive his degree at Swansea University, no longer the rebellious teenager, but an upright young man anxious to get on in the world.

Within a short time, Barry, obtained a teaching post in Oxford at the Architectural college, to lecture in Architectural Psychology, the study of the effect of colour in rooms, while he pursued his Master's degree at the university.

After a futile search for accommodation, Lally and I decided to purchase a property for Barry, which he would share with fellow students to add to his income; we settled on a townhouse – in a comparatively recent development near to the college – which we refurbished on a tight budget: garage and one room on the ground floor, lounge and kitchen on the middle floor and three bedrooms on the top floor. Oxford became a family commitment as Lally and I travelled up each weekend with Barry and Chris, (a lad who usually assisted Lally in the garden), carrying out the decorating and furnishing.

All the walls were painted white; in the open-plan lounge, wall-hung white units stretched along the length of one wall, holding the hi-fi, TV, records, books and bric-a-brac; two settees and four easy chairs provided the seating. Barry chose to tile the worktop to renovate the kitchen units; the central dining area of the kitchen benefited from an early morning visit to the Caledonian Trade Market where we purchased a Victorian pine table and six rush-seated pine chairs. The four bedrooms were all done with the same format: a bed, wall shelves above a desk, one or two chairs, a hanging wardrobe and drawers. I made a bedcover with co-ordinating curtains for each of the rooms.

Barry settled like a fish into water, fulfilling his lectureship at one college and studying for his Master's degree at the other, basking in the camaraderie and comfort of his home.

Six months later, due to government cuts in expenditure, the Psychology course, as it was the most recent addition, was cut from the curriculum. Barry's world was turned upside-down. The devastating news was bewildering, as he felt that the previous three years were a complete waste and his study of colour useless. Of course they weren't, but sadly, Barry didn't reap the benefit. The senior lecturer used Barry's notes to produce a book, from which we all benefit, especially in such places as waiting rooms and hospitals, which pander to our mood: relaxed, stimulated and so forth. Barry was adamant about selling the house, although I begged him to keep it as an investment. He was determined to cut all ties with Oxford.

As I had a lot of design work on hand for Hanover Grand, I persuaded Barry to join me at the Cliffs Hotel in Blackpool. He proved to be an excellent assistant. His specifications and drawings were exemplary. The liaison was first-rate. Additionally, he took a course which gave him the status of electrical and heating engineer. Barry's collaboration with large projects which were to follow, was invaluable.

In the meantime, Marcia was completing a very successful pre-Diploma Art course at Sir John Cass, in Whitechapel, which, in tandem with Naomi Marks, had resulted in a close friendship, with interesting holidays and joint working projects, which occasionally benefited with photography by the staff at Marks and Spencer.

Marcia chose Liverpool Art College to follow, egged on by Pamela Rose, daughter of our next-door neighbour, who was at the University. We had assumed that Marcia would live in the same shared house as Pamela, so the last-minute problem of finding accommodation took us by surprise.

On making enquiries at the police station, we were told that some of the roads were not advisable for young girls on their own; one police officer even recommended: "Carry a steel comb in your pocket and use it if you are attacked."

Finally we did find a pleasant room and mentioned it to the waitress in the Adelphi Hotel as she served our coffee.

"Oh no, not in Upper Parliament Street!" she blurted out. "I wouldn't let my daughter live there. It's the worst street in the area."

Finally, after searching solidly for a week, the task of finding somewhere suitable ended in frustration.

Pamela had arranged for us to meet at her friends' house. They listened as I told Pamela that unless something turned up, Marcia would have to give up her place at the college.

"We have a box room full of junk, but we can clear it up," said a large, fair haired young man called Ian. "You're welcome to use it until you find something."

"That is a most generous offer," I replied. "I shall be happy to know that Marcia is with kind and considerate people."

And so Marcia moved into 1A Sunnyside, the annex of a delightful Edwardian end-of-terrace, by the entrance to a park.

As Marcia settled in, they told her that there was no need for her to look for other accommodation, if she was happy staying there, which was so. It came as a surprise to learn from the address printed at the bottom of one of her letters that 1a Sunnyside was the Communist and British Marxist-Leninist Headquarters.

Marcia made good progress and enjoyed being at the college. Liverpool was a long drive from London so visits home were few and far between, mainly during in-between term breaks. Christmas-time heralded an enormous party, with the house overflowing with fellow students from Liverpool and chums Barry had made in Swansea, mingling with local friends.

At one party Lally was drawn to one side by one of Marcia's Liverpudlian friends who told him, "I'm a member of the PLO and when the revolution comes you've no need to worry. I'll make sure no harm comes to you."

That pleased Lally no end!

Renee heard the screams. Wondering what had happened, she opened her front door and gasped with the realization that the screams were coming from the front of our house!

"What's going on?" she shouted.

The screams continued and she ran out, heading towards Marcia's car; a shadowy figure brushed silently past her.

Marcia was sobbing, her dishevelled body slumped over the steering wheel, utterly distressed.

"Oh, my God," cried Renee, as she rang the doorbell to alert us.

Marcia's face and neck were bruised; her long hair had been caught round her face in the tussle and stuck together with the chewing gum she had in her mouth, as the attacker tried to stifle her cries.

The police tried to piece together what happened; the conclusion was that the attacker must have been stalking her. He was obviously waiting in the shadow of the archway, in the knowledge that Marcia would park by the front door, in the middle of the three arches.

There was little else they could do without any clues or evidence. Their advice was that she could have counselling, but the best thing was to try to forget it. A tall order for a vulnerable victim!

Marcia went back to Liverpool, but during the latter half of her second year, she began having problems with her hands. The art materials she had been using created a virus which spread to all her fingers. The painful treatment failed to arrest the progressive, virulent form and eventually affected her hands to the extent that, with regret, she was unable to continue at the college.

Marcia had originally considered doing teacher training as an option and so, under the circumstances, came to the conclusion that it would be the most appropriate course to follow. It was proving to be very successful. She soon discovered that she had a natural empathy to gain the confidence of truants, which interested her.

"If they're truants, you can't have any pupils," was the obvious quip when she spoke about it, but calls like, "Please, can I speak to Miss Leigh," brought forth a smile and sense of pride in how she gained their confidence.

She was settling into the course reasonably well, but was finding it difficult to get enthusiastic, as it was second-best.

The doorbell rang! I was surprised to see a handsome young man standing there, dark hair contrasting with deep-blue eyes in a chiselled face, with a disarming smile.

"Does Marcia Leigh live here?" he asked.

"Why do you want to know?" I queried.

"My brother met her in Canada last summer and asked me to look her up while I was in London."

"No, I'm sorry. She's at school," and as he seemed to be very surprised, added, "She's doing teacher's training."

"Perhaps I could leave my name and telephone number," he suggested, taking out a notepad and pen. He began writing as he explained, "My name is Robbie Baker. I'm a medical student doing a short course at Guy's Hospital and shall be here about a month."

His explanation made me more hospitable. "Come for dinner. Marcia will be home then and I'm sure she'll be pleased to meet you. Tell me your brother's name and come around seven."

Marcia was not pleased when I told her what I'd done and blurted out, "I wish you wouldn't try to run my life for me."

"I thought I was doing you a favour," I said. "Anyway, he's coming here for dinner."

"Well, you can talk to him," she replied.

"As you wish, but I expect you to be civil," I warned.

We decided not to wait for dinner and were sitting around the table when the bell rang.

"Will you go?" I asked.

"No!" was her reply.

He had brought flowers and my heart sank as I thanked him.

"Come in," I said, leading him into the kitchen.

Marcia took one look and I could see the confusion as she realized that he was something special. Sweetness oozed out and I could see my lovely Marcia returning.

They spent a lot of time together, as much as Robbie could spare. But within a few weeks the course ended and he returned to Winnipeg. They corresponded and that summer, Marcia again went to Canada, this time to Winnipeg. As Lally and I saw her off at the airport, we wondered if she would be returning. It was in the lap of the gods and only time would tell.

Marcia returned from her Canadian holiday, minus Robbie, and I was secretly pleased to have her back and shelved the thought of her living so far away. She was still going though the difficult period of growing up.

When the opportunity arose for her to share a flat in St John's Wood with four girls, we gave her our blessing. The unfurnished, five-bedroom flat in Hall Road had a communal kitchen and a large hall which served as the lounge. Each girl had to decorate and furnish her own carpeted room which gave them a sense of responsibility. It was a good arrangement.

Marcia was happy with her newly found independence and had loads of friends; it also made travelling to work much easier. The other girls were similarly employed, one on the threshold of journalism, another doing administration. They discussed and helped each other.

"Mummy, I'm blind. I can't see anything!"

"Were you in an accident?" I asked.

"No, I just can't see. I don't know why," she cried.

"Marcia, don't worry. You'll be all right. I'm coming to help."

The journey from Edgware to St John's Wood seemed to take forever, as I hurried up to the flat. One of the girls let me in. Marcia looked awful.

"I'm taking you to Moorfields," I said as I bundled her into my car.

The department was quite crowded, but I explained the problem to the person in charge and she was hurried through to see a doctor. They diagnosed tricoma and after treating both eyes, bound her head in bandage to cover one eye, leaving her one eye with restored sight. She was assured that the other eye would be all right.

Not knowing what to do, I decided to take her somewhere special and remembered an unusual restaurant by Shepherd's Market, in the West End. Tiddy Dolls was just right. I didn't expect to have a band at lunch-time, but it was an additional bonus. The staff were wonderful in showing their concern as Marcia continued crying. It turned to laughter when the violinist came to our table and continued to serenade her.

Her normal sight was restored within a short time.

With the passing of time, she began to tell me about her hopes and aspirations. I was no longer just "Mummy". I was her confidante and friend.

~ *Beefeater By The Tower* ~

"Don't take off your coat, we're going out." Joe Lewis's pronouncement took me by surprise.

"Where to?" I asked.

"You'll see," he replied.

Joe didn't give much information away, preferring to fire questions at you and wait for answers. I knew a new project was in the pipeline because he had hinted that I would shortly have something to think about. Obviously this was it.

The route from the middle of Mayfair took us through the city, passing St Paul's Cathedral, the Tower of London and Tower Bridge. Surroundings began to deteriorate as we came to a stop beside a derelict building, surrounded by water, in Dockland.

"There it is, Ivory House," said Joe proudly.

We made our way towards it, treading carefully on the uneven rubble underfoot, entering the building on the right. The rough stone staircase led downstairs to a vast area. The basic building was interesting; double vaulted brickwork was supported by steel girders down the centre, lined up with walls dividing both sides into separate cavernous arches.

The floor, as such, was non-existent, as services for the entire building were being laid below; open areas had planks laid across to give access. The building had been partially submerged under water for years and grimy walls were coated with lime scale. Despite the condition, it had an aura, though it was obviously a warehouse and had in fact housed ivory.

Joe, as excited as a schoolboy, asked, “What do you think?”

I was surprised and lost for words, replying, “It’s fascinating and very large. You must have something specific in mind.”

“I want a first-class restaurant. The World Trade Centre have their headquarters here and there are plans for a marina in the dock, so there should be a good lunchtime trade.” Words came tumbling out as he continued, “I want something interesting for tourists at night.”

I could understand his excitement. As for me, it was a wonderful project and I was ready to take it on.

The first thing I did was to delve into the history of the site; it dates back to the reign of the Norman kings. In the year 1148, Queen Matilda, or Maud as she was then known, founded the Hospital of St Katharine. The legend of St Katharine comes from the tenth century. She was tied to a spiked wheel to be burned on the stake, symbolised by the Katherine Wheel and remembered on Firework Night, an interesting bit of history, which I sought out with the possibility that it could prove useful.

All that existed of the building was a shell. There was much planning and preparatory work that needed to be done for the basic layout. Meetings followed with architects for the contractors responsible for the restoration of the building, as well as meetings for specifications by kitchen consultants and chefs. Other meetings included Rex Gray, who provided entertainment for the group. The staff quarters and kitchens were positioned at the far end; facilities were needed for staff and changing rooms for entertainers, who had to have clear access to the restaurant without impeding kitchen staff; the kitchen included the positioning of In and Out service doorways. When all their requirements were met, the actual area for the restaurant was defined.

The reception area continued through the central aisle, with five arched bays leading off on each side. The vast subterranean cavern, meandering in different directions, was awesome, but not welcoming. The brickwork of each bay ended abruptly with a bulkhead built into the blank wall, two of which had openings through which the ivory was delivered. Each bay could seat approximately fifty people. The task facing me was to make the ambience so exciting that everyone would clamour for a place. Each bay, and especially the end wall, would have to be an important focal point.

Sandblasting of the grimy walls restored the natural patina of age to the beautifully vaulted brickwork, which dated back to 1825. I was advised that the contractors were scheduled to lay a slate floor. I then drew a plan featuring inset brickwork, to add interest and gave instructions for a raised dais to elevate the end of each bay, so that the top table would be on a higher plane.

Seating was the next consideration, with the problem of linking the bays. The solution came with forming a continuous line, like a serpent, with settle-seating in dark oak, with carved detail panelling on high backs, clinging close to the wall, in and out of each bay. Tables and chairs in front joined it all together and were distressed to show age. The settle-seating of the top table in each bay, a little higher than the rest, had additional carving, denoting that they were for the Lord and Lady of the evening.

A wrought-iron chandelier provided overhead lighting in each bay, but the central area lacked atmosphere. It needed more interest to overcome the monotony of the cavernous brickwork.

I sought advice from the architects who were restoring the building, with the query, "Could we put gas torches on the side walls of the centre aisle?"

"You'd have to speak to a combustion engineer for that," was their reply, and they gave me the name of one.

The combustion engineer's comment was encouraging: "I could certainly give you gas burners, but I'm not a designer. Give me a suitable design and I can have it made."

I made drawings of flambeaux, adding protective plates for the brickwork, which won everyone's approval and were ably executed. The flaming torches on the side walls created the excitement of a baronial hall.

My thoughts now focused on the reception area. The wall opposite the entrance staircase would be another challenge for the combustion engineer.

"Are you game to try something else?" I asked.

He laughed. "Why not? I'm willing to try anything as long as it's practical."

"What I have in mind is to have a boar, roasting on a spit, in front of a fire," I declared.

A deathly silence followed, while he absorbed my statement, then asked, "Are you serious?"

"Definitely about the fire," I replied. "An antique rotating spit is available from Architectural Salvage . . . if it's viable," I added.

"It is possible to construct a fire. A simple cage could hold small jets. The problem will be to find non-combustible material that looks like burning coals. I'll make some enquiries." He went on, "If we can create the fire, mounting your boar in front won't be a problem."

The quest for material that looked good and met with all the safety standards, proved difficult and several were abandoned before a satisfactory one was found. The end result was stupendous and in conjunction with the flambeaux, added character to the building and presented a welcoming, warm greeting. Initially, a boar was roasted on it daily for the lunchtime trade.

(Without doubt, this was possibly the prototype for gas fires now installed in private homes.)

The steel girders down the centre were out of character. I resorted to fibrous plaster cladding, aligned to the curve of the vaulted brickwork, fitted around each girder; Gothic moulding at the top concealed lighting which gave a glow to the vaulted brick-work. Dark oak service-tables were built around the base.

Somewhere along the way the idea of operating a lunchtime trade was dropped.

"What subject should I concentrate on for the banquet?" I asked Joe, as I hadn't been given any lead, and added, "The build ing lends itself to a medieval banquet, but it needs a theme that captures their imagination."

Joe was not interested in discussing the subject, dismissing me with, "That's your problem. That's why you've got the job."

"Fine, now I know where I stand," I replied.

He strode off leaving me with my thoughts.

My decision was that royal monarchs in their palaces would interest tourists more than anything else and I put the idea to Joe.

A slow smile crossed his face. "Yes! I like the sound of that. Get on with it!" he replied.

I set about getting the information I needed and smiled to myself contemplating the reaction I would get from the National Portrait Gallery. They had been helpful with information for the Caledonian project, but I suspected that they found my constant enquiries tiresome. Actually, they were great!

They recognised and greeted me with, "What are you looking for this time?"

"I'm not sure, but I'm planning to use the lineage of royal kings as a theme. I plan to link each one with a palace, preferably in London," and added, "I thought I'd start with suitable portraits."

"You probably know that early ones are death masks. The first painted portrait is of Henry the Fifth. How many portraits do you need?" they enquired.

"I have ten walls to fill."

"Goodness! That's a tall order."

"That's why I've come to ask your help. I'll have a look at that portrait and let you know what I think."

They pointed me in the right direction and I found myself face to face with a sombre image of the heroic king who won the famous Battle of Agincourt on St Crispin's Day. This was the Plantagenet King Henry V, immortalized by Shakespeare's play and Laurence Olivier's film! Excitement welled up within me. It was perfect. The Palace of Westminster, the original Royal residence that now forms part of the Houses of Parliament, would be the first bay, with the portrait on the end wall.

I made my way back to the desk to thank them and followed through to Richard III. This monarch was slain on Bosworth Field, thereby ending the War of the Roses; he was the wicked King, accused of murdering the Princes in the Tower. What could be more suitable than for him to reside in The Tower, in the shadow of the Tower of London.

"What about Henry the Eighth? You can't go wrong with him," suggested the girls at the desk, who were interested in my project.

I selected a handsome portrait of the Tudor king and felt that everyone would recognise the larger than life king.

"Do you want his six wives?" they asked.

"No, I don't think there will be enough room," I replied, amid their giggles.

There was no problem in selecting his residence: Hampton Court, one of the finest specimens of Tudor architecture, was presented to King Henry VIII by Cardinal Wolsey when the King expressed his displeasure that anyone should have a home more grand than his own. His portrait hanging on the end wall, flanked by large tapestries of hunting scenes, would reflect the decoration of the period.

"Queen Elizabeth the First?"

"Yes, indeed, but before that I have to deal with the fourth bay which doesn't lend itself to a portrait."

"Why not?" they asked.

I explained about the opening in the brick wall.

"It sounds like Traitor's Gate," remarked one of the girls, laughingly adding, "You could have the ghost of Anne Boleyn, with her head tucked underneath her arm."

"That's a wonderful idea. Not the ghost, but Traitor's Gate. Brilliant!"

As an afterthought someone added, "Not all who entered the Tower of London through this gate were executed. Important prisoners dined in some affluence as befitted their station."

Visions of the portcullis across the opening flashed through my mind. I would follow that idea through.

For the Elizabethan period I chose an extravagant and elegant portrait of the Virgin Queen Elizabeth. To join her I added two of her favourite courtiers: Robert Devereux, Second Earl of Essex and Robert Dudley, Earl of Leicester, who fell out of favour on the axe man's block.

Brocades and Genoese velvets would portray one of the greatest periods of English history. Nonesuch Palace echoed that era. When first I heard the name Nonesuch, I thought that someone was pulling my leg, but research revealed that in Tudor days Nonesuch meant "without equal". The Palace, built by Henry VIII near Ewell in Surrey, was a flamboyant building much favoured by Queen Elizabeth and her court. Unfortunately, Nonesuch

Palace was destroyed, down to the ground and only an outline of the foundation can still be seen.

I came now to the bay opposite Traitor's Gate. Following in the same trend, this bay became Newgate, the Debtors' Prison. The old City Wall near the Old Bailey was used for debtors and felons from 1188, one of the gateways that led into the walled city of London in the Middle Ages. Iron bars across the opening and rough, stone-faced walls scrawled with names and dates carved into their surface, reflected poor wretches thrown in there for as little as stealing a crust of bread. Many an evening I spent with a crochet hook and black cotton to make gigantic cobwebs.

"Charles the Second is well-known and historically interesting," suggested one of the girls. It was good advice. His reign after Oliver Cromwell was the period of the Restoration; his reign saw The Great Plague, the Fire of London and the rebuilding of London with Christopher Wren. Added to his portrait was Nell Gwynn, the King's favourite and the Duke of Buckingham, to hang either side of King Charles II in the Court of St James.

"William and Mary, the only joint rulers in our island's history, should be included," was the next suggestion.

"I don't know anything about their reign, but I recall that we had William and Mary furniture in our home when I was a child," I laughingly responded, remembering the elegant room, adding, "William and Mary will certainly be included."

"That is the most unbelievable reason I've ever heard!" The wry remark of one of the girls made everyone laugh and she continued, "Nevertheless, it's a good choice!"

History of the period had eluded me, but I now know that Mary, the daughter of King James II, married William, Prince of Orange; and the victory of the Battle of Blenheim was during their reign. Their portraits hang in Kensington Palace, where they held Court.

I considered it amusing artistic licence to include the House of Hanover although there is no royal residence of that name. The Hanoverians were the royal family during the rule of the four Georges. The Prince Regent, a leader of fashion, created what is now known as the Regency Period, famed for beautiful architecture and furniture. There was dismay when I selected his portrait.

"It will be more suitable to show them as King George the Fourth and Queen Caroline," they advised. I heeded their guidance; their portraits were added to the list.

"You must include Queen Victoria."

It sounded like an order, but of course they were right.

Queen Victoria was probably the best known of all the monarchs. Her long reign was marked by great commercial progress and social reform. I chose a mature portrait of the Queen and added the portraits of four politicians of her time: William Gladstone, Benjamin Disraeli, the Marquess of Salisbury and Joseph Chamberlain. Osborne House, in the Isle of Wight, was her favourite home and a palace most people would associate with the Queen.

The task now was to make the fantasy come to life, creating a pageant in history which would reflect the era of each of the reigning monarchs.

Architectural Salvage was a good source for finding decorative memorabilia; faded, gold braid-trimmed velvet hangings were formed into a coronet above the throne of King Richard III in The Tower.

I sought out the firm in Primrose Hill who made decorative plaster, and was taken under the wing of the elderly principal who had formed the company some generations before. Though in his eighties, he put in an appearance every day.

I told him about the end wall in each bay, explaining one of my ideas of putting a canopy in the centre, under which I would hang a portrait or put a coat-of-arms.

"That's easy enough and a good idea," he replied, adding, "Have a look in the attic and it will give you some ideas."

The storeroom and attic were crammed with designs accumulated through the years and they allowed me to delve through models that had been stacked away for years. He taught me the rudiments of working with old models and I learnt that with a little ingenuity, anything can be accomplished. They catered to my every whim to bring glamour to what could have been nondescript. Fibrous plaster is a fabulous medium; in the right hands it can create magic.

A number of enquiries led me to a firm near Nottingham who made heraldry, armaments and chain mail for film sets. They proved to be very helpful by suggesting and supplying pennants, shields and armour suitable for the Palace of Westminster and for The Tower. They fabricated an effective portcullis for Traitor's Gate together with torture implements as well as providing a wall of hanging pennants, figures in suits of armour and flags on long poles for the entrance.

Fabrics for each bay were chosen to convey the period and either covered the wall or were draped over a canopy. Full credit is due to the specialist firms who carried out the work. The sign writer was a nonpareil; he executed scrolls, beautifully painted with each name, to hang across the entrance to each bay.

The "Ladies of the Court" were given the luxury befitting a Queen: to retire and toilette amid walls draped across in rose-coloured silk; crystal lights fitted into softly etched mirrors over the long, marble-topped gilt dressing tables.

A lot of time and discussion was spent planning the evening operation. Meetings, which included directors, managers, PRs, chefs and entertainers, were held weekly, first at Hanover Grand headquarters and, as work progressed for food tasting and trial entertainment, at the Beefeater. Serving five hundred people simultaneously takes planning and co-ordination. It was agreed that food had to be taken to tables in quantity and served there.

I scoured around markets and sorted through Architectural Salvage looking for something suitable. I came across the black pot at a remote farm in Sussex, where they had a barn full of memorabilia. It had interesting markings which made me think of Shakespeare's witches dancing around a fire. When tested, the size was right to hold sufficient food for six people. The carrying handle was a bonus. The casting of the pots was put on order.

To have pewter place plates was deemed too expensive an option by the purchasing manager, who suggested an aluminium plate, which resembled a reject pot lid. I thought it had potential.

"Let me have the plate, John. I think I can do something to improve it."

Using a little innovation I made a border with clay which, when cast in aluminium, was perfect. Additionally, I made an impressive-looking goblet which, at Joe's request, held a minimum of wine and a small serving dish. They were approved and put on order.

Manufacturers were happy to assist with supplying samples of crockery. The meetings for testing them were hilarious. Cups and plates were thrown about the room to see what stress they could take. The final choice was plain dark brown and practically impossible to break. They were suitable and looked good.

Many more trial evenings were held with alternative meals. Votes were taken for the final decisions. Cutlery got the thumbs down in favour of daggers. Steel liners, which just slipped into the black pots, were suggested, thereby the same black pot could be used to serve two courses. Rex Gray entertained us with show-people who were resting and many were becoming efficient "wenches".

The work was nearing completion when I was approached by Cecil, who did the printing for the group:

"Gwen, can I have a word about the graphics for the Beefeater?" he asked.

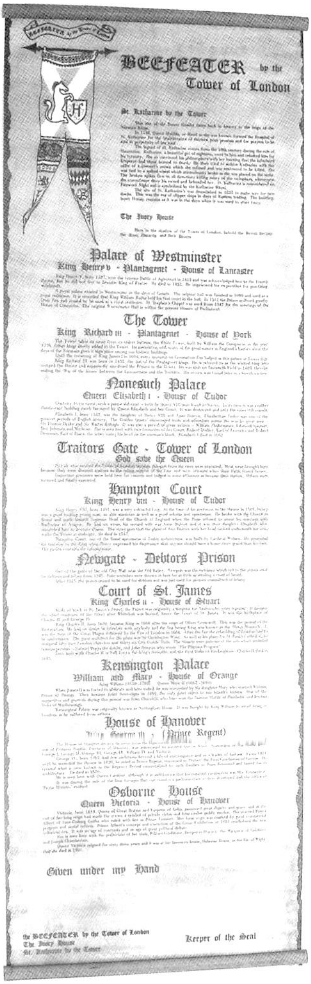

"Yes, of course, what do you want to know?" I replied.

"Joe told me to give the job to someone else, but I think he's wrong. I think you should do it, unless, of course, you don't want to," he added.

"He probably thinks I have enough to do," I replied.

"Do you want to do it?" he asked.

"Of course I want to do it!" I replied.

"Good. I'll let you know what's required, but don't tell Joe."

"I'm glad you asked me, Cecil. I would have been upset if you had given the graphics to someone else."

It did entail a lot of extra work, but Cecil was right; the graphics were an integral part of the project, which embodied the menus, the certificates, the signs, and in fact, the whole concept of the Beefeater, which was mine alone.

The Beefeater by the Tower of London is steeped in history. As one enters, large flags, a figure in a suit of armour standing guard and heraldic emblems on banners hanging across the wall, exude a sense of grandeur as one descends into the vast baronial hall ablaze with flaming torches. Scrolls hanging at the entrance to each bay convey the grandeur of British Heritage.

Each guest is greeted with bread and salt and traditional mead, a token of hospitality. During the reception, a couple are chosen to be Lord and Lady of the evening. They are robed, escorted to and seated on the raised dais of their Palace and their subjects summoned to join them. (I visualized costumes relevant to each bay, but they considered it too much trouble.) A Keeper of the Wine is delegated to keep the goblets at his table constantly topped up. The Keeper of Food is responsible for seeing that guests at his table do not go hungry. The ceremony is repeated until every Lord and Lady and their subjects are seated. At the end of the evening, each "performer" receives a certificate to verify that their task was well done.

A narrative with the history of the residence and that of the Royal Monarch is placed at each setting. A galaxy of strolling players provide non-stop entertainment, performing at the entrances or within each bay. Serving wenches are potential "stars" resting.

A visit to the Beefeater by the Tower of London is an experience. Your every need is planned and catered for: good food, entertainment and a superb atmosphere.

It took two years from start to finish to rescue Ivory House from decay and turn it into the Beefeater by the Tower of London.

The most significant reward for me on completion of this project is the award of Professional Status, granted to me by the Institute of Interior Design and also by the Interior Design and Decorators' Association, with the honour of membership in recognition and acknowledgement of my work.

I also give thanks to my son Barry, whose help was invaluable.

The Beefeater by the Tower was completed in 1975; since then it has changed hands at least three times, but I'm informed that the format remains the same.

Even more incredible is the fact told to me by Cecil just a year or so ago, whose firm continues to do the printing: "It's unbelievable, Gwen, but they still use your menu."

~ *It must be very, very beautiful* ~

I recognised the gruff voice and smiled as Frank carried on without a preliminary greeting. "Gwen, I need your help. I've just been to see a client about an unusual marble bathroom. He tried to explain what he wants. I'm no artist, but I know enough to realize that it would be a disaster. I've told him about your work and he would like to meet you. Interested?"

Frank was the specialist marble contractor who did the installation at the Beefeater. He had his own marble workshop and knew his trade well. I was a little surprised, because although he had executed quite complex installations according to the designs, he had never been complimentary.

"Why me?" I asked, unable to hide my suspicion.

"I think it's just up your street. It's a toughie and I know how you like difficult jobs."

"Come on now, flattery is not your scene," I parried.

"No kidding, it's no walkover. It needs someone with a vivid imagination. You know I'm not one to give praise, but you usually come up with something good, especially when it seems impossible," he continued. "Will you meet him?"

"Well, yes. What can I lose by meeting him ? Set it up; mornings are best for me and thanks for the vote of confidence."

I rang off, inwardly very excited with the surprise conversation; I did like a challenge.

Frank was waiting as I pulled up in front of the house in Kensington and gazed at the beautiful, large late-Georgian building, and we entered the house together.

Mr Hakim was a dapper man, moderately tall with sleeked black hair and large brown eyes. I noted that he was immaculately dressed and wafting in an aura of aftershave. He smiled a lot, oozing with charm. He presented his drawing to me and I asked to see the actual room. We made our way up the graceful staircase, through the master bedroom, into the existing bathroom.

I studied the drawing to see what Mr Hakim had in mind for the long narrow room. I could now understand Frank's reaction to his plan. It indicated a marble wall halfway down the room, with narrow stairs in the middle, leading up to a platform at the top. An oblong area, cut out in the centre of the marble, formed the bath.

The involuntary words came out instinctively: "Oh no! It would look like a mausoleum!" I bluntly remarked.

The two men stared at me and I realized that I had been too blunt. By way of explanation, I continued, "There should be gentleness and softness in a personal bathroom. Let me check the measurements of the room, tell me what you require and allow me to put forward my suggestions."

They agreed and I took down the details. Mr Hakim insisted that it had to be marble, not marble trimming. The basins and the shower box were to be scooped out of marble.

Surprised, I asked, "Solid marble?"

Mr Hakim seemed bewildered at the question. "Yes, of course and it must be a beautiful colour. I want everything to be very, very beautiful."

"I'll do my best," and I smiled to show confidence, but with amusement.

Frank and I discussed the project briefly as he helped me into my car. "Tell me, Frank, is it possible to make a bath that large?"

"With money you can do anything. I knew you'd have good ideas. Here, I have made a plan of the room, so that will save you time. Call me if you need any information. I've indicated the size of the bath, in which he wants an L-shaped seat. It's a sort of communal bath. It seems they actually entertain in the bathroom, so bear that in mind."

I smiled as I took the plans, saying, "To tell you the truth, it's mind boggling, but I like the sound of it. You were right, this is a challenge and there'll be a lot of problems. I can't wait to get started."

I anticipated a sleepless night. Ideas were whizzing through my head; this was going to be exciting.

Though at first sight the room seemed to be quite large, the list of requisites was equally large. It was going to be a struggle. I went through the list and picked out the priorities. The bath was going to take up a large proportion of the room and coupled with that, was the thought that it had to be graceful and elegant.

I drew a curved line across the room and then added another. These steps would form the raised split level for the bath area. Picturing the sunken bath in soft carpet, I decided that the walk-in shower should be on the same level. By curving the platform to accommodate the shower cubicle, it worked perfectly, continuing the wall line on the lower level to the enclosed toilet and bidet; the double basins would be on the opposite wall. It formed the perfect balance with the Georgian window between.

Now I could consider finer details as I resorted to an artist's impression. Drawing the curved steps to form the platform with the bath showing the L-shaped seat set to one side, columns at the four corners with decorative cornice on the ceiling emphasized the square area. On the back wall, I drew a flower trough with plants growing up against an antiqued mirror wall, softly lit by small downlighters in a lowered soffit. In the recess formed by the depth of the shower unit were a display niche and cupboards for towels.

The finished drawing looked good and contrasted with Mr Hakim's sketch. Another meeting was arranged. The suggested design was approved and work was set in motion.

Layout drawings with approximate sizes of the units were drawn up to calculate and determine the weight of the marble. The next important consideration was to assure that the structure was able to support the marble. This was put in the hands of a reputable structural engineer. Before the project could proceed, a lot of preparatory work had to be done. The whole building had to be reinforced from the foundations in the basement up to the first floor to take the weight of the marble, which was estimated at five tons.

Then the work began in earnest. Scale drawings and details for the marble had to be worked out with great precision. The exact design of the bath had to be determined, with concern as to how the bath would be filled. Conventional taps were ruled out as the water would be cold by the time the bath was filled. It was decided to have inlets on four sides. Central heating under the bath was also considered necessary as marble is such a cold material. The three marble sides around the scooped-out shower tray, as well as the hand shower, were detailed with body jets. The two oval basins scooped out of the nine-inch marble vanity unit required special taps and wastes, and various other areas required wall cladding.

Frank went to Carrera, in Italy, with all the finalised details, to make his selection at the quarry and to supervise its execution and transportation. Breche Rose, a clear white marble, with large patches of rose pink and green veining, was the choice of marble. I had visited Carrera the previous year while on holiday in Italy, little thinking at that time that I would be responsible for taking a huge chunk out of the mountain.

Frank kept in touch while I got all the structure prepared. The split level for the bath area had to be ready and plumbing in position, with accuracy in every detail. Secondary areas included the vanity unit and shower; all had to be made ready and waiting. Daily visits were a must. Mr Hakim was always there watching the progress. He took an immense interest in everything that was going on, which was very helpful if there were any problems. He was meticulous and kept the workmen on their toes, not tolerating anything shoddy. He had a poor opinion of English workmen's "sweeping everything under the carpet" attitude. Before any work could be done, he insisted that the whole area below the floorboards had to be vacuumed. The workmen respected and actually liked him. Mrs Hakim did not interfere at all. She was content to let her husband make all the decisions, the only exception being to say what conveniences she would like in the vanity unit.

At last the day came for the marble delivery. First on the scene was an enormous crane. A scaffolding was put around the building and everything was to be hauled through a back window which was taken out in preparation. The road was closed to traffic as the crane lifted and carried each enormous box around and over the tall building and set it by the window opening. All the pieces fitted as they were put in place. Frank had chosen a very good, clear-veined section of marble.

Now all the refinements could be added. The waste for the bath was a big problem in coping with the nine-inch depth of marble and had to be specially made. The problem was doubled when it fell out of the courier's bag as it was being delivered. Every effort to try to find it was made by retracing the route taken; but it had to be made again. Due to the thickness of the marble, a pop-up waste was not possible.

Mr Hakim was not pleased. "Mrs. Leigh, doing this by hand is very inconvenient. It will not do. You'll have to do something about it."

A special tool was made with a long handle to reach down to link with the waste plug and twist it open and closed.

It wasn't perfect, but Mr Hakim accepted the difficulty.

Details of the original artist's impression were refined, adding a cocktail cabinet and fridge next to the display niche, circular shelves to hold drinks revolving over the bath and a television was mounted so it could be viewed from the L-shaped seat.

The lower area was more feminine. Decorative cornice, soft lighting in the lowered soffit above the vanity unit, acid-treated bordered mirrors, panelled walls and double-panelled doors to the concealed toilet and bidet. Ivory silk walls, shot-silk rose curtains and pale-green, deep-pile carpet added delicacy.

It had been a challenge and it *was very, very* beautiful.

As the work neared completion, I was approached by Mrs Hakim. "Could I ask your advice?" she queried.

"Yes, of course," I replied.

"I've bought a series of pictures in auction and I don't know what to do with them," she explained.

"It doesn't sound too serious. Can I see them?" I asked.

She took me into the study and produced the portfolio, saying, "There are a hundred and one paintings."

I took out one or two of the paintings and could see at once that they were wonderfully detailed watercolours of flora.

"I can see that you have a problem," I laughingly remarked, "but there must be a way to overcome it."

My thoughts raced ahead as I stated categorically, "The hundred and one paintings must be kept intact as a series," and added, "I'll find a place for them!"

Mr Hakim had obviously been told of our meeting and approached me with, "Mrs Leigh, thank you for your offer of help for my wife. I would be interested to hear what you have in mind."

"I was impressed with the wonderful collection that your wife bought and feel that they should be shown to advantage. The one thought I had was the hundred and one paintings mounted on the curved wall of the staircase from the ground floor up to the top floor, would be an outstanding feature."

"I like your idea very much, Mrs Leigh." I was stunned as he continued, "In fact I've been impressed with all the ideas you have put forward. Would you consider doing the rest of the house?"

And so it came to be that I was involved in the most fascinating project: designing four floors of a home where detail and quality were the priority. Everything had to be "the best". Details of built-in furniture were hand-carved. The utility room of the top floor nursery was tanked, lest the washing machine leak. Security was planned to the last detail. Everything had to be planned and discussed meticulously. A major difficulty was to always find the balance and agreement between East and West culture.

The firm of contractors carrying out the work were first-rate. Nothing was too much trouble. The retired managing director, in his nineties, came out of retirement to supervise the work. He was a craftsman of the old school and he made sure the work was done to perfection.

Following on from this project, Mr Hakim presented me with the model of a house in Saudi Arabia, to design the interior details. I made drawings and included suggestions of fabrics and colours. I was invited to go there to supervise the work, but I was not interested in pursuing the matter further.

~ *Barry Flees The Nest* ~

The bombshell came out of the blue. "Mom, I'm going to branch out on my own."

I stared at Barry in disbelief and finally managed to ask, "Why? I thought you liked the work and you're so good at it."

"I'm fed up with being Mama's boy. This is your business. You don't need me. People like you and they trust you. I'm just your son."

It was true. I relied on Barry and gave him responsibility, but clients did tend to treat him like an office boy. He'd go on site and they'd ask, "When is your mother coming?"

"You must have given this a lot of thought. What do you plan to do?" I asked.

"I'm going to do the services, electrical and heating installations. There's a shortage of good contractors and there seems to be a lot of work around." He had obviously done his homework.

"I shall miss your help, but I can understand how you feel. Have you spoken to Dad?" I asked.

"Not yet, but I'm sure he'll agree that it's time I did something myself," he replied.

I did regret that the collaboration with Barry was coming to an end. His assistance had been exemplary and would be sorely missed, but I could understand his motivation in setting up on his own and I admired his courage. Good contractors in the services field were at a premium. His expertise would be coveted.

To break his ties with home and avoid being influenced by us, he chose to move into shared accommodation to work things out by himself. He began by tendering for small contracts which involved a lot of heavy physical work.

"Perhaps Eddie would be interested in working for you," I suggested, naming an experienced plumber who had carried out several jobs for me.

Sure enough, Eddie was pleased at the prospect and before long Barry took on a young boy; he now had two people working for him. Recommendations followed and contracts became larger, which involved more and more money for equipment, as he balanced his investment with the anticipated return from the contract. He acquired business premises and equipment and took pride in purchasing a truck. Lally and I went with when he bought his truck, so he could drive it home.

He was like a child with a new toy as he explained, "This will be so useful – the tail lift is a motorized rear platform for loading large, heavy items."

It was during this period that he found a soulmate and brought her round to meet us, announcing, "This is Kathleen."

She was obviously of his ilk. He was proud of the fact that she was highly intellectual and spoke several languages, which included Chinese. She also delved into other cultures in which they shared an interest: the occult, astrology and various cults.

Among the cults was one based on following the tradition of ancient Japan in Zen Buddhist monasteries. Zen involved balancing Yin and Yang, the foundation based on a macrobiotic diet as a way of life.

This was the cult they chose to follow. Barry gave me a cookery book and I became versed with the Yin and Yang, but it had to be kept separate as it was contrary to our normal western style of eating. It was literally impossible to keep to the diet and have a meal in a restaurant.

I liked Kathleen despite the fact that she was odd. She was a frequent and welcome visitor to our home and usually came with Barry. By the same token, Barry accompanied Kathy to Newcastle when she visited her music-teacher mother. He formed a bond with her father, an eminent angler, whose books and fly-fishing hooks were considered the best in the country, especially by the Queen Mother and Prince Charles.

Kathy was certainly mixed up, but to give her credit, she was trying to sort herself out. She blamed part of her problems on her name and insisted that she wanted to be known by her middle name. I was into making jewellery at the time, so I made a silver bangle for her with HILARY formed in silver letters. I don't know if it did any good for her morale.

Their liaison lasted over quite a long period, so I was shocked when Barry told me that Kathy had been lured into ta Japanese Budhist sect and was now dedicated to their chanting.

By this time Barry was well-established, having progressed from small domestic work to larger developments. He felt he had "arrived" when he succeeded in taking on and completing a large housing development for a property developer. Unfortunately, misfortune struck when the ruthless developer delayed payment for work carried out and materials provided for the development and fled to another country. Barry lost everything he had worked so hard to build up. He had been too honest and conscientious. Nothing could be salvaged. Barry was so sad to part with his truck; it languished in a side street until Lally took it to the factory and sold it. It was the last thing to go.

Friends, to this day, sing his praises. Their problematical heating systems that could not be rectified by countless servicemen, were put right by Barry in one short examination.

Now Barry had another useless qualification. Disillusioned, Barry drifted, not knowing which way to turn.

"Continue with accountancy," was Lally's sound advice.

As a teenager, Barry had been articled to a reputable London firm of accountants who were sorry to lose him, so we were overjoyed when he finally agreed to return to accountancy. He sailed through with flying colours and became a Chartered Accountant.

He was articled to a large London firm with clients all over the country and found himself being sent away to do audits He enjoyed the variety of clients and staying in good hotel accommodation for weeks on end. He was meeting interesting people and exploring the countryside, which stimulated his curiosity. It was a new phase, with status and free of financial worry.

It was no secret that I was prejudiced and held strong views on girls having children out of wedlock, so when Barry moved in with Suzie, it came as a surprise to learn that she was an unmarried mother. I steeled myself for the meeting and despite my bigoted opinion, found myself liking her warm and friendly personality. She was attractive and her reserved manner lessened some of my hostility which vanished as I was captivated by handsome and confident four-year-old Alex

Suzie, for all her show of independence, was really one of the "flower people" without a grain of malice in her being. Alex was a product of her love and echoed her gentleness.

The union was beneficial for all of them; Suzie needed someone who cared for her, and Barry had the capacity to give her the love, devotion and guidance she needed. Alex now had a father figure who not only disciplined him, but took an interest in his development. He brought order into their lives with love. His taking on the master role gave them the opportunity and encouragement to develop in a stable atmosphere, develop a routine with stability.

The prestigious house in the heart of Hampstead was neglected, but Suzie seemed unaware of how dilapidated it was.

Taking Barry to one side, I suggested, "All it really needs is a coat of paint to smarten it up, except for the kitchen. I don't know how she manages to cook in it."

Barry laughed. "She doesn't. Most things are takeaway."

"I'm not surprised," I replied and continued, "It wouldn't take much to bring it up-to-date."

Barry looked surprised and answered, "Probably not."

"Why not have a word with Suzie about it?"

Suzie was overwhelmed. "What a wonderful idea. Barry says we can all join in doing it. It will be fun."

Barry came with and we chose kitchen units to go across one wall, which included a sink, cooker and fridge, with wall cupboards above, together with gallons of paint.

As we made our way back, I told him, "This is a present from Daddy and me. The installation and decoration is up to you."

The house was turned into a home by the improvements. Additionally, the downstairs loo was rescued from being used as a cycle shed and renovated.

Suzie was gushing in her gratitude. "I can't thank you enough for being so kind."

I felt that I was the one to be grateful. Barry had never been so happy. He had found his niche, his home and ready-made family.

The refurbishment did have an effect on Suzie. She kept the house spic and span. And even excelled in the culinary art of having a meal ready every evening for her two men.

There was one serious period when Alex was mixed up with a group of boys who were involved with gambling in a local shop; the under-aged boys were not discouraged. Barry made sure that the management were taken to task. The shop was closed down and Alex didn't fall into a trap like that again.

When Barry was a child, my father singled him out from all his grandchildren as a companion. Papa instilled in Barry the love of knowledge, to include the universe and nature as well as books. I could see in Barry the image of Papa as he imparted his knowledge to Alex, coached him and encouraged him with his studies. It paid off when Alex won a scholarship to Mill Hill Public

School. No father could be more proud of his son. Alex recognised the relationship and requested that the school listed Barry as his father for any problems while he was at the school. He did well at school, through to his A-levels, when Barry presented him with a car for his achievement.

Unfortunately, Suzie eventually reverted back to her old ways; her addiction to alcohol escalated. Barry's attempt to help her fell on deaf ears.

The time had come for Barry to move on; he decided on a spacious basement flat in Hampstead, but he still continued to care for them and their welfare.

~ *Marcia Ties the Knot* ~

There were many would-be suitors vying for Marcia's hand but none that she took seriously. John was a good friend, destined to be a musician; her introduction into the entertainment world meant late nights spent listening to arrangements and consorting with professionals from overseas. True, not many had a dedicated song in the hit parade, an embarrassment that wasn't a great success. Paul no doubt became a college professor; he was eccentric in the extreme, bringing exotic gifts and an introduction into Oxford society. Keith was held in high regard, but he lost favour when he failed to visit her in hospital when she had her appendectomy. Tom is remembered for his persistence.

The serious contenders came into being on the occasion of Gillian's wedding. Marcia was seated between two eligible bachelors: Robert, and Russell. Each time Russell turned to ask her to dance, Robert was leading her on to the floor, but before the evening was over he had secured her phone number. Robert had already dated Marcia when Russell phoned and he had to settle for second choice. However, a single red rose arrived with a note stating that he was thinking about her. A bunch of roses arrived on the next date thwarted in Robert's favour.

Russell had planned a special treat for Marcia's birthday, so he was taken aback to discover that Robert had arranged to take her out.

Marcia's "terribly sorry" was not at all comforting.

To her astonishment, twenty-four red roses arrived by special delivery, one for each of her years, to wish her "Happy Birthday". All the girls, laughing, helped in looking for containers, jars, milk bottles, anything they could find. The flat was in a state of confusion when Robert's arrival with yet another rose made everyone burst out laughing, much to his embarrassment; the chagrin continued during the evening when Marcia kept apologizing for calling him Russell.

Marcia was exhausted as both boys battled for her hand. She knew Robert was serious when he proposed introducing her to his parents. I received a cry for help. "Mummy, what shall I do ? I can't go on like this."

"You'll have to choose," was my advice.

"I like them both," she said.

"Never mind about the flowers. Which one do you find yourself thinking about more? There's usually some special attraction," I suggested, and added, "Which of them would you want to spend the rest of your life with?"

"I think it's Russell," she whispered.

"That's your answer," I said, adding, "You realize that he may just be having a fling if his reputation is anything to go by. But that's a chance you'll have to take."

I began to doubt my advice when Helen, my sister-in-law, seemed to take issue regarding Russell's reliability. I found it disconcerting that on the one hand she had seated Marcia next to Russell at Gillian's wedding and was now criticizing him. But the die was cast! There was nothing I could do but let the situation take its course.

The courtship progressed as their romance continued. A month or so passed when Marcia phoned and excitedly spoke to Lally. "Daddy, I have wonderful news for you."

"You have a ring," he suggested.

"Better than that. Russell's bought me a horse!" she said.

Russell was anything but conventional. The time had arrived for Marcia to be introduced to Russell's parents. Great thought was given to what she would wear and I offered to take her to my hairdresser to trim her normally unruly mop of hair. I dropped her off while I attended to one of my current projects and returned to find her sitting on the pavement of the West End Mews, crying her eyes out.

"You've ruined my life!" she cried.

They didn't reject her, despite the hairstyle.

Next came the formality of Russell asking for her hand in marriage. Russell came to dinner, after which we'd arranged for Lally and Russell to go into the lounge, giving Russell the opportunity to state his case. Sadly, we didn't brief Barry, who followed them in. The ritual had to be repeated the following week.

More formality followed as we were invited to meet Russell's parents to discuss wedding arrangements. Russell and Marcia wanted a small private wedding. Russell's parents were in agreement. Lally felt that wasn't enough and said so. Victor's warning was that if he had to provide a list there would be at least a thousand people. At last we agreed to have a family lunch. They had no objection to our having open house in the evening for our friends. They left the date up to us.

Russell had a preference for the rabbi he wanted to officiate. He was offered two alternatives: in two weeks' time or in six months, when the rabbi returned from Australia. Russell phoned me and asked if I could do it with just two weeks' notice. I said I'd let him know.

Many years earlier, I had given Mrs Smith, who was now a reputable caterer, her start in catering, by having her assist me in catering Barry's bar mitzvah. She had repeatedly expressed a wish to do Marcia's wedding and of course, the answer was yes. I phoned Russell and said okay. Three days later I was told it would have to be catered under the Beth Din as the Haham Rabbi Gaon and his wife were coming to lunch. There were now only ten days left. Another friend, Jack Anthony, who was in catering, came to our assistance by putting us in touch with a suitable caterer who was able to do it.

I lost no time in phoning Helen to let her know that Marcia and Russell were getting married and that the sceptical opinion she had of Russell's intentions had been unfounded. Helen was surprised, but no more than I, when she added, "I still don't think it will last."

Cecil printed invitations advising friends of the impending wedding and inviting them to "open house" in the evening, but we were asked not to send them for fear of offending those omitted. Phone calls had to suffice. Additionally, friends not invited to the lunch were asked not to come to the ceremony, as others thinking they were invited could be offended.

The two weeks were indeed a challenge. During the first weekend Marcia was thrown from her horse. She wasn't badly hurt, but Russell insisted that she should recuperate in Norfolk. So she wasn't available for several days. In the meantime I sorted out my wedding gown and arranged for a couturier in Mayfair to attend to it. It was cleaned and ready for Marcia's fitting when she returned to London. They suggested making a Juliet cap to hold the Posnansky family lace veil loaned by Russell's grandmother.

In the meantime, I'd managed to put together a reasonable trousseau, but felt it was lacking something special. By chance, I caught sight of an evening gown displayed in a shop window which I thought was just right, and managed to persuade the proprietor to let me have it on approval. It looked stunning on Marcia and it proved to be a winner.

Time was running short when Marcia had a recurring problem with her eyes. She was adamant that she would not wear spectacles:

"I'm not walking down the aisle wearing glasses!"

Mr Mackie treated her every day and on the last day managed to get her eyes conditioned to wearing contact lenses.

There were a few hiccups. The veteran Rolls Royce arrived and Lally left with Marcia and her bridesmaid, Rhoda, forgetting that Barry and I were going to follow the car as we didn't know where the synagogue in Holland Park was. The caterers had arrived and our Japanese au pair was left to help. When we arrived back for lunch the caterers told us that she packed her bags and left soon after us, offended at not being invited. Additionally, the highly recommended photographer arrived drunk; a meagre selection of inferior photographs were submitted, few of a reasonable standard. Certainly not enough to fill an album.

The caterers had worked magic and our home had been transformed into an elegant banqueting hall: in the dining room the U-shaped Top Table was garlanded with flowers and enhanced by the softly lit decorative niche, with the windows either side giving an additional glow to the turquoise walls.

The curved table symbolically linked the families, with Russell and Marcia in the centre. Mishcons were seated to the left, Victor and "B" as she liked to be called, and next to them, the Haham Rabbi Gaon and his wife. Leighs were seated on the right: Lally and me, with Rabbi Michael Leigh and his wife, Sonia. It was apt to have Michael next to me; many years ago I collaborated with Michael in illustrating his book, *Jewish Observance In The Home*. The Haham took the service and Michael, who held the Haham in high esteem, was overwhelmed to be given the honour of partaking with him.

There was no formality at the lunch as family members took their seats at the round tables situated in the lounge and hall.

There wasn't room to accommodate younger members of the family for the lunch, which was just as well, as the cousins were pleased with just being invited to the party in the evening.

The wedding party or open house, call it what you will, was sensational! Everyone who was invited and those who heard about it from friends, came to celebrate the union. All our musician friends brought their instruments which had the whole place rocking. The caterers surpassed themselves; they heeded my request for it to be fabulous and they went to great lengths to make a spectacular display by providing a buffet the entire evening set up in the dining room. Though Russell and Marcia said they wouldn't be staying, they changed their minds and joined in the party, remaining nearly the whole evening. It was a wonderful day!

Marcia became Mrs Russell Mishcon on 6th November, 1976.

It is regrettable that this happy family union was to undergo a change from this day on; Helen broke up the family for reasons unknown, unexplained and unrelenting; her daughters Cheryl and Gillian were compelled to sever relations with Marcia, Russell and Barry and eliminate them from family functions, or she wouldn't attend. No amount of apologies would suffice. I've no doubt that I would have been included if she could have broken the strong bond my brother has with me, but she couldn't break that; I cherish the bond we share and love my brother dearly.

~ *Move to Hampstead* ~

"I'm going to look at houses in Hampstead. When I find something suitable we can put this house on the market."

"Over my dead body!" Lally's reply took me by surprise. Lally hated change.

"So be it!" I quipped, "but that's not what I had in mind. Anyway, I am going to look. We don't need a big house anymore."

At that point Lally's car arrived to take him to the factory, putting an end to the conversation. My enthusiasm began to wane as I got ready; it wasn't going to be easy to convince Lally that another house would be more suitable than our home.

A call on the phone had Lally asking, "Are you still going?"

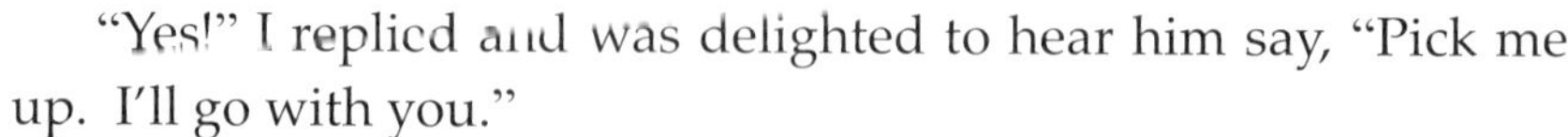

"Yes!" I replied and was delighted to hear him say, "Pick me up. I'll go with you."

I had with me the list I had received that morning from the estate agent and headed for the house in Church Row. The odd house protruded over the pavement and though it may have been very nice inside, it did not appeal to either of us.

The next house was listed as an "1830 Cottage in need of modernization". We pulled up into the entrance of a recently modernised townhouse development and gazed at the shoddy building.

My first comment was, "If you buy a house in bad condition you can do it up to suit yourself. Shall we try to see inside?" I asked.

"All right," he replied.

Lally waited in the car as I walked up the road to the estate agent. He phoned through to the occupants who told him, "If they come right away."

The girl who let us in was Miss Sweden and she brightened the interior, the condition of which was worse than the exterior. It was obvious that the developers had anticipated demolishing the cottage, but a conservation order resulted with them patching up what they had destroyed. We viewed the house without saying a word, each of us just absorbing what we saw.

Back in the car I remarked, "It has all the potential to make it a wonderful home."

To which Lally replied, "Yes, I agree, I could live there."

Leaving the car where it was, we walked up to the estate agents. Lally put forward his offer on the house and was told that it would be accepted.

We drove home and as we neared Canons Drive, Lally said, "Drop me off at the bottom of the road; I'll ask the estate agent to call up."

The next day the estate agent came to assess the house and our home was put on the market.

The following day was a Saturday; I was involved with a design project which dragged on until mid-afternoon. I could see that Lally was excited as I walked in and I asked, "Is anything the matter?"

"I've had such a busy time. Several people have been here viewing the property. I think I've sold the house!"

I looked at Lally in amazement, absorbing the news; and we both burst out laughing.

A search about the cottage revealed that it was Two Prince Arthur Mews. Number One was the derelict piece of land on the corner at the entrance to the mews with planning permission for a three-storey house. If that house was built it would blight the cottage. Lally negotiated the purchase of the plot, which we converted into a garden. As each plot had been allocated parking space, we had the advantage of parking for two cars.

Major constructional work had to be done before we could contemplate moving; this was carried out by a reputable firm of builders. A porch, incorporating old doors found searching through Architectural Salvage, was built in front of the enlarged entrance opening; double-casement doors replaced the window to give more light. We were told that the cottage had been used as a laundry for the mews, which were previously stables, which explained the reason for the enormous fireplace and chimney which had to be removed, including the fireplace on the upper floor and chimney to the roof. The two medium-sized bedrooms on the middle floor were made into one with a doorway opening into the enlarged bathroom. Much of the interior was gutted; replacements would be carried out by specialist contractors.

The top floor was made habitable to serve as a refuge while renovation of the cottage was being carried out. Shelves, a plan chest and storage trays for art materials would be my studio and give me adequate working facilities; a new bathroom en-suite, with built-in cupboards, with the bedroom featuring the black-and-white wall-hung units rescued from Oxford, would contribute to our basic comforts. All that needed to be added was our bed and a few personal items to tide us over.

The best laid plans can go awry, none more so than our disastrous move, delayed for three weeks due to the flare-up of Lally's back problem, with the doctor's decision that he couldn't be moved.

Pickfords were chosen for the complicated removal which involved four destinations: the Cottage, Barry's flat in Hampstead Garden Suburb, Marcia's house in Bedford Park and the storage depository for the remaining furniture.

It was obvious that the estimator did not do a preliminary check about the area, or he would have been aware of the difficulty of access to the mews and arranged for the one-way street to be temporarily closed to traffic. As it was, after delivering the few articles to the top floor, the removal van was unable to exit from the mews; the huge vehicle was restricted by the large bollard from manoeuvring out of the turning. In the end he had no alternative but to force his way, ripping through the entire side of the van. (The offending bollard has since been moved.)

The next stop, in pouring rain, was to Barry's third-floor flat. They delivered the dining room suite, large lounge settees and two beds. By this time the wheels of the van were stuck in the mud of the grass verge and had to be dug out.

On arrival at Marcia's in West London, they discovered that they had neglected to bring the shoe to move the piano. The removal van had to be kept in their warehouse overnight. The storms caused flooding, which made road conditions difficult the next day, but the delivery was made. The remaining contents were put into storage.

The delayed move brought us up to Christmas. Nothing would be happening until the festive season was over. We booked to spend Christmas at Selsdon Park. Christmas Eve, as we were getting ready to leave, Lally's back problem struck again.

I called the doctor who came straight over; after a thorough examination, he announced, "You'll just have to rest up again."

"We've booked to go to Selsdon Park for Christmas," I explained.

"I can book an ambulance to take him there," he offered.

But Lally was adamant. "I'm not going away in an ambulance to spend Christmas in an hotel bedroom."

Marcia and Russell had gone to spend Christmas in Norfolk, but I managed to catch Barry as he was about to leave for Newcastle. He came over to see if he could help. We cleared the room and Barry set up the television set. He couldn't get a picture.

"I'll bring mine over. In the meantime I suggest you do something about getting some food and some way of heating it up," he advised.

There was a hire shop in Heath Street. They offered a dilapidated cooker and fridge on a three-month contract and delivered it.

It was difficult to find shops open who had any fresh food left. I had to beg the butcher to let me have something, grateful for his kindness.

I came back to find Barry struggling with his television. In the end the two televisions were set in unison: one with the picture, the other underneath for the sound.

And so Christmas was spent on the top floor with little other than a bed, a defunct television and dodgy cooking facilities. Strangely, we look back at that incredible Christmas with affection.

Work in the house began with the rising damp reported by the surveyor. Countless holes were drilled in the walls, with countless readings, but in the end they conceded that the damp was not rising but coming down. Investigation revealed that the problem had been caused by Miss Sweden who regularly showered down the bathroom floor in keeping with the custom of her country. The walls were stripped, plastered and left to set overnight, but the plaster gradually slid downwards, settling in a heap on the floor. Removing the dry plaster created dust which pervaded the whole place for ages. The exercise was successfully repeated. Installations followed to renew the electrical and plumbing systems.

It didn't take us long to realize that there were periods when living on the top floor was unacceptable and we booked into the Hendon Hall Hotel. We had a weekly arrangement; occasionally they would ask if we could vacate the room as they were regularly booked up at the weekends. It suited us as well as we appreciated the change

It was essential to have a carpenter on site and I had the good fortune to engage two capable brothers. The "old boys" were set in their ways; no matter what, at 9.00 a.m. to 9.30, they made coffee on their primus stove. Lunch was timed to the minute and a delivery on site would have to wait until "time was up", but their work was good and they were reliable.

I have only praise for the support given by specialist contractors for taking up the challenge of restoring character into the cottage. Terry Bedford's joinery shop catered for jobbing carpenters. He welcomed the challenge and diversion of doing something special; he ably executed detailed architraves, panelled doors, brass-trimmed radiator covers and bookshelves. He produced special skirtings to curve with the line of the staircase. A slim hardwood moulding made for the wardrobe doors carried my name when added to the company samples. Fitments in the marble bathroom were made with the same details.

Ron Butcher had worked with me on the Beefeater; he provided cornices throughout the cottage and as a special favour he allowed me to use a design in the bedroom which was withdrawn from the range because of its complexity. I understood why when the work dragged on and on, and told Ron, "He'll be due for his pension by the time he's finished."

Boxed-out cornice above the windows hid the curtain rails; a lowered soffit to form a coronet over the bed with inset downlighters became a popular feature with all my clients.

The marble bathroom displayed everything that one would covet; panelled walls, antique brass taps, mirrors, lowered soffits over the bath and vanity unit, varied lighting; inset cabinets and wall-hung fitments.

The staircase had to be renewed; Lewis were the best in the trade and they sent Tom and Jerry to carry out the work. Their work was exceptional; the graceful polished handrail skimmed by the wall, weaving in over the gracefully turned balusters and then out again in line with the wall, to finish with a flourish in a wreath over the circlet of balusters on the curved bottom step.

Decorating was put in the hands of Jim Baldwin, the doyen of decorators. Our association dated back to the early years; his advice had stood me in good stead. The decoration was the same throughout; with neutral tones of fabric, walls, ceilings and skirtings; when they were added, curtains and carpets contributed to the background. The simplicity gave elegance and emphasized the quality and detail. Doors and built-in furniture were French polished, except for the bathroom.

I chose Poggenpohl rosewood units for the galley kitchen, which blended well with the mahogany polished wood. Surprisingly, the tiny kitchen was able to accommodate all the appliances; with the bonus of their hideaway table and fold-away chairs, it converted into a live-in kitchen.

Finally, the plot of land came in for attention. I recalled seeing railings in keeping with the period of the cottage at Architectural Salvage. A search resulted in buying a large bundle and also acquiring the front of an old conservatory. I drew up plans for the wall and what can only be called a garden shed and put the work in the hands of an able landscape gardener. The result was magic! The addition of window boxes and railings, with a Portman stone terrace, all added up to the creation of a desirable 1830 residence in the heart of Hampstead Village.

July 17th heralded the arrival of Joel, our first grandchild! We had been patiently anticipating the day, with preparation for the nursery, searching for and finding an antique cradle and nursing chair, then frantically stitching muslin frills and covers to have the antique cradle ready.

Visits to Bedford Park became the norm, with long journeys each way added onto Lally's journey from Borehamwood, the Hendon Hall hotel and the cottage.

"Why don't you stay here?" Marcia asked. " We have an empty flat on the top floor. You'd be more comfortable and I'd feel happy to have you around."

It didn't take much to persuade us to move in. It added a lot of travel time into our day, but it was well worth it.

~ *Eilat and the Consequences* ~

The flight on El Al had been amusing. Lally had no chance to concentrate on his panic because the woman passenger next to him on the plane kept him from thinking about himself or, for that matter, about the trip. We had been allocated aisle seats. The couple were seated to Lally's left, the husband by the window and his wife between the two men.

We had not been long in flight when the lady sitting next to Lally began rummaging through her handbag. She took out a few items and placed them in a plastic bag. Then, standing up, she reached for her hand luggage on the overhead shelf. Lally, watching her struggle, offered to help, taking down the small case. She smiled with a grateful "thank you" and balancing the case on her knees, attempted to open it, only to discover it was locked. Reaching down into her handbag at the side of her feet, she located her leather key-case. It took a little time to sort out the relevant key, unlock the case and put the plastic bag inside, at the same time taking out items from that case. She locked the case and with apologies to Lally, began to reach up to replace it on to the overhead shelf. Gallant as he is, Lally took the case from her struggling hands and put it back. For a while she sat rigidly twisting her fingers and after an interval, she reached for the second case. She spent the entire journey moving the contents of one case into another, with the problem of unlocking, locking and either putting a case up or taking it down. If Lally didn't get up to help, he suffered the pressure of her bum in his face as she stood on the seat. Every so often he'd look across the aisle and smile at me, obviously sympathetic to this poor woman's nervousness.

As we disembarked at Eilat, her husband apologised to Lally for his wife's behaviour. It apparently was her normal way to cope with flying.

The courier from the travel agency greeted us at the airport and led us to the waiting hotel car. The hotel, La Rhome, five miles out of Eilat, had appealed to us the previous year when we visited friends who were staying there. We eagerly looked around as the car sped along the sea road. The hotel was perched on a hill and looked welcoming as we were driven up to the front entrance.

We were delighted with the ground-floor room we had requested, just a stone's throw away from the pool. It didn't take long to unpack. We donned swimsuits and made our way to the pool. This was heaven. Umbrella-sheltered beds and long, cool drinks. We relaxed, breathing in the sea air and soaking up the beauty of the surroundings. The glistening pool was very inviting and pretty soon Lally roused himself and announced that he was going in. I told him I'd soon join him and watched as he felt the water with his toe and slowly let himself down into the water. He waved and beckoned me to join him, calling out, "Come in, the water's great."

I waved back and replied, "Coming!"

I can swim, but I'm not crazy about it. I hate getting my head wet, especially my ears and so I never really relax in the water. Eilat is the exception. It's the only place that draws me into a pool. I looked around and could see that Lally was standing on the opposite side. I plucked up my courage and swam across. It was lovely, refreshingly cool and not too crowded.

I reached Lally who was standing holding on to the side hand-rail and asked, "Are you all right?"

"I'm a bit tired. I'm going out," he replied.

"Fine. We can go out there." I indicated the steps about six feet away and we began easing our way along the edge of the pool. There was no hurry and as we slowly made our way, I casually looked around scanning the faces around the pool on the chance that I might see a familiar one; although October is not a popular month for holidays, it is good weather-wise in Eilat.

I turned back to Lally. He had his head in the water and it made me smile. He always ducked his head under water to rinse off in the bath and here he was doing the same to cool off. Suddenly I felt something was wrong and realized that he was under too long. I pulled his head out and looked into an absolutely blank face with wide-open, staring, glazed eyes.

With horror I shouted out, "HELP! HELP!"

People were all around, laughing, talking, but no one paid any attention.

"FOR GOD'S SAKE, WON'T SOMEBODY PLEASE HELP ME?" I shouted, hysterically.

Help did come. They pulled Lally out and laid him at the side of the pool.

Two French doctors appeared. They examined him and agreed, "No pulse."

They began as a team giving him resuscitation, one pressing on his chest with two hands, down, up, down, up, down, up and the other giving the kiss of life. They changed places and began again, down, up, down, up, down, up.

I was still in the water, numb with fear, watching from the edge of the pool. A crowd had gathered around, necks craning to see what was going on. Two people helped me out of the water.

I implored the doctors to do something more. "He has heart trouble. Is there not something you can do?"

"There's no pulse," one answered.

There was a noise at the back of the crowd as someone shouted, "What's going on?" The young Israeli boy who had shown us to our beds pushed his way through the crowd. He knelt down. "What happened?" he asked.

"There's no pulse," stated one doctor.

The boy put his ear to my husband's chest. He looked up, his large dark eyes filled with surprise. "No pulse," he said.

I was speechless. I looked on, my head in a daze, "This can't be happening," I kept telling myself.

Suddenly the boy raised his arm and brought his fist down firmly on Lally's chest. "You'll break a rib," one of the doctors called out.

The boy stared at the doctor, his large dark eyes opened wide in amazement. "Better a broken rib than a dead man," was his curt reply. His arm came down again with a resounding blow.

Suddenly, "COUGH . . .COUGH . . .SPLUTTER . . .SPLUTTER. HE HAD STARTED UP LALLY'S HEART!

They rolled him over and he coughed up the water he'd swallowed. He opened his eyes and looked around, surprised to see all the faces looking down at him. He turned around, attempting to sit up, wondering what it was all about. Shaking with fear and shock, all I could do was muster a wan smile.

Someone told me to get dressed. They'd phoned for an ambulance which would be there any minute. I ran to my room flinging off my swimsuit and putting on the first thing that came to hand, running out doing up buttons as I went. The ambulance had just arrived as I got back and they were putting Lally on a stretcher. I held his hand as they carried him to the ambulance.

I could see the printing on the side, MDA, Magen David Adom. My heart swelled with joy. We were active fund-raisers for MDA. It had never occurred to me that we would personally benefit from the work we did for the committee.

One ambulance man was administering medical aid while the other drove. We had gone about half-way when he called to the driver:

"Alert intensive care to be ready and speed up. He's fading."

I felt the spurt forward as he turned on the whine of the siren, the two-note droning sound steeling every sinew in my body. Five miles seemed to take an eternity. They had to drive through traffic to reach the hospital on the far side of the town. One has to admire the ambulance men who have to manoeuvre through small streets with unaware car drivers. The five miles seemed endless, but at last we reached the gates of the hospital, a rambling, one-storey structure.

"Is this it?" I asked, taking in the primitive surroundings.

"Don't worry," the young medic assured me in his Israeli English, "it's good! It's very well equipped, especially for emergencies."

We pulled up to the emergency entrance where two white-clothed men were waiting with a trolley. In no time at all they'd moved Lally on to it and were running through the corridor – crowded with people lying on beds either side – to the intensive care unit. I waited outside while they wired him up to all the monitors. After a while the doctor came out to tell me he would be all right and I was allowed to go in to see him. They gave me a bed so that I could stay with him although the hospital was filled to capacity.

My day took on a regular routine. I slept at the hospital; in the morning I returned to the hotel to shower, change and have breakfast. I'd collect a picnic lunch and take a taxi back to the hospital and spent the day at Lally's bedside.

I digress here to mention my hobby involving eight silver asparagus eaters that required hours of filing; I brought them on holiday to keep me occupied while sitting around and found them to be a blessing in disguise.

I'd have dinner at the hotel and then return to the hospital for the night. Nights were harrowing, as the machine frequently recorded danger, but the nurse would readjust it saying that it was always playing up.

Over two weeks were spent in intensive care. I cannot praise the staff of the hospital enough. Their care and consideration were faultless. The same applies to the hotel staff who were concerned and understanding.

The last five days found us back at the hotel. They changed our room to one closer to the dining room and swimming pool. A special lilo which received a refreshing breeze from the sea was reserved for Lally. On our last day they set up a table near us.

"What is the table for?" Lally asked.

"It's to celebrate your birthday," was the reply.

"But my birthday is in May," said Lally.

"Mr Leigh, you've just had your birthday!"

Everyone drank his health in champagne or whatever.

With hindsight I can only say that if this had to happen on holiday, I was happy that it happened in Israel. I cannot express my gratitude for the warmth, love and consideration given to us. Shalom.

Lally was not well when we returned from our holiday. He could barely walk and we immediately attended a consultant. Tests at the Harley Street Clinic showed that he needed surgery.

"All right, but I want a ground floor room here," replied Lally.

"There isn't one available here," said Mr Parker.

"I'll wait," said Lally.

"I won't be responsible for you longer than forty-eight hours," warned Mr Parker.

The next day, Lally was operated on with a quadruple bypass at the Princess Grace Hospital.

~ *Shakespeare's Tavern and Playhouse* ~

"Robert! What a surprise!" It was truly a surprise to see Robert Earl on my doorstep. My mind raced ahead wondering what he was doing there. "Come in," I said, opening the door wide, ushering him in. "Tell me why you're here."

It sounds callous, but I suspected an ulterior motive. Robert had a way of buttering someone up when he wanted something. He was made junior manager for the Beefeater in the finishing stages of embellishment, watching intently as I supervised work being carried out, constantly asking "Why" and "How?"

"Are you still with the group?" I asked.

"No," he answered, " I'm setting out on my own. I have someone backing me and the premises. That's why I'm here. I know you're the best person to take it on."

"That's quite a compliment. Tell me about it," I replied.

He began, "I want to turn a disused wine warehouse into a Shakespearian tavern. No one can do it as well as you. Would you be interested?"

"You've aroused my curiosity," I replied. "I'd certainly think about it."

The following day found us within sight of Blackfriars Bridge, parallel to the main road. He pulled up in Blackfriars Lane and waved his arm in the direction of the railway arches.

"These two arches are ours," he said, pointing to them. "I'll show you the one on the right first because it also leads to the lower floor."

Robert struggled with the padlock on the door and we stepped inside. The vast open space with curved ceiling was unmistakably an underground station. "Nice big room, eh?" said Robert.

"Well, there's no mistaking what it was," I replied.

"Wait till you see downstairs!" enthused Robert excitedly, leading the way.

Narrow stone steps at the far wall led to the lower floor. I clung to the wall as we made our way down to a cavernous underworld. It was bleak and cold; I could see that it was large and had been used as a warehouse. Rough brick walls divided the space into areas, some large, some small. The condition was abysmal and perilous, with ramps linking uneven floors. Here and there some wine-racking remained.

Nevertheless, the vast underworld had an air of mystery, with the promise that potential existed in the squalor. Needless to say, the project looked so impossible, that I took on the challenge.

Robert emphasized that work should be done on the lowest possible budget. My thoughts raced ahead with the theory that if one could find suitable items in Architectural Salvage, they would cost a fraction of the price for having new ones made and distressed. That, in the main, was the line I intended to follow.

I was given scale drawings of the building which showed the two arched areas on the ground floor; the floor below stretched beneath both areas with access confined to the narrow stone steps I had to manoeuvre with Robert.

Meetings were held with the contractors to determine the layout. It was agreed that the offices and entertainers would be in the second arch with their costumes stored to the rear. A staircase would give access to the banqueting hall and the kitchens positioned below, at the far end of the banqueting area. Facilities would be required for the staff.

I now concentrated on the format of Shakespeare's Tavern and Playhouse. The Underground Station appearance was a giveaway. No matter what one did, there would be no escaping the fact, unless something radical was done. I reverted to the scale drawing and toyed with drawing a timbered barn. I drew a beam the length of the room through the centre of the curved ceiling; four more beams divided the curve into four sections. This provided the framework to create a beamed roof. Suitable beams were found and the conversion to an Elizabethan room was miraculous.

A substantial staircase to provide access to the lower floor for five hundred guests was the next priority. Listed by Architectural Salvage was a convent near Birmingham, due for demolition. I viewed the premises and took measurements, which presented the perfect answer. A stairwell was constructed to accommodate the impressive oak staircase. It was superb; the size was right and the period suitable.

Architectural Salvage then advised me about a pub in Croydon due to be demolished; it proved to be a godsend. The entrance doors, when adapted, fitted perfectly within the arches of the two entrances. The entire bar and surrounding area was carefully dismantled and re-assembled on the lower floor at the bottom of the palatial staircase; the surrounding walls were clad in the panelling.

Spacious cloakrooms were installed on the lower floor by the staircase. The Men's provided basic necessities while the Powder Room had marble-topped carved wood dressing tables, soft lighting and mirrored walls.

I turned my attention now to the banqueting. It wasn't straightforward, but a pattern evolved in creating theatrical settings, with a painted mural forming a backdrop for the top table and tables either side, accommodating approximately fifty guests; a scroll sign at the entrance would bear the name of the play and relate to the seating plan.

As a last resort, I would have undertaken the task of painting the murals, but I was of the opinion that art students would jump at the opportunity; we were inundated with volunteers.

There were ten areas, namely: 'As You Like It', 'A Midsummer Nights Dream', 'The Comedy of Errors', 'Much Ado About Nothing', 'Hamlet', 'Anthony and Cleopatra', 'The Taming of the Shrew', 'Macbeth', 'The Merchant of Venice' and 'Othello'.

Around this time, Marcia and Russell had a cottage in Norfolk and many of our weekends were spent there. Nearby were two large warehouses with four floors stacked high with second-hand furniture, bric-a-brac and memorabilia.

Architectural Salvage recommended only authentic antiques, whereas many of the items on sale at the warehouses could be just as suitable for our needs. My time was spent measuring and eventually purchasing, vast quantities of church pews. They were sent to Bedfords' joinery shop to be adapted with made-to-measure Elizabethan seating and matching trestle tables.

By now most of the basic work was in hand but I was still looking for something to create an interesting and exciting atmosphere. The walls were bare, but for the embellishment of beams, which did add warmth. By chance, a length of balustrading caught my attention and on closer examination, discovered that it was part of a balcony. In my mind's eye, I envisaged it stretched across the far wall of the Elizabethan barn. Rummaging around, I found two lengths of staircase, sufficient to create an accessible source of entertainment from either end. It was just what was needed, to create added interest during the reception.

But the pièce de résistance was a beautifully carved, decorative pulpit; the fact that it was mobile is what made it so special. It could be moved to anywhere in the reception hall, from which the Master of Ceremonies could address his guests from an elevated height to invite them to take their seats for the evening performance. It was truly a wonderful find!

I did not have carte blanche to purchase at will and so I phoned Robert.

I told him about my find, saying, "I can't place this on order, so will you deal with it?" I asked.

"Fine, leave it to me," he replied, and I turned the phone over to the salesman.

Robert gave instruction for a truckload of chairs, together with the balcony and pulpit, to be delivered COD.

Everything began to fall into place and most of the work was near completion. On the day of delivery, I made a point of being there to make sure that it arrived intact. I was in the office discussing a problem when one of the girls came in and whispered something to Robert. He jumped up, alerted his partner and they both disappeared.

Almost simultaneously, the man from Norfolk walked in; he handed her the statement, asking for his money.

"There's no one here at the moment to pay," he was told.

"But this was ordered cash on delivery; I hired the van specially," he explained.

"I'm sorry, but I can't help you. You can leave it and we'll send the money on to you," he was told.

The man was devastated but in the end he unloaded the goods.

Not until then did I become aware of the problem with payment that the specialist contractors were having. Bedford was threatening to withhold delivery of the tables; Ron was threatening to take away the signs; and Jack said that he would personally go in and smash the marble. I was livid! Robert should have kept me in the picture to let me know that he was in difficulties. As it was, Robert had jeopardized the trust the specialist contractors had in me. Fortunately, they recognized that I, too, was a victim.

In the end, all was settled amicably and we were seated with Robert's parents at the trial evening…which was fantastic!

Shakespeare's Tavern and Playhouse was a huge success and a serious threat to the Beefeater by the Tower. So much so that Joe Lewis negotiated with Robert Earl and Shakespeare's Tavern became part of the Hanover Grand Group. So did Robert Earl.

Shakespeare's Tavern is no more. It made way for a new development scheme in Blackfriars.

I dare to mention my belief that this project was probably influential in Robert's attaining millionaire status, following in the footsteps of Joseph Lewis.

~ *Concerning Marcia* ~

"Mummy, can you spare the time to come and look at a house?" queried Marcia.

"Yes, if you want me to," I replied.

"It's not in London, but Russell thinks it's worth looking at. He's drawn a map, " she added.

The "little way" turned out to be near Windsor, but Russell's map was vague and we drove up and down looking for the turning in Englefield Green, until we were directed to the driveway leading to Sandylands. We had a surprise as we came across several bulls who were roaming freely across the drive.

"I don't like this!" gasped Marcia.

But I could only laugh; it was so preposterous.

Sandylands stood at the end of the drive. We were stunned by the stately manor house. Not very large, but beautiful proportions, just on two floors, with a turreted roof.

"Wow!" was all I could utter in admiration.

A pull of the bell brought an elderly lady, who was obviously waiting, to greet us. We entered into the large entrance hall, doors leading off to the left and straight ahead; there was a passage behind the sturdy, polished-mahogany staircase on the right, which led up to the bedrooms. She imparted interesting history, telling us about the manor house and showing us the charter and various relevant details.

We viewed the house in silence, overwhelmed by the grandeur: spacious rooms, high ceilings, large windows with internal shutters, parquet floors. An original Victorian kitchen and a terrace overlooked spectacular gardens. In addition, a swimming pool, tennis court, stables, paddock and a dower house.

We were both confused as Marcia drove us back to London but eventually I broke the silence saying, "You can't fault that house; it's almost unreal, but it is very isolated. How do you think you would feel about living there?"

"I think Russell was playing a joke on us," she replied.

But Russell was serious and it wasn't long before they moved to Sandylands.

Marcia phoned to say they'd moved in. I had a sudden premonition that something was wrong; I knew why when she said Joel wasn't well.

"Take him to see a doctor," was my immediate response.

"We have, Mummy, we've been to the group practice."

"I don't think that's good enough. He ought to be seen by a paediatrician."

Russell was annoyed, saying, "Tell your mother not to interfere."

I was sufficiently concerned to contact a paediatrician, who was a friend, asking if he would go to see Joel.

"I can't do that, but I have a colleague in Windsor. I'll give you his number."

I called the doctor in Windsor, explained my worry about Joel and asked him if he would go to see my grandson.

He acknowledged my concern, but explained, "I can't ring somebody's doorbell and say 'I've come to examine your son'. Give them my number and I will be on call if they want me."

The fact is that Joel did get worse and they did phone the paediatrician. When the symptoms were explained he quickly responded with, "We won't waste any time; take him to the hospital right away and I'll see him there."

The alerted staff were waiting for Joel who was immediately put on a drip and kept on it for two weeks.

Marcia and Russell soon settled into Sandylands. Their two horses, Glen and Fanny, were brought down from Norfolk and riding in Windsor Great Park became the norm. By the summer, Marcia was expecting another baby. As the date drew near, Lally and I went to Sandylands to look after Joel.

When Marcia went into labour there was panic.

I was taken aback by Russell saying, "Gwen, the horses need to be fed," adding, "All you have to do is take the feed bags down," he pointed to them, "and give one to each of the horses."

I was left there completely stunned. I'm not used to being with horses and usually tend to keep my distance, but this seemed a small request, not really involved with being with horses.

With horror, I discovered on entering the stable that the horses were back to front; and confronting me were two enormous rear-ends ready to kick should I do something wrong. I had to squeeze past to reach the feed bags. How I did it I'll never know.

We did enjoy being with Joel. There were many interesting places to go but he liked going to Windsor Castle most of all. Wearing the Guardsman fancy dress, he delighted in marching back and forth with the Grenadier Guard, stamping his feet and turning about. The guards are not permitted to deviate from their vigil, not smile nor talk. They must have considered him a pest, but we loved it.

Portia arrived on Joel's birthday, making it a joint celebration. Needless to say, she was beautiful, as she is to this day.

Russell was initiated into the world of polo; Russell's name was put forward and he became a member of Guards Polo club. The two enormous horses returned to the hunt in Norfolk, where they belonged and were replaced by polo ponies.

Thereafter, much time was spent at the polo grounds, where they soon made friends. Russell was a natural for the sport and became an avid polo player, eventually captaining his own team, sponsored by Perrier and playing in important matches, sometimes with, or against, Prince Charles, and mixing with the celebrities.

I was pleased to get back to London and start on an interesting project. The Chatwani brothers had purchased their first hotel. They had been impressed by the project I had done in Holland Park and offered and assigned to me the updating and upgrading of the Bedford Corner Hotel, by Bedford Square.

I was taken aback when Marcia sensibly remarked, "Mummy, you're going to miss out so much of Joel's growing up. It's a pity you don't see much of him."

She was right. We arranged that Joel would spend one day a week with me. At seven in the morning Russell brought Joel to London and collected him either at four o'clock or at seven, to miss the rush hour.

It was a good arrangement. We planned different things; Brent Cross was one attraction as it had a splendid play area, with a giant wooden horse and crawl-through caterpillar. We then joined a play group in Hampstead Community Centre where they could make things, play games and mix with other children. It prepared him to go to school.

Portia followed in his footsteps and did the same, but not for as long, as she was able to go to the play group in the same school as Joel.

I returned home to be greeted by Lally, his face thunderous.

"What's the matter?" I asked.

"Dr Groves, from the Royal Free Hospital, phoned!" was his terse reply.

"Oh yes, what did he want?" I asked.

"He wants to know why you haven't been back. He told me you have a tumour and are not doing anything about it," said Lally, angrily.

"He only suspected it," I said.

"So why haven't you checked it out?" Lally asked.

"I had X-rays and a brain scan before going to Israel," I explained. "After that other things had priority."

I thought back to that appointment. I had driven myself to the Imaging Centre in Harley Street, expecting to have a simple X-ray, not realizing that I should have arranged for someone to drive me home. The furore in Israel put the matter right out of my head.

Mr Groves was more like a friend than a consultant. He sensed my indifference and went to great pains to explain the necessity to follow it through. For a second opinion, he sent me to the surgeon he had trained under, who corroborated his suspicion. Another scan was necessary to ascertain the exact size and position of what appeared to be a tumour in my middle ear. I had it done at the London Hospital.

Marcia was the first to notice that something was wrong and alerted the sister to check her suspicion. Though she noted that my condition was worsening, the alarm was not raised until well into the night, when the doctor was called. There was panic as a crew arrived and put me on a stretcher, then hurriedly carried me downstairs where I was transferred to a trolley and bundled up with blankets; they opened the heavy front doors and lowered me down into the clammy, clinging darkness that enveloped me like a shroud. Then they ran by the side, pushing the trolley to the black building, barely visible in the eerie light of the main hospital.

The entire team were standing by. I was now wide-awake and aware of what was happening as I was put into the tunnel to reduce the pressure on my brain. A nurse told me to keep very still in the tunnel but it was an unnecessary warning; I couldn't move.

From the X-ray department I was moved to an intensive care ward. I can't remember anything else until I awoke to find a nurse sitting by my bed monitoring various tubes attached to me. I sensed that something was radically wrong. I didn't realize until later that I was unable to move or speak. I was totally dependant on the nurse sitting by my side to deal with all my physical needs. That does not convey the whole picture; it encompasses being totally incapable, the inability to feed oneself; having to depend on someone to brush your teeth or give you a drink of water. Add losing the ability to communicate and the trauma is incomprehensible.

I didn't actually lose my speech; words did come out, but not the words I had intended. I heard myself talking gibberish. The harder I tried, the more muddled the emitted words became. In the end it became too distressing and I stopped talking; I had lost the ability to communicate.

In an open ward, one could watch in awe how patients with head injuries and similar problems, accepted and coped with their situation. That, combined with admiration for the dedication of the nurses who tended them, relieved one's own trauma. I gained strength from a wan smile and nod of head which made me feel I wasn't alone.

Marcia bore the brunt of responsibility, hovering over me like a mother hen, helpless, but trying to understand. Circumstances were such that there was no-one else to relieve her.

Lally was the victim of the dreaded agoraphobia, which made him a prisoner in his own home; it was difficult for him to venture out. Marcia insisted that Lally came to visit and brought him to my bedside despite his acute agoraphobia, which made it a mammoth task for both of them. It was a sensible thing to do, of no actual benefit, but a comfort to all

Barry was distressed because he couldn't help. His gout was the problem. It had spread from his foot to his knee with pain so intense that he could not move his leg nor put his foot on the ground, which made it impossible for him to venture out.

Additionally, what should have been a pleasant visit by my brother and his wife turned into a fiasco. Marcia's face lit up as she alerted me that my brother Albert and his wife, Helen, had come to visit. She greeted them with arms outstretched and a big smile saying, "How nice of you to come to see Mummy."

Marcia was devastated by her rebuff as Helen turned away saying, "I don't speak to her."

I couldn't speak, but if I could I wouldn't have known what to say. To tell you the truth, it would have been better if they had not come. The irony is that we didn't know and will never know, why she bore such a grudge.

A disrupting factor in the hospital was the political situation, with the unions taking over the country. I was a private patient, now in a national health ward, though a patient was allocated to take my place in the private wing, a daily inspection was made by the head porter to assess my condition. My speech was returning to normal and I was due to have the tubes removed.

"You'll be returning to your private room tomorrow," said the consultant.

"I'd rather stay here in the ward. It gives me more confidence," I replied.

"I would prefer to keep you here but my hands are tied. Do you see that porter who's watching us very closely? If you are not returned to your room when the drip is removed, they will all go out on strike. They run the hospital now!" was his reply.

The next day I was moved back to the private sector; I felt very cut off and missed the smiling faces.

I didn't delve into the reason why this happened and though I had the symptoms of a stroke, implications were that it was probably due to an allergy to the iodine injection which caused my brain to swell. They were confident that I would improve. It took close to three weeks to return to normal.

It's thanks to Marcia's keen observation that I'm here to tell the tale.

The results of the scan revealed a large tumour in my left middle-ear. It was inoperable and I was referred back to the Royal Free Hospital. As the condition was rare, Mr Groves asked permission to video my ear before treatment started, as it would be useful for the medical students.

A course of radio therapy followed. A mask was made of my face and fixed to a flat table; to ensure absolute accuracy,

I was strapped into position and revolved to two positions. The treatment every day for six weeks left me feeling disoriented and unwell. I will always be grateful for the support of Georgie, Helena and Gina, wonderful friends who made a rota to take me each day.

By the end of the course, my energy was depleted and I was despondent. My state of health was low and I wasn't responding. It was then John and Gina took me to a faith healer. It did help and I began to feel better.

I mentioned the faith healing and the improvement at a regular check-up at the hospital. "Well, I hope you give us a little credit, too," was the doctor's response.

The medical students laughed, but I was serious with my reply,

"I can never thank you enough for all you've done!"

The recuperation period was speeded up by getting back to work. I concentrated on helping my friends. I drew up plans for Georgie's marble bathroom and bedroom; Helena had a helping hand for a new kitchen; and Gina's kitchen and breakfast room had a complete facelift.

I was now ready for something new. I had had enough of big projects. I wanted change.

The long-term effect of the treatment was not favourable. It weakened the left eardrum, which eventually disintegrated, culminating with loss of hearing. In the normal way this would not have been too serious, but now it was coupled with the fact that as a child I lost the hearing in my right ear. I'm fortunate to have and am dependant on, digital hearing aids to rescue me from the silent world of the deaf.

~ *My Design Studio in Hampstead* ~

The uninitiated would not be aware of its existence and only the very curious would dare to venture in, but once one had knowledge of the Hampstead Antique Emporium, visiting became compulsive. Open antique gates revealed a cobblestone pathway; the first door on the left, just in front of the three shops, ushered the way in, to reveal a bevy of antique traders displaying their wares, each with their own area, either side of the long centre aisle.

My introduction to the emporium was when I assisted my friend Jean in setting up her stand to display bric-a-brac. Thereafter, it became my favourite haunt. And so, when four adjoining stalls at the far end became vacant, it occurred to me that it could be an interesting venue for a design studio.

Gerald Smith, the property dealer whose late wife had set up the antique market several years earlier, was surprised, amused and sceptical at my suggestion. "I can't help you," he stated categorically. "The stands are available for antique dealers, not designers."

I stood my ground, replying, "Mr Smith, an interior design studio could add interest for people with antiques."

"What do you mean?" he asked.

"I specialize in restoration of buildings. My work includes replacing decorative features which have been damaged or removed. Also, the coming trend is for decorative finishes such as cornices and marble. It would surely be of interest to an antique clientèle."

After much persuasion, together with drawings which illustrated the point, he conceded and a lease was drawn up.

My aim was to simulate domestic areas and display specialist trades, to show how, with a little ingenuity, an ordinary room could be transformed. With this I was in the enviable position of having the co-operation of the specialist contractors who had supported and assisted me in previous projects. I owe much to their assistance in setting up the studio, but none more so than to Ron Butcher, who helped set the standard with the Corinthian columns made for use in a film.

"Ron, let me have them for the entrance," I begged.

"You're joking, of course!" he responded.

"No, I'm not. They will look magnificent," I replied.

He looked at me as if I had gone berserk, then smiled and laughingly consented. "Yes, all right! I know you won't be satisfied till I agree."

GWEN LEIGH DÉCOR CONSULTANTS supported by Corinthian columns at the entrance, was impressive. As work began, it became evident, on the removal of the dividing walls, that each space was different in shape and depth and the area was open up to the rafters. Contrary to being a handicap, the uneven walls and lack of ceiling provided interest, which turned out to be advantageous. Seven cornices, each one shown to advantage, were displayed in the ceiling,

Fibrous plaster was one of the most versatile in the specialist trades; it can be adapted to enhance any room. Flat columns supported a large arch on the antiqued mirrored wall behind my antique desk, imparting a subtle illusion of space, as did the decorative niche with softly lit shaped shelves and displayed ornaments.

The first item to catch the eye on as one entered was a section of staircase. It jutted out from the wall leading to nowhere and displayed a fine example of a French-polished handrail ending in a curved wreath and curved bottom step. To the right of the staircase was an example of inner entrance doors in polished mahogany, with bevelled glazing, through which one could see a display of brass handles and knockers. Left of the staircase, were additional samples of cornice behind a pair of wallpapered, mahogany-edged wardrobe doors; next to it, a marble bathroom setting with inset basin and antique taps. Antique wall lights and low voltage downlighters inset in a lowered ceiling provided some of the lighting.

On the opposite wall there were a marble-topped Regency-styled radiator cover and built-in traditional bookshelves. Handmade carpet was also included in the display of Specialist Trades. The addition of a drawing board completed the picture.

Hampstead in the 80s was still regarded as a village, a place to meet friends and spend a few casual hours, walking over the Heath, lunching or having tea at one of the many restaurants and browsing. In the Emporium, visitors could linger undisturbed amid the variety of antiques on display. People who would never venture into a design studio were attracted and fascinated. The concept was interesting and effective, the question being, "What is for sale?"

Partial room settings had to be explained, which was good because it gave immediate rapport, which captured their interest. I would point out the different cornices explaining how the designs would suit certain rooms. Talk about bathrooms, kitchens and bedrooms became important topics as I explained differing aspects of approach to each area. I soon discovered that the general public are reluctant to change and have little imagination as to how something would look in a different setting. Artist's impressions helped but the usual response was that they would think about it or talk to their husband or decorator.

Interior designers were generally viewed with suspicion, with the fear that their home would be taken over and attuned to someone else's taste. This is, of course, true for designers of note who are commissioned solely for that reason; they take complete charge of the project, with publicity that promotes both the artist and the client.

The role of an interior designer is often underrated, with the concept that all they do is select colours for decorating; in fact it gets the publicity but plays a minor role. I did my best to try to convince them that a bona fide interior designer's role is to ascertain the needs and personal preference of the client and provide the most advantageous plan to meet those requirements.

Having our cottage nearby was an advantage and led to several small projects. Clients were convinced by the built-in wall of wardrobes and panelled walls in the marble bathroom; several houses now have a lowered soffit with downlighters over the bed. I also had many enquiries for kitchens.

Enquiries entailed going on site, taking measurements and submitting drawings of suggested schemes or alterations, for which I charged a nominal fee. I enjoyed the challenge of small projects but I was disappointed at the lack of interest in the specialist trades. Clients used their own building contractors who preferred doing work themselves, reluctant to have anyone passing comment on what they did. The occasional sizeable project involving specialist work did turn up but they were few and far between.

The most interesting one I recall is the bathroom I designed and had executed in Totteridge Lane. Originally a priory, the minute bathroom, with steeply sloping ceiling at one side of the house, was like an attic room. It required a sunken bath to allow for headroom; the vanity unit was inset into an alcove and a shower, toilet and bidet were miraculously all fitted in and the finished room, with marble and hand-blocked wallpaper, blended in perfectly with their Jacobean four-poster bed.

During that period I participated in a government scheme. I took on a young lad interested in interior design and taught him the rudiments of interpretation and making drawings. He stayed with me for six months and with his portfolio attained a place at Art College

A welcome diversion from the studio was the intimation that Marcia and Russell would not be averse to moving back to London. Following a social visit to friends, Joan and Steven in Hampstead Garden Suburb, they were quite taken with the area. The possibility that they would consider moving to London was "on the cards". I needed no more! My challenge was to make enquiries and see what was available to meet their requirements.

Estate agents abound in Hampstead but the result with each one I approached was negative. However, I persevered in looking at properties that did not fill the bill and retraced my steps with repeated visits to the agents.

At last an agent had a possibility; a house was on offer but the purchaser was unable to complete; everything was on hold.

"Go and view it," he suggested, "and we'll see if anything comes of it."

The house was in chaos. Though they were advised that we were coming, the owner seemed surprised to see us and remarked brusquely, "We're moving tomorrow. I can't see how coming at this stage can be much use."

"I'll try not to be a nuisance. I'm looking on behalf of my daughter who would like to move to London and I can see that this would be perfect," adding, "It must be a trying time for you."

"Yes," she replied, "we've lived here since I came to work for the London County Council."

"Really! Did you know Victor Mishcon?" I asked.

"Of course!" she said emphatically. " He was the head."

"My daughter is married to his son!" I exclaimed.

Perhaps the mention of Victor's name struck a chord but her attitude changed with her saying, "If they're interested, they can come tomorrow morning."

Marcia was astonished with the news, saying, "Reynolds Close was the turning we liked best of all."

They loved the house and Russell's charm prevailed, with the promise that she would give them first option should the deal fall through. Four days later she phoned and the deal was done.

Needless to say, I got the job of doing the interior design.

Lally's physical condition continued to deteriorate and three years later he was forced to retire from his brush business, bereft of hobbies to turn to; golf and fishing were previous pastimes he had abandoned due to ill health.

"Help me in the Emporium," I suggested.

"Doing what?" he asked.

"We can take the empty stand next to ours. We'll sell bits and pieces. We have lots of bric-a-brac," I said.

After some discussion, we took the adjoining stall and called it HAMMOND LEIGH. The bric-a-brac consisted of brass hooks, knobs, brass taps and a medley of assorted items for the home.

By chance, as I was setting up the place, someone came in and attracted my attention. I looked around to see a young girl carrying a heavy holdall.

"Excuse me," she said. "Would you be interested in buying prints of London?"

"Perhaps, I'll have a look." I replied. The prints were good and I selected about six.

"One of the other dealers would probably be interested," I told her, taking her to Jean Austin's stand; Jean was the old friend I had helped in setting up her stand years earlier.

It suddenly occurred to me that it would be sensible to get more prints and went back to tell the girl, "When you've finished, come back and see me."

She explained that she was selling the prints for a friend who was closing down his shop.

"Tell him I'm interested in buying the lot."

We did the deal and I filled the walls of our second stand with beautifully framed prints of London.

Jean was not pleased. She came, looked and exclaimed, "With friends like you, who needs enemies?"

That was the end of a beautiful friendship!

To say Lally found the Emporium boring is an understatement. After being at the helm of one of the largest brush companies, dealing with large Government contracts, supplying the Air Ministry and making special rollers and brushes for use on *Concord,* the pace at the Emporium was tedious. He recalls his first customer. "Can I help you, madam?"

"Yes, how much is this?" she said, pointing to a brass knocker.

"Five pounds, madam," he replied, adding, "Would you like me to wrap it for you?"

"No, thank you. I may bring my husband to look at it on Saturday."

A holiday in the Cotswolds was the catalyst to changing our lives, when a silver frame in an antique shop in Chipping Camden caught my eye. "Look, Lally," I said, pointing to it, "that's exactly like one we have on our dressing table,"

"So it is," he agreed.

The lady in the shop was very helpful as I asked for a discount, explaining that I had a new shop in Hampstead.

"It's reproduction," she told me.

"It's very good. Are they all reproduction?" I asked.

"Most of them. A firm calls on me regularly. I'll give you their name and you can get in touch with them," she volunteered.

I gratefully accepted her offer, adding, "I'll buy the frame anyway."

We invested in a small second-hand glass cabinet; the supplier came to see us and we bought a few things.

The addition of a glass display cabinet and a few silver frames made the shop much more interesting, especially for Lally. This was our first taste of retailing and we liked it. An invitation to attend the Gift Fair in Birmingham, where the supplier was exhibiting, changed our life. It was new and exciting. We bought a proper display cabinet at the exhibition, more silver frames and added jewellery and small silver items. Hammond Leigh was attracting customers and proving to be of more interest. We decided to move the cabinets into the design studio and combine the two.

Converting the wardrobe was the first alteration. Sliding glass replaced the timber doors, the inside walls were clad in suede and adjustable glass shelves were fitted. Following on, glass shelves and suede walls were fitted behind the glazed mahogany doors, but eventually they were replaced with sliding glass doors and the doors were given to Marcia to fulfil their proper use as inner entrance doors.

So as not to step on any one of the dealers' toes, we decided to specialize generally in presents. A freestanding glass display cabinet replaced the drawing board at the entrance; the sign GWEN LEIGH DÉCOR CONSULTANTS was removed. HAMMOND LEIGH had taken over.

As a customer approached our shop, it came as a shock to hear Jean Austin's voice ring out loud and clear:

"It's a travesty of truth. There isn't an antique article in the shop. They should be forced to leave."

Gerald Smith approached me, saying, "I don't want trouble. Can you do something to appease her?"

And so Present-Day Presents was added to the sign, clearly stating that we did not sell antiques.

"With friends like that who needs enemies?"

~ *Hammond Leigh* ~

It was my honest opinion that having a shop was a doddle. "Open the shop, wait for a customer, close the shop and go home." Believe me, that's a far cry from actuality. Running an efficient shop takes up every minute of the working day and continues with planning and preparation for the rest of the twenty-four hours. I soon learnt that the path wasn't going to be easy. If one takes it seriously, it's exciting, stimulating and interesting.

Converting the studio to a shop had not been difficult; in fact, the decorative features turned out to be an advantage; one entered between Corinthian columns to perceive an antiqued mirrored wall, illuminated shelves in a decorative niche and a section of staircase going nowhere. Customers found it fascinating and amusing, which created a relaxed atmosphere.

My first visit to the Gift Fair was an eye-opener, when I became aware of the power of presentation and display that marked the difference between being mediocre or distinctive, I knew which category I wanted it to be. The voluminous exhibition added to the confusion; I was amazed that so many avenues were open to us. The small selection of silver frames and jewellery which formed the contents of our shop were lost in the enormous variety displayed by countless exhibitors, each more wonderful than the other.

I gingerly absorbed what was on offer, hesitant to commit myself. I was overawed and confused by the complexity, variety and comparative quality, by the innumerable exhibitors in a field hitherto unknown to me. I realized that I had a lot to learn as I delved into everything being displayed.

Going from stand to stand, I discovered that by intuition, one's attention links onto something that triggers the imagination and becomes interesting. I limited purchases, but ordered enough to add to the selection we already had, thereby initiating a new trend.

We decided to specialize in presents, mainly silver. Gradually, as we became more established, more changes were made to improve the display. Eventually every inch of available wall was fitted with a glass cabinet, except for the panelled wall, where the mirror was retained and proved to be useful for the sale of jewellery.

Presents turned out to be a fortuitous choice, encompassing everyone and everything by catering for every occasion, every age group and every price bracket. Our one stipulation was that everything we stocked had to be well-made and useful.

Items were displayed in groups, silver and marcasite jewellery in one cabinet. The large cabinet next to it held choice presents in hallmarked silver, suitable for weddings and similar occasions, as well as unusual items for the person who has everything. Gold jewellery had pride of place in the centre of the shop, while shelves below displayed personal silver articles: a hand mirror, brush and comb and birthday book. Silver charms individually hanging